Moral
Conflict

Moral Conflict
When Social Worlds Collide

W. Barnett Pearce
Stephen W. Littlejohn

SAGE Publications
International Educational and Professional Publisher
Thousand Oaks London New Delhi

For information address:

SAGE Publications, Inc.
2455 Teller Road
Thousand Oaks, California 91320
E-mail: order@sagepub.com

SAGE Publications Ltd.
6 Bonhill Street
London EC2A 4PU
United Kingdom

SAGE Publications India Pvt. Ltd.
M-32 Market
Greater Kailash I
New Delhi 110 048 India

Printed in the United States of America

Library of Congress Cataloging-in-Publication Data

Pearce, W. Barnett.
  Moral conflict: when social worlds collide / W. Barnett Pearce
and Stephen W. Littlejohn.
    p. cm.
  Includes bibliographical references (p.) and index.
  ISBN 0-7619-0052-7 (cloth: acid-free paper). — ISBN
0-7619-0053-5 (pbk.: acid-free paper)
    1. Interpersonal conflict. 2. Interpersonal communication.
3. Culture conflict. 4. Conflict management. 5. Ethical problems-
-Social aspects.   I. Littlejohn, Stephen W. II. Title.
BF637.I48P43 1997
303.6—dc21   96-51308

97 98 99 00 01 02 03 10 9 8 7 6 5 4 3 2

Acquiring Editor:	Margaret Seawell
Editorial Assistant:	Renée Piernot
Production Editor:	Diana E. Axelsen
Production Assistant:	Karen Wiley
Typesetter/Designer:	Danielle Dillahunt
Cover Designer:	Lesa Valdez
Print Buyer:	Anna Chin

Contents

Preface

Moral Conflict is a book about one of the most serious problems of our time. Although many other labels would work as well, we use this term because it captures the depth and moral drive of many disputes in the world today. Our concern arises from watching people clash mercilessly over the question of what it means to be a human being, always a moral question.

This book focuses on communication, the subject of our research, teaching, and practice for 30 years. Our chief aim in this book is to assert the inevitable link between the quality of communication and the outcome of communication.

Conflict is usually treated as something that happens to people and communication as a tool for managing it. For us, in contrast, the nature and course of a conflict are made *in communication*. People produce conflicts through interaction. Communication is not a class name for a type of human action but a way of looking at any form of human activity. All human activities, from our movements within the economic system to those that sustain our religious institutions, whatever else they may be, are also patterns of communication that express and suppress certain ideas, include and exclude certain people, and facilitate or constrain certain forms of human life.

This approach to conflict stems from our social constructionist orientation. Social constructionism as a movement views human realities as a product of social interaction. Human beings live in a world of communication, a world made through communication. This perspective leads us to look for the ways in which our worlds are built in social life and to seek forms of social life in which better worlds might be created. Our approach contrasts sharply with traditional ways of studying conflict. Instead of viewing communication as one part or aspect of conflict, we see it as the essence of all forms of conflict. The constructionist frame leads us to look for new forms of communication in which to bridge incommensurate social worlds.

We have been studying moral conflicts for more than a decade. We do not want ours to be the "final word" on the topic and are under no illusion that others will treat it so. Because we have found the idea of moral conflict illuminating and our studies of various ways of managing moral conflict provocative, we hope that this book will stimulate and contribute to a conversation about what can and should be done when "social worlds collide."

As authors, we see our most important task in this book as the promotion of new forms of discourse. Suggesting new ways of communicating, especially in the volatile arena of moral clash, presents a challenge to all of us who care deeply about the issues affecting our lives. We will not find one best form of discourse, we are sure, but we are searching for a repertoire of possibilities.

We emphasize new forms of communication that facilitate peacemaking, an endeavor taken by some as a distraction from their goals. Many people who are committed activists see peacemaking as a sellout. We do not disparage the efforts of activists because, as we later explain in the book, "going to war" is sometimes the appropriate thing to do. But it is not the only thing to do, and often it is the worst thing to do.

Although this book presents a particular point of view on conflict, we have been eclectic in using insights from many sources. For starters, the literatures on the history and philosophy of science, the sociology of knowledge, and moral philosophy have helped us see how contrasting traditions and moral orders can come to clash. From the ideas in these fields, we developed the term *moral conflict* to designate situations in which the social worlds or moral orders of the participants are incommensurate.

We have relied on moral philosophy to help explain the problem of moral difference. The works of critical theory and cultural studies have been helpful in showing how unexpressed differences can lead to silencing and marginalizing certain groups and their interests. For us, the problem requires the expression of difference without the oppressive consequences of verbal and physical violence. We believe there are forms of public discourse in which this type of achievement can be made.

Consequently, the emerging literature on public discourse has been a crucial building block in our work. Several scholars and practitioners have been writing about the poverty of public discourse or the way issues are explored through the media and other public forums. The idea of the "public sphere" from critical theory, including its critique of "liberal democratic" processes, has been immensely useful for understanding this problem. Many of these authors argue, as do we, for the improvement of public discourse.

Another field that has influenced our thinking in this book is American pragmatism, especially the work of John Dewey, and Ludwig Wittgenstein. In different ways, both these authors proposed a radical reorientation of Western social theory. Instead of trying to identify lawlike, causal relations among variables, Dewey and Wittgenstein emphasized the description of continuous, unfinished patterns of social actions. We have taken this move seriously and have found it a thread that when tugged persistently enough leads to a useful way of understanding human communication.

Taking a pragmatic perspective, then, we face the limitations of the dominant focus of the Western intellectual tradition, the truth value of propositions, expressed in the "ocular" metaphor of knowing. In this tradition, to know something is to see it. Efforts to work out an ocular metaphor have achieved a great deal, but its limitations are becoming apparent, particularly when applied to human social life. Our work, therefore, has been influenced more by alternative metaphors such as *text, game, drama,* and *conversation.*

We are interested less in making analytical truth claims than in being able to discern the possibilities in any given situation. We advocate *practical judgment,* or knowing how to act in situations in which the outcome is uncertain, labeled by Aristotle (1962) in *Nicomachean Ethics* as *phronesis.*

The approach we adopt in this book, then, looks at specific human activities, not psychic variables. We are more interested in how the conflict on national health care is something the participants make rather than the site of variables such as attitude change, ego involvement, or polarization. We view such activities as inherently contingent and incomplete, in the process of being worked out by the participants who are moving into an uncertain future. Our interest is to illumine the particularities of the activity, not to predict the relationship between variables in some abstract world of generalized persons.

Readers will open the book for various reasons. Some will be interested in the theory of communication and moral conflict presented here. Others will be attracted to the case studies. Still others may concentrate on the philosophical problems and puzzles addressed. We think many readers will look with special interest at the idea of transcendent discourse and the pragmatic programs of conflict intervention described here. Personally, we hope most of our readers will gain from the blend of all these features.

This book has been written for anyone interested in conflict and the quality of discourse. We believe it will interest researchers, teachers, and practitioners in a variety of disciplines concerned with communication and conflict. We invite readers to consider adding the work to their bookcases as well as adopting it as a textbook in relevant courses.

Although we must be held responsible for what we have written in the following pages, we cannot take credit for all the work that has led to this book. Indeed, we have been blessed by an especially talented group of collaborators and coauthors. These include Alison Alexander, Warren Bean, Robert Branham, Carlos Cano, Victoria Chen, Sara Cobb, Mark Higgins, Suzanna Hines, Roz Leppington, Z. M. Mess, Jonathan Shailor, Melinda Stone, Michael Weiler, Maureen Williams, Janis Wright, and many others who have provided counsel, insight, and support. We wish especially to acknowledge the assistance of Sally Freeman, who collaborated on an early version of this manuscript, and Glen Gordon, Dean of the Faculty of Social and Behavioral Sciences at the University of Massachusetts, for his support of the Kaleidoscope Project.

PART I

Moral Conflict

1

Discovering Moral Conflict

In 1985, a regularly scheduled campus visit by recruiters for the Central
Intelligence Agency (CIA) at the University of Massachusetts at Amherst provoked a torrid sequence of events. The clash that occurred
disrupted normal university operations, attracted the attention of the
national news media, elicited the participation of news makers Abbie
Hoffman and Amy Carter, brought hundreds of state police officers and
canine auxiliaries to campus, and ultimately resulted in a nationally
televised trial (see Freeman, Littlejohn, & Pearce, 1992).

A group of self-identified liberal students protested the impending
visit of the CIA. In an attempt to settle the conflict, university authorities
agreed to deny the CIA access to campus facilities, offering an alternative site off-campus, while refusing to endorse the students' anti-CIA
position or to schedule a meeting between the students and the university president.

Citing their dissatisfaction with the way they had been treated by
the university, these students organized a demonstration. They planned
to occupy Whitmore Administration Building but were blocked by the
combination of the building's fortresslike design and a tip to security

officers, who locked all doors to the building. Improvising, the student demonstrators took over Munson Hall, a small adjacent building.

Reacting to this sequence of events, a group of politically conservative students organized a counterdemonstration. They complained that their rights had been violated by requiring them to leave campus if they wanted to meet with CIA recruiters, objected loudly and publicly to infringements on their freedom of speech by the liberal protesters, and criticized the university administration for being unable to control the liberal students. These conservative demonstrators circled Munson Hall and, as a countermove, occupied the headquarters of the liberal student organization.

Fearing violence, a group of faculty and staff interposed themselves between the occupied Munson Hall and the encircling demonstrators. Wearing white armbands for identification, they created an adult presence and a human buffer zone between the rival camps of demonstrators.

Those who occupied Munson Hall shouted slogans such as "No way, CIA! Out of Nicaragua!" and the besiegers replied with "Rambo, Rambo, he's our man!" When such rhetorical possibilities were exhausted, the groups began to sing the lyrics of "We Shall Overcome," counterposed with "America, the Beautiful." Throughout the day, these messages were enlivened by more personal comments such as "Fuck you, commie bastard!" and "Up yours, fascist pig!"

The administration set a deadline for the occupiers to leave the building. Instead of leaving, the protesters let it be known that Amy Carter and Abbie Hoffman had somehow (!) been smuggled into the building, undetected by the envelope of counterdemonstrators, the adult presence, and the more sporadic attention of reporters from the media.

When the deadline passed, after dark, approximately 200 state police and their dogs ringed the building. Never previously the center of campus attention, venerable Munson Hall was now thoroughly encased by people.

After some tense hours (and after the deadlines for the evening news), the state police entered the building and, using "pain-compliance techniques," arrested and removed the occupants. In the melee, at least one officer and a demonstrator were injured.

We were working at the University of Massachusetts at the time and, in the days following the incident, talked with many of the participants on all sides. We proposed facilitating a conversation between the two groups of students but were repeatedly told by both that they had nothing that they wanted to say to or hear from the other group. The party line on both sides was that the other had forfeited its right to participate in civilized society.

The quality of public discourse was an early casualty in this dramatic conflict. Positions potentially capable of interesting, eloquent elaboration were truncated into obscene slogans and semantically simplistic actions. We were struck by the difference between the slogans and taunting songs that occurred when the two sides faced each other and the eloquent elaboration that each side gave us when we talked with them separately. Whatever else might have been achieved by this demonstration and its aftermath, the way the conflict was managed diminished, rather than enhanced, the quality of public life on campus.

▧ A Hard Learning

We have a deep appreciation for the arts of persuasion and debate. Our professional training led us to expect that if disputants are sufficiently willing and able to present their cases and respond to others thoughtfully and logically, they could achieve a mutually satisfactory resolution. We assumed that plain old-fashioned persuasion and debate would lead eventually to truth—or at least to communal judgment. We presumed that failures to reach a decision or settle a dispute were caused by unskilled communication, poor debate technique, or selfishness.

Events such as the CIA demonstration, however, taught us that not all conflicts have resolutions and that the rhetorically eloquent presentation of one's case sometimes intensifies, rather than settles, the conflict. They taught us that the use of the best argumentation sometimes widens, rather than narrows, the breach. This was a hard lesson to learn because we had much professional stake in our view of the power of persuasion and critical thinking.

Moral conflicts are vexing disputes that ordinary discourse will not resolve. In this chapter, we report our own learning—the data that we found most convincing—that led us to adopt this term. In subsequent chapters, we show how what we learned fits into the literature on conflict, and we introduce some of the technical terms useful in describing particular features of moral conflict.

The ability of people from different social worlds to manage their differences is one of the most important issues of our time. Moral conflicts—sometimes termed *culture wars, ethnic conflicts, ideological conflicts,* and *intractable conflicts*—occur on issues such as which textbooks to use in elementary schools, whether creation science should be taught, whether abortion should be legal, how the environment should be protected, what rights gays and lesbians should have, what the role of women and men should be, what place religion should take in society, and how justice should be served. Moral conflicts are difficult to manage and, if mishandled, produce particularly costly and painful patterns of social relations. When social worlds collide,

> each side considers its own position to be so vital, and that of the adversary to be so dangerous, that neither seems mindful of the costs of the battle. Allegiance to one side or the other often requires individuals to set aside feelings and beliefs that do not fit easily with the official positions and statements associated with their "side." Those who join neither side are devalued as uncaring or muddle-headed. The whole system suffers as valid concerns on both sides are belittled and important values are denigrated. Passion, energy, and material resources are depleted in fruitless and redundant battles. Participants in the battle, as well as many bystanders to it, are left frustrated, turned-off, or sometimes despairing. (Becker, Chasin, Chasin, Herzig, & Roth, 1992, p. 1)

The problem is all the more confusing because suppressing moral conflict can be just as damaging as fighting it out. When important moral differences are left unexpressed, points of view and perspectives on the world go unheard, and the interests of entire groups become marginalized in the process. The difficulty, then, is managing moral disputes in a way that allows expression and without the violent, disrespectful, and demeaning outcomes of open clash.

℞ Developing New Forms of Communication

Our central interest in this book is to explore new ways of expressing moral difference. Ours is an invitation to those who are involved in conflict to step back a bit, look again, and consider different forms of discourse that might be used in the face of moral difference. That new way will be found not in one best form of communication but in a repertoire of constructive ones.

People who are deeply enmeshed in a moral conflict, those whose civic virtue compels them to oppose, confront, and destroy their enemies, might dismiss what we have to say as a naive, sentimental appeal to civility, as if we were saying that everybody should just talk nicely to one another. Nothing could be further from our purpose.

We do not equate forms of communication with talking, whether nicely or not. There are many forms of communication. Indeed, anything we might do in the presence of others can constitute communication (Pearce, 1989). Although talk is important to most of what we cover in this book, we take into our sights all forms of human activity as expressions of moral positions that sometimes come to clash.

And our purposes are not well described by the adjective *nice*. By definition, it is usually impossible in a moral conflict to "talk nicely" because the participants usually have different definitions of what *nicely* means. Indeed, in these conflicts, the participants often lack the ability to understand or communicate well with each other at all. Using the best rhetoric available within one's repertoire, no matter how polite it might be, does not ensure understanding and respect across rhetorical traditions.

Indeed, moral conflicts have a peculiar way of making "normal" communication tactics impotent. That participants in moral conflict use different languages and symbols is a relatively minor part of the problem. The greater problem is that they use the same language and symbols in incompatible ways. But the greatest problem of all is that each side is compelled by its highest and best motives to act in ways that are repugnant to the other.

This type of communication is difficult because neither side will find within its rhetorical tradition the resources to make a bridge to the other side. The participants will need to go to some new place to reach one another. We are convinced that these other places can be found, or, more accurately, created. Perhaps if we were dealing with aliens who did not live in the same physical universe as we do—who were not born, did not need to eat and excrete, did not reproduce sexually, and did not die—we would be unable to communicate across worlds. At issue, therefore, is not whether differences are so great that they cannot be bridged but whether participants in moral struggles choose to develop and exercise a wide range of ways of relating to one another.

New forms of constructive communication can be achieved if participants change their ways of relating and risk the consequences of understanding their own assumptions and taking other worldviews seriously. They must forgo the comfort of unreflective fanaticism in exchange for the more subtle pleasures of self-doubt and open-minded discovery. Perhaps they might develop more sophisticated and subtle abilities to relate to their own positions as well as those of others. It is possible that such new abilities come packaged with a deeper knowledge of self and a broader understanding of other people and other cultures.

The type of communication needed in moral conflict does occur. Luckily, we are not required to create unprecedented patterns of communication ex nihilo. Such forms of communication, however—which elsewhere we have called *cosmopolitan communication* (Pearce, 1989) and *transcendent discourse* (Freeman et al., 1992)—have almost always been the exception rather than the rule, characteristic of saints and sages rather than ordinary folk.

Our analysis of moral conflict leads us to believe that the times are here when new forms of communication should be clearly identified, the requisite skills inscribed and taught, and the preconditions for their practice institutionalized so that they are regularly, normally used in appropriate situations. As we explain our perspective in the chapters of this book, we refer to and borrow from many others who share our concerns.

Like any society, ours uses a language that is richer in some ways than in others. We have an extensive repertoire of terms for describing physical shapes and sizes, for example. At the same time, however, our vocabulary for naming, describing, and comparing forms of communication is not nearly so rich. The very idea of distinguishing forms of communication seems a peculiar notion to many people. The language used to talk about communication is usually simplistic, used mostly to distinguish forms of communication such as television, radio, print, speech, and nonverbal cues. After that, people have a mixed bag of names such as *argument, interview, lecture, speech, memo,* and the like.

In other words, as a society, we have a laissez-faire attitude toward and an underdeveloped vocabulary for discussing communication. Not surprisingly, then, we do not seem inclined to create communication situations that will have new features but are more likely to work to protect those forms of communication with which we are already quite familiar. We assume that if free speech is guaranteed, then all will be well, when our speech is really quite constrained.

The problem is that the First Amendment guarantees that people can say what they want, but it does not in any way guarantee that all points of view will be heard, that they will be listened to in ways that promote our common interests, or that there will be an appropriate response to what is said. Freedom of speech is an essential foundation for open communication but by itself does not promote salutary forms of expression. The quality of public discourse cannot be guaranteed by statute; it must be made by citizens in the ways in which they address the important issues of the day. And our society does not do a good job of helping people communicate creatively about their differences.

In recent years, however, a considerable number of people have joined in a process of developing new and better ways of communicating. For example, Kolb (1994) described the *alternative dispute resolution* movement as a worldwide confederation of people united by their belief that it is both possible and necessary to "bring a different kind of process to the problems of overcrowded and unsympathetic courts; to changing, conflict-ridden communities; and to the stalemates that accompany long and contentious struggles over public policy and international affairs" (p. 2). Later in this book, we describe some of these efforts. In the remainder of this chapter, we tell our own story.

℞ On the Way to Discovering Moral Conflict

Our interest in moral conflict grew from our observations and reflections during the past decade. We wish to describe the process by which we came to these insights without suggesting that every observer would or should come to the same conclusions.

We have engaged in three long-term research projects that led us to reexamine some of our basic assumptions about conflict and to search the literature for help in understanding what we were seeing in these studies. One project focused on the interaction between the Religious Right and its opponents, sometimes called *culture wars* (Hunter, 1991). The second project involved our studies of mediation and, through that, the alternative dispute resolution movement. We have been participant-observers in a third project, which we called Kaleidoscope. The purpose of Kaleidoscope was to bring to public discourse some of what we learned about conflict resolution. As it turned out, this project taught us a lot about the way people become enmeshed in conflict.

Culture Wars: The Religious
Right and the Secular Humanists

The case of the Religious Right and its critics is a powerful symbol of moral conflict in our society. It demonstrates the chasm between deeply held views of the true and the good, which, when they come to clash, frustrate and anger both participants and observers. This moral conflict, which seems to appear regularly these days, is persistent and patterned. Since the late 1970s, it has been especially ugly.

In the turn of the political tide in the early Reagan years, many conservative Christians became involved in American politics in a new way. Previously, most conservative and evangelical Christians had defined their primary task as the otherworldly mission of saving souls, and they expressed little interest in politics. For whatever reasons, however, a significant number of leaders began to take more seriously the affairs of this world, especially legalized abortion, and they linked their concern for practical politics and their evangelical mission. The movement was strengthened by televangelism. With these changes, the "New" Christian Right was born.

Jerry Falwell, who as late as the mid-1970s had preached against his colleagues who entered politics, organized and became president of the Moral Majority, Inc. He explained his new interest in politics by claiming that the United States was the nation God chose to be the base for worldwide evangelism. He opposed national policies that weakened military strength, economic prosperity, and moral rectitude because such policies threatened the security of the missionary base camp.

Well-organized, well-financed, and skillful in the use of broadcast media direct mail campaigns, organizations such as the Moral Majority and the Christian Roundtable successfully brought their agenda to the forefront of mainstream politics in the 1980 and 1982 elections. They credibly claimed responsibility for defeating many of their targeted elected high officials, including George McGovern, Birch Bayh, and Frank Church, and thereby gained a prominent access to the Reagan administration.

Today, the New Christian Right is known more commonly simply as the Christian Right or the Religious Right. Although it became known for its national political clout during the Reagan years, in the 1990s the movement has made inroads in state and local politics, on initiatives, in school board elections, and on issues such as gay and lesbian rights and creation science (Yoachum & Tuller, 1993).

The issue that catalyzed the movement in 1979 was abortion, and this issue remained its cause célèbre well into the 1990s. During the Reagan years, the antiabortion movement was fueled by the hope of reversing *Roe v. Wade* (1973). The battle came to a feverish peak during the Bush years, when changing Supreme Court personnel made reversal possible. *Roe v. Wade* was not overturned, however, and after Bush's defeat in 1992, the election of a pro-choice president, and certain court decisions that reduced the likelihood of a complete reversal, many wondered if the abortion battle would abate. The early 1990s, however, proved to be just as hot on abortion as were the 1980s.

The organizational structure of the Religious Right has changed since the early 1980s. In the beginning, Jerry Falwell of the now defunct Moral Majority and Heritage Foundation was the most well known leader, but later such names as Lou Sheldon of the Traditional Values Coalition, Pat Robertson of the Christian Coalition, Robert Simonds of the Citizens for Excellence in Education, and Beverly LaHaye of Concerned Women for America became more familiar (Yoachum & Tuller, 1993). The efforts of the Religious Right were less centralized in the 1990s than they had been a decade earlier because they concentrated on various causes in local communities.

From the beginning, the Religious Right elicited a strong response from liberal opponents. Perhaps the most visible opposition has been People for the American Way, founded by television producer Norman Lear to combat the Moral Majority. Most of the opposition to the Religious Right in the 1990s occurred on an issue-by-issue basis. For example, when the anti-gay rights issues were put on the ballot in Oregon and Colorado in 1992, strong statewide organizations arose to combat them.

We became interested in the New Christian Right early in the movement when we viewed a particular television program. Then Senator Lowell Weicker (R-Connecticut) debated a representative from the New Christian Right (whose name we have long forgotten) on an early-morning news program. We were struck by the extent to which the arguments made by the debaters went past each other; in particular, we were surprised that so articulate and experienced a politician as Senator Weicker was unable to hear, much less respond to, the arguments of his opponent in this debate. As we interpreted the exchange, both speakers were sincerely and eloquently expressing their positions on the issues. What each considered a "good argument," however, was heard by the other as further proof that the speaker was mad, bad, or sick. The debate shed little light but reflected much of the heat of misunderstood sincerity.

Whatever one's politics, the public's interest is not served when opportunities such as this result in escalation of misunderstandings and demonization. We suspect that those whose sympathies lay with the Christian Right were convinced that Senator Weicker and the "liberals" with whom he was identified did not understand them at all. On the other hand, those whose sympathies lay with Senator Weicker probably were convinced that their religious conservative opponents and the spokesperson on this program were ignorant, naive buffoons who should not be allowed near the reins of political power.

Because we are academics concerned with the quality of public discourse, regardless of our opinion on this issue, we decided that the interactions of the Religious Right and those whom they call secular humanists were an important part of the public discourse of our times and set ourselves to understand them better (Branham & Pearce, 1987; Littlejohn, 1993, 1994b; Pearce, Littlejohn, & Alexander, 1987, 1989).

Initially, our research strategy led us to focus on public discourse in two types of situations. First, we analyzed the talk and writings of each group when members were speaking or writing to those who already agreed with them. These texts include sermons, lectures, newsletters, and conversations. During this part of the project, we worked to hear each group within the contexts of its own worldviews; we took our task as elucidating the rationality of each group rather than criticizing or responding to it. Second, we analyzed the talk and writings that occurred when members of each group were addressing the other side or third parties who might be persuaded to agree with them. In this part of the project, we focused on how the parties "constructed" one another in their discourse and how each understood and responded to what the other side said and did.

We were struck by a radical discontinuity between these two discourses. In each case, we were impressed by the rationality, intelligibility, humanity, and compassion of intramural discourse. We were equally *un*impressed, however, with the intermural discourse that occurred when members of these groups talked or wrote about members of the other group.

We found that both the Religious Right and its opponents had rich ways of describing their own worldviews and followed strict codes of reasoning and argumentation. Taking a hermeneutic perspective toward these groups, we found it was clear that "natives" of both could live lives of dignity and honor within the moral orders of their groups.

The public discourse between them, however, was much more barren, and we doubted whether there were sufficient resources for rational argument, much less a life of dignity and honor, in that discourse. In public, the normal discourse consisted of reciprocated diatribe, in which the more liberal members of the economic-political establishment told the newly active politicians of the Christian Right that they were ridiculous, irrelevant, and uninformed and advised them to leave politics to their betters.

Not surprisingly, this message was not received gladly. The Religious Right members pejoratively labeled their opponents as secular humanists, defined secular humanism as a covert religion that hypocritically preaches tolerance and pluralism but reacts intolerantly and imperialistically toward conservative Christians, characterized the morality of secular humanists as "making it up as you go along," and attributed to that rootless ethic all of what they cited as the problems of contemporary society—including, at times, crime, divorce, abortion on demand, declining standards in education, feminism, homosexuality, pornography, inflation, declining standard of living, and declining American influence and military strength.

The third part of our project consisted of looking at the pattern of public discourse that was produced when spokespersons for each side addressed each other. As we analyzed a series of these episodes, we found that the conflict was not simply a disagreement about particular issues, such as the proposed Equal Rights Amendment. Rather, each group's worldview constituted clusters of stories that were incommensurate with the other group's stories.

One way of characterizing the Religious Right's social world focuses on the importance of morality. For the Religious Right, morality is a clear-cut category so fundamental that it structures everything else. "Moral sanity" consists of submitting one's own thinking to divinely ordained principles: "Man must choose or invent his own ethics; secular humanism makes man the measure of all things" (Shaeffer, 1982, p. 24). In their set of stories, conservative Christians are seldom if ever in doubt about what they should do. Whatever the topic, it is ultimately a moral issue, and, because right and wrong are clearly established, the issue takes the form of whether one has sufficient courage to do what one already knows is right.

Things are not nearly so clear-cut in the worldview of those labeled secular humanists. The opponents of the Religious Right are not monolithic in worldview or organization. They are a rather loosely affiliated set of groups espousing academic freedom, liberal education, free press, scientific and technical approaches to social issues, and relativistic and/or pluralistic concepts of society. "Reason and intelligence," not morality, are the key concepts organizing this worldview (Kurtz, 1973, p. 17).

When these social worlds collide, whether in casual conversation or in political activity, each finds that the other constitutes a repudiation of that which it holds most dear. This finding is not merely epistemic but also moral. That which each side holds most sacred compels it to oppose the other, and to the extent that the other resists *and justifies that resistance within its own moral vocabulary,* each is compelled to redouble its efforts to obstruct, eliminate, and disempower the other. The results are familiar patterns of reciprocated diatribe, in which each side rudely tells the other what is wrong with it. Useful discussion of the ostensible issues becomes a casualty of the bickering.

In their video documentary *The Great Divide,* Fort and Skinner-Jones (1993) describe the 1992 gay rights battles stimulated by ballot proposals in Oregon and Colorado. This video clearly traces the attenuation of eloquence as the social worlds of the supporters and opponents of the ballot proposals clashed, with all the dehumanization and verbal violence that characterize this case (Littlejohn, 1994a). This conflict is remarkable not only because it contains so clearly the dynamics of moral conflict that we have come to expect but also because it is so profoundly important in the lives of the disputants. Because this conflict is a signpost of our times, we will come back to this story again in Chapter 6.

Hunter (1991) suggested that these conflicts are symptoms of a historical culture war between those he calls "orthodox" and "progressives." The shape of this war has been obscured because it does not follow traditional institutional lines. Instead of the conflicts among relatively discrete groups of Protestants, Catholics, and Jews that were typical of the early U.S. history, this conflict divides each of these groups, resulting in sometimes curious alignments of those who are committed "to an external, definable, and transcendent authority" (the orthodox) and those who have "a tendency to resymbolize historic faiths according to the prevailing assumptions of cultural life" (the progressives; p. 44).[1]

How should this conflict be conducted? In the mid-1980s, recognizing that the reciprocated diatribe was not achieving anyone's purposes, two agreed-on leaders of the two sides, Reverend Jerry Falwell and Senator Edward Kennedy, sought to instill civility in their discourse. They joined each other in a series of debates, in the process becoming, in columnist Cal Thomas's bemused observation, the "Traveling Odd Couple" (Branham & Pearce, 1987, p. 424).

Reflecting a similar faith in the efficacy of civility, Hunter (1994) called for a "renewal of substantive democracy" (p. 244). The steps toward this renewal include accepting more modest political objectives; redefining the public as involving smaller, face-to-face groups rather than equating it only with national movements; "reviving the art of argument and persuasion" (pp. 238-241); and revitalizing politics "within the practical boundaries of its sphere of activity" (pp. 241-243). Hunter cited the Williamsburg Charter, a document produced as part of the bicentennial celebration of the writing of the Constitution. This charter identifies four guidelines for civil public debate "as a central part of the mutual compact implicit in democratic pluralism":

1. Those who claim the right to dissent should assume responsibility to debate.
2. Those who claim the right to criticize should assume responsibility to comprehend.
3. Those who claim the right to influence should accept the responsibility not to inflame.
4. Those who claim the right to participate should accept the responsibility to persuade. (p. 239)

These guidelines are helpful, but if our analysis of the case of the New Christian Right is on track, civility is just a small part of the solution. In exploring possible expansions of civility, we found Bernstein's (1985) concept of incommensurability and Rorty's (1979) concept of abnormal discourse helpful.

Bernstein used the term *incommensurate* to describe a relationship between two worldviews or social realities that differ such that one cannot be "mapped onto," expressed as, or reduced to the other. For example, measurements of distance in miles and kilometers differ, but these systems are commensurate; kilometers can be expressed, however awkwardly, as a precise number of miles. In contrast, an interior decorator might evaluate a book's worth by its size, shape, and attractiveness in a bookcase, but this standard of value is incommensurate with that used by a scholar, whose library means something entirely different.

In his historical studies of science, Kuhn (1970) showed that scientific paradigms are incommensurate. As a result, the criteria for "good reasons" differ among paradigms, making it difficult to reach rational agreement about which paradigm is correct. What seems like a good argument within one paradigm sounds like foolishness in another. Drawing explicitly on Kuhn's distinction between "normal" and "revolutionary" science, Rorty (1979) said that

> normal discourse is that which is conducted within an agreed-upon set of conventions about what counts as a relevant contribution, what counts as answering a question, what counts as having a good argument for answer or a good criticism of it. (p. 320)

But when various normal discourses are incommensurate with one another, people do not agree about what counts as data or whether a particular piece of data supports, refutes, or is irrelevant to a hypothesis. In such situations, only those who are deeply enmeshed in a shared paradigm can wholeheartedly agree on truth claims or ways of making truth claims. Those with sufficiently open minds to understand that there is another paradigm and that the "other" paradigm is incommensurate are faced with a crisis of confidence, a problem in communication, and, often, a shift to a new paradigm.

Rorty (1979) described *abnormal discourse* as "what happens when someone joins in the discourse who is ignorant of these conventions or who sets them aside." Although normal discourse produces "the sort of statement which can be agreed to be true by all participants whom the other participants count as 'rational,' " abnormal discourse functions differently. Its products "can be anything from nonsense to intellectual revolution" (p. 320).

Abnormal discourse is a necessary, but not sufficient, requirement for handling moral conflict. If the participants in a moral conflict only act in ways prefigured by their own social worlds, they cannot transform the situation in which they find themselves; they can only add fuel to the fire by doing "more of the same," and nothing changes.

We believe that the continuing skirmishes between the Religious Right and progressives are parts of a conflict between incommensurate worldviews. As such, the good reasons that either side puts forth in its own normal discourse will only exacerbate the conflict. With this in mind, we began to look for forms of abnormal discourse that would create spaces for the gaps between the worldviews to be bridged.

Such abnormal discourse is not easy to achieve, in part because those working within a particular worldview feel morally compelled to sacrifice to advance their own cause. In his autobiographical *The De-Valuing of America,* William Bennett (1992) presents himself as a fighter. One of his first acts as chairman of the National Endowment for the Humanities (NEH) was to review a film supported by an NEH grant called *From the Ashes . . . Nicaragua.* He characterized it as "not an educational documentary, but a politically tendentious pro-Sandinista film" (p. 17).

Bennett (1992) took it on himself to fight against such objectionable pieces of work and was somewhat surprised to see that not everyone agreed with this view of the role of the NEH. "So began my entry into the culture wars," he reminisced (pp. 18-19). He easily adopted the position of fighter in this war, to suppress perceived illegitimate and dangerous "left wing" forces of society.

Bennett displayed a certain courage in this fight, but there is no evidence in his writings that he ever considered developing abnormal discourse. Rather, he engaged in normal discourse by using standard conservative rhetoric to denounce those who held opinions other than the official Reagan administration line; he put the filmmakers' expressions into his own vocabulary, without any sense of the limitations of that vocabulary. Bennett was in turn denounced by those on the other side, and the moral conflict displayed the degraded public discourse that we have come to expect.

What would have happened if Bennett and his detractors had engaged in an abnormal discourse? Would greater light have been shed on U.S. Central America policy? Would the Reagan administration have escaped the damage caused by the Iran-Contra scandal? Would the people of Nicaragua have been better off? What would that discourse have looked like anyway, and where would it have occurred?

Those deeply enmeshed as participants in a moral conflict see their role as difficult, and it is. But the difficulty they confront is having their interests and views expressed without suppression, fighting on, perhaps without hope of winning, and sometimes incurring great personal costs. The question for them is whether one has sufficient willpower to persevere.

We respect those with this commitment and courage, but we suggest that another type of courage is necessary in managing moral conflict. This is the courage of confronting one's own assumptions, questioning whether the issue deserves the sacrifice that has been offered to it, and opening oneself up to the possibility of engaging in a different pattern of relationships with enemies. All of us need to exhibit this new type of courage at least some of the time, not because it would be nice to do so but because it is a realistic response to the characteristics of the contemporary world.

Many people are living in different social worlds all together on a relatively small planet. We bump into each other with increasing frequency because of the contemporary economic, political, transportation, and communication infrastructures. In such conditions, "The task of a rational being is to see beyond his own prejudices, not to deride the prejudices of another" (Wheelwright, 1954, p. 4).

But how do we develop the ability to do that? Where do we find places to do it in? Who shall we do it with? We must give some thought to creating contexts in which rational beings are helped to see beyond their own prejudices and in which deriding the prejudices of others is ineffectual. We should create the preconditions for new patterns of communication that have the potential for managing moral conflict.

One place to look for new forms that might be applied to public discourse is in relatively safer, more contained settings of private conflict. One such setting is mediation.

Conflicting Realities in Mediation

In 1984, we were invited to work with the recently established University of Massachusetts Mediation Project. Our participation took the form of observing live and videotaped mediation sessions, analyzing them from a communication perspective, presenting a report to the mediators, and then discussing our findings with the mediators and with the director of the project. This set up a rolling research project in which our findings were incorporated into the practices of the mediators and used for other research purposes (Cobb, 1994; Cobb & Rifkin, 1991; Littlejohn, Pearce, Hines, & Bean, 1986; Littlejohn & Shailor, 1986; Littlejohn, Shailor, & Pearce, 1994; Millen, 1992; Shailor, 1994).

All the members of our research team were generally familiar with mediation and had read the project's training manual. Some of our researchers went through the training process and became mediators.

Ours was an interpretive and critical research project. We did not attempt to measure the outcomes of the mediation sessions that we observed (although we took note, of course, of whether the disputants signed an agreement) or systematically to relate various measures of outcome to specific mediator strategies or practices. As a result, our project did not address, let alone answer, certain questions typical of much of the burgeoning literature about the effectiveness of mediation.

Our choice was to focus on the ways in which the mediators and the disputants put together the conversation called mediation. We worked from a communication theory, the *coordinated management of meaning* (Pearce & Cronen, 1980), that is interested less in generalizations about what usually happens than in describing what particular patterns of communication afford and constrain. In the mediation research, as with other studies done under this rubric, we asked how the participants understood the patterns of communication that they were creating with each other (*coherence*) and how they meshed their actions together (*coordination*).

With this as background, we looked at the mediations as events that were being co-constructed by the participants, including the mediators and disputants. In our analysis, we viewed each statement in a mediation as a move performed from the worldview of the speaker and entering into the worldview of the listeners. That is, each turn in the conversation was an act, and each act came from one's own set of beliefs. Each move was also a response to and elicitation of moves from others. In other words, mediations involve interactions on a small scale not unlike larger societal conflicts.

Several things quickly became apparent from our mediation research. First, the meanings of messages (such as *fairness*) changed when they moved from the social reality of one disputant to that of the other. For example, if one disputant understood *justice* as retributive and the other disputant understood it as equity, any statement would be understood differently by each party, preventing the formation of a coherent and coordinated action on the part of both. One of the cases we observed illustrates this problem. The case is sufficiently informative to present in some detail. This is the story of the divorce mediation of Jane and Roy.

After 14 years of marriage, Jane and Roy were divorced. Although the early years of the relationship were relatively happy, the last several were dominated by tension over a variety of issues. Roy had put a great deal of energy into restoring and remodeling the couple's country home, and Jane resented the time he spent on this project. Feeling restless and unfulfilled, Jane began attending college at a nearby university. There she met interesting people and began to long for more stimulation and freedom, but her plan to sell the house and move to town was unacceptable to Roy.

Jane left home, and in the ensuing divorce, Roy got possession of the house and custody of their two children until the 21st birthday of the youngest child, then three. Shortly after the divorce, Roy remarried, and the newly constituted family lived in the home that Roy had built.

Needless to say, Jane was pretty unhappy with this arrangement and the court order and filed an appeal. At the same time, she wanted to avoid the expense and hassles of another trial and so suggested to Roy that they try to settle the matter in mediation. He agreed, and they made an appointment at the local mediation center.

The mediators were Ellen, who had considerable experience as a mediator, and Tim, a novice. The first session was taken up with a lot of talk about the marriage and the details of the divorce. The mediators perceived Roy as angry, even dangerously so, and decided to have a private caucus with him so that he could vent his emotions. This private session turned into an exercise in self-justification for Roy, and in their brief private follow-up meeting with Jane, the mediators had no concrete proposals from Roy to report. At that point, the first session came to an end.

In the second session, the mediators continued to work with the couple, attempting to help Jane and Roy understand one another's perspective. No movement was achieved.

In a rather dynamic third session, the mediators worked hard to get the couple to move in the direction of settlement, and Jane and Roy did make proposals. Sensing that they were still far from agreement and that feelings were still running high, the mediators asked the couple to think about their positions and suggested a fourth meeting to take place in about a month. In just two weeks, Roy informed the mediators that he did not want to participate further, and the mediation was terminated before that fourth session could occur.

These details tell just a small part of the story of Roy and Jane's mediation. This case displays certain characteristics of moral conflict outlined in the previous chapters. The two disputants framed their lives in entirely different moral orders. The mediators, like all third-party interveners, had a moral order of their own; in the end, these three versions of reality could not be sufficiently coordinated to achieve resolution of the conflict.

Roy told the story of how hard he had worked to make a home for the family. His many hours of hard work on the house were not only personally satisfying but also a display of the love he felt for the family.

Consequently, when problems began to happen, Roy "felt used, and not particularly appreciated." He felt as though Jane was out doing her own thing, and he came to resent that. And in his words, "Jane grew to hate my resentment."

Roy's story is about a family and a home. It is a story of frustration and pain resulting from the personal "hedonism" that, from his perspective, obstructed his naturally salutary goals. His sense of righteousness was reinforced because he had won in court. As far as he was concerned, Jane had received her comeuppance. She had left and essentially forfeited her rights as a parent and partner and should just "learn to take her medicine."

Jane, on the other hand, framed her world with individual rights, and her frustration was that her husband's simple-minded vision had obstructed her ability to fulfill herself as a person. After the divorce, in Jane's view, Roy had prevented her from seeing the children and refused to live up to his part of the court-ordered financial arrangement. Hers was a world in which equality, connectedness, and responsibility governed relationships. Relationships for her were negotiated to meet the needs of both partners.

In some of the cases we observed, the disputants and mediators shared a common frame of understanding and were able to make use of shared forms of communication (normal discourse) to resolve the issue. In others, such as the case of Jane and Roy, no common frame was found. Jane and Roy were embroiled in a moral conflict not unlike many larger disputes in society as a whole.

Our second insight from our work on mediation was that the standardized practices of mediation themselves have a deep structure of assumptions about morality, conflict, and justice. These assumptions are often clearly articulated when the virtues of alternative dispute resolution are being championed, but in mediation sessions, in training programs, and in private discussions among mediators, this social reality was presented as neutral.

The myth of the neutral mediator is a useful fiction that really means something more like *impartiality.* Mediators are impartial toward the outcome but never toward the process, and the process mediators advocate is part of their own social reality regarding persons, conflict, and how differences should be resolved.

In his own practice, Lawrence Susskind, a well-known public policy mediator and a professor of urban and environmental studies at MIT, shares our suspicion of neutrality:

> I'm not neutral with regard to the outcome. I'm *nonpartisan.* That's a big difference. I refuse to adopt the interest of one side as being more important than the interest of any others. I will not side with any party, including the least powerful. If only for pragmatic reasons—I wouldn't be able to maintain my role in a dispute if I'm viewed as partisan.
>
> But I'm not neutral with regard to the quality of the outcome that maximizes mutual gain, that doesn't leave joint gains unclaimed. I want an outcome that takes the least amount of time and that saves the most money for the parties. Maximizing joint gains means that you haven't left something on the table that would have been better for both sides, even if the parties didn't propose it. (Kolb, 1994, pp. 328-329)

Widely shared by individuals who volunteer to become mediators and reinforced by basic mediation training, the mediation view consists of several ideas: Individuals in disputes have conflicting interests, those interests should be discussed, creative solutions should be sought, and win-win agreements should be negotiated. Bush and Folger (1994) describe this orientation as a problem-solving ideology that leads to the practices of (a) finding and defining problems in the dispute, (b) aiming for settlement or solution to the problem, and (c) ignoring concerns that cannot be defined as tangible problems. Shailor (1994) summarizes the mediation reality in these terms:

> In simplified form, the story that mediators tell and retell is this: As neutral third parties, we empower disputants to negotiate their own mutually acceptable agreement. Mediators claim to empower disputants by providing them with (1) a forum for self-determination and (2) a model for cooperation and compromise. (p. 15)

We are not saying that all mediators hold this reality all the time, but it is widely disseminated in the mediation community. There are potentially many alternative realities that mediators could adopt. Bush and Folger (1994), for example, suggest a *transformative* model in which the goal is never settlement or satisfaction for its own sake but transformation of the relationship between the parties through a dual process of empowerment and recognition. In accomplishing transformation, a mediator engages in practices rather different from customary problem-solving interventions.

Some mediators may fail to recognize their deep biases, but that is generally true of everybody. People tend to be struck by a cultural blindness regarding their own ways of viewing the world, and they tend to think that their own ways of knowing are objective and neutral. People are not usually conscious of their deeply held assumptions, and they are often oblivious to the limits of their own worldviews.

Likewise, and this is our third insight from our work on mediation, mediators for the most part do not deal with the deep structures of the social worlds that the disputants bring into the sessions. Rather, the mediators control the pace and structure of the conversations according to their own reality and invite the disputants to join them. Sometimes this is successful, and sometimes it is not.

Mediations are episodes of communication. They can further the conversation between the disputants and thereby strengthen the sociality being created between them, they can engage one party in a type of conversation of affirmation and thereby align with that party, or they can create a new type of conversation in which all three parties together create a third culture and a new reality for viewing the dispute.

One unfortunate consequence of failing to take the social reality of the disputants into account is that it sometimes makes possible an inadvertent and unknowing coalition with one disputant (whose social world was closer to that of the mediator or who accepted the mediator's invitation to join the process) against the other (whose social world differed from that of the mediator). This finding, of course, was distressing to mediators who were genuinely trying to be helpful. In our analysis, this outcome was not the result of mistakes or the lack of skill as mediators. Rather, it was the product of the institutionalized procedures inscribed in their training manual and rehearsed in their training sessions. These procedures directed them to focus, in Lovins's (1977) terms, on "conflicting interests, not conflicting views of reality" (p. 12).

This type of unwitting alignment occurred in the case of Jane and Roy. Jane's world was similar to that of the mediators, and Ellen and Tim identified readily with Jane's view. As an eager negotiator, Jane was an ideal mediation client. Roy's behavior, however, was viewed as problematic because he failed to respond with counteroffers and refused to move toward settlement in good faith. Jane articulated her wants and needs clearly, but Roy was more emotive and less clear about what he wanted and needed. Jane was willing to try to compromise; Roy appeared intransigent. In the end, the mediators concluded that he was either love-struck or stupid.

This is a negative example of what can happen when the social reality of the mediators varies from that of the disputants. But in many cases, the social realities of the parties, including those of the mediators, are close enough that the process works with little difficulty.

Early in our investigations, we realized that our studies of mediation had something in common with those of the New Christian Right. We realized that we were looking at the larger question of how people express their differences, privately and in public. Much of our work in recent years has been directed to developing a perspective for understanding this bigger concern, and that is the subject of this book. We found, too, that we shared with mediators the search for new forms of discourse with which these differences might be explored more creatively and constructively. There are many brands of mediation, of course (Kolb, 1994), and through the years, we have borrowed techniques from mediation in our own public issues work.

Since our early involvement with mediation described in this section, we have become mediators ourselves and have incorporated many of the techniques we have learned elsewhere into our practice of this art. One of the opportunities we have had to develop and learn new forms of communication for conflict situations is our continuing experiments in the Kaleidoscope project.

The Kaleidoscope Project

In the mid-1980s, the regional director of the National Conference of Christians and Jews, Dan Nussbaum, approached a group of faculty and staff at the University of Massachusetts with a proposal to support a "Kaleidoscope Program" to promote good public discussion of difficult public issues. Dissatisfied with the conventional model of a controversial speakers series, this group decided to create a way to discuss "undiscussable" issues (Carbaugh, Chen, Cobb, & Shailor, 1986; Leppington, 1987; Littlejohn, 1986).

We identified two types of issues as undiscussable. The most obvious are those in which the conflict is so hot that the speakers believe that they have nothing useful to say to each other and believe that broaching the subject would set off a dangerously intense conflict. Other issues are undiscussable because one side takes its position to be so obvious and true that discussing it would be seen as giving credence to a clearly inferior position.

One topic taken as undiscussable by many at the University of Massachusetts at that time was homosexuality and AIDS. This topic was considered undiscussable for both the reasons stated above. The issue was made salient when a student group invited Dr. Paul Cameron to speak on campus. Cameron had a reputation as a person who blamed AIDS on homosexuals, proposed castration of male homosexuals, and called for a quarantine for all homosexuals, whether or not they were infected with HIV. This was an admittedly outrageous position, and many critics considered it undiscussable precisely because unreasonable positions had been expressed. The question, of course, was whether the issue could be explored in new, less inflammatory, more educational ways. This was the problem of "discussing the undiscussable."

One part of the work of the Kaleidoscope group was to develop a process that created the preconditions for better communication in a moral conflict. We describe this work in more detail later in the book. Perhaps our most important finding emerged from our own private group meetings as we talked about topics, speakers, and ways of managing moral conflicts in public discourse. To put it bluntly: We found that we ourselves were not immune to the effects of moral conflicts.

The Kaleidoscope planning committee was composed of people from all over the university who were, by any relevant standard, tolerant and active in attempts to create a civil and nourishing community. The group included therapists, the university ombudsperson, and staff and administrators who had sought positions in which they could help resolve conflict. To our great surprise, we learned that everyone in this group had some topic about which his or her otherwise impressive tolerance vanished, supplanted by assumptions that could not be challenged, interpersonal hostility, and general obstinacy!

The discovery that there were undiscussable issues for all of us caused a great deal of embarrassment, pain, and soul-searching. The composition of the committee changed as some people dropped out because they could not support a public discussion of a particular topic by a particular speaker.

Those of us who remained or returned were a bit more humble and even more fascinated by the inability of our usual communication practices to come to grips with moral conflict. We were amazed at the extent to which our good natures and professional skills were subverted by topics that we personally found undiscussable.

We drew several conclusion from the finding that all of us had undiscussable topics. First, we realized that it was not the topic itself that made it undiscussable. An issue that barely raised an eyebrow from one member of our working group would lead another to withdraw as an act of conscience.

Second, we generalized from our own experience to the conclusion that all people are vulnerable to being enmeshed in moral conflicts. It is not that there are two types of people, those whose personalities or beliefs conduce to conflict and others who do not. Although some personalities and belief systems make persons more prone than others to get caught up in unproductive, intractable conflicts, none of us is immune.

Third, we became convinced that there are communication skills that make us susceptible in different ways to becoming involved in moral conflict and that enable us to manage these conflicts with greater facility. The purpose of the Kaleidoscope project was to develop an interventionist strategy, and it sometimes worked. By inviting those involved in a moral conflict into the communication pattern that we developed, we were (sometimes!) able to help people find ways of talking more productively with those with whom they did not (and should not!) agree.

In later reflections on what we learned from participation in the Kaleidoscope group, we were helped by Kegan's (1994) suggestion that contemporary society is a school whose curriculum demands a complexity of thinking not commonly available. Kegan says that most people are able to recognize different forms of thought, realize that these create difficulty between people, and even adapt messages to be understood by those who think differently than they do. The problem is that most people are not able to step out of their own system of thinking to see it as a social construction. Most people do not realize that "reality" is not immutable truth but a complex and contradictory set of forces between and among systems of thought. Without the ability to undertake what Kegan calls *trans-system* thinking, individuals are incapable of seeing the limits of their own worldviews and creating new forms of discourse that incorporate or synthesize otherwise incommensurate realities.

Moral conflict itself is inevitable in a postmodern world, in which there is no universally shared sense of foundational truth. One of the reasons our responses to moral difference are limited is that we are stuck in our own ways of seeing things, unable to rise above these, and incapable of manufacturing new synthetic positions.

Kegan (1994) outlines five levels of consciousness, increasing in complexity. The fifth level of thought, which Kegan calls *reconstructive postmodernism*, helps us with moral conflict in a number of ways:

In essence, the postmodern view bids disputants to do several things: (1) consider that your protracted conflict is a signal that you and your opponent have probably become identified with the poles of the conflict; (2) consider that the relationship in which you find yourself is not the inconvenient result of the existence of an opposing view but the expression of your own incompleteness taken as completeness; (3) value the relationship, miserable though it might feel, as an opportunity to live out your own multiplicity; and thus, (4) focus on ways to let the conflictual relationship transform the parties rather than on the parties resolving the conflict. Postmodernism suggests a kind of "conflict resolution" in which the Palestinian discovers her own Israeliness, the rich man discovers his poverty, the woman discovers the man inside her. (pp. 320-321)[2]

This form of thinking is for most people more a challenge than a reality. Although we can function perfectly well without it most of the time, society today increasingly requires this more complex way of thinking about the world.

We began to think about people's performance in conflict as a matter of their *abilities* to relate to their own beliefs, to the beliefs of other people, and to other people as well as their positions on the relevant issues. Among other things, this helped us understand how people who agree on issues sometimes participate in the conflict differently.

These abilities are learned, and they are unequally distributed in the population. Kegan argues that learning is always done when there is some optimal ratio of challenge and support. We began wondering about the social structures of our society and the amount of challenge and support they offer and if we could create situations in which an optimal ratio of challenge and support was present.

The Kaleidoscope project has come a long way since its early days. We will have much to say about Kaleidoscope later in the book, when we present some of the techniques that we have learned from this experience.

◊ Forward

The perspective developed in this book is not taken from any single intellectual heritage but borrows from several. We think of our work as a building project, a *bricolage*, which Stout (1988) defined as putting "assorted odds and ends . . . together to serve the purposes of the moment" (p. 294). In this sense, we are postmodernists because we share "the conviction that big problems in a philosophical tradition need to be replaced by lots of little pragmatic questions about which bits of that tradition might be used for some current purpose" (p. 294).

The operating philosophy in all our work is that theory can never really be separated from practice. Practice is always guided by theory, explicit or implicit, and theory is always produced, reproduced, and changed in light of practice.

As in life, our movement in this text will be a tacking back and forth between these two indivisible things. As the book evolves, our theory of moral conflict and peacemaking will become increasingly apparent, but the practices we observe and teach here will at the same time be tightly tied to our ways of understanding human experience.

▧ Notes

1. From *Culture Wars*, by J. D. Hunter (New York: HarperCollins Publishers). Copyright 1991 by HarperCollins Publishers. Reprinted by permission.
2. From *In Over Our Heads: The Mental Demands of Modern Life*, by Robert Kegan (Cambridge, MA: Harvard University Press). Copyright © 1994 by the President and Fellows of Harvard College. All rights reserved. Reprinted by permission.

2

Understanding Conflict

On April 19, 1994, the people of the United States were shocked by one of the worst acts of internal terrorism in the history of the nation. One hundred seventy people were killed, some instantly, others after suffering hours and days in agonizing injury, when the Federal Building in Oklahoma City was split in half by a car bomb.

Although two individuals have been arrested, at the time of this writing, the details and motives are yet to be proved. One thing is clear, however: Somebody was mad and wanted to make a statement that would be heard. Somebody was unhappy about some group and its actions and decided to do something about it.

There are those who will attribute the bombing to insanity, and maybe the guilty party was crazy. Mental health aside, however, acts such as this occur worldwide when one group decides to stop the actions of another. For whatever reason, many people do not deal with their differences humanely.

Since Adam and Eve argued about who was at fault for eating the forbidden fruit and getting kicked out of the Garden, conflict has been a part of human society. But is it necessary? Is it inherent in the structure of human social life, or is it an aberration, a needless breakdown of peaceful structures, to be eliminated as quickly and finally as possible? Should our interest focus on how to win, eliminate, or manage conflict? Questions such as these have a long history in the Western intellectual tradition, but never have they seemed so important to so many people as they do today.

℘ Traditional Orientations Toward Conflict

Humans have thought about conflict in a variety of ways in different times and places. In their recent review, Nicotera, Rodriguez, Hall, and Jackson (1995) outline three popular approaches. The first is game theory, which looks at conflict arising from rational decision making in competitive and cooperative systems. The second, the cognitive approach, focuses on individual differences such as conflict style. The third way of looking at conflict is institutional and concentrates on societal structures and processes in the generation and expression of conflict. All these approaches are useful, and each draws our attention to something important about conflict. With our social theoretical bent, we are inclined to begin looking at traditional orientations from an institutional perspective.

Within the system of liberal democracy that has governed the United States since its founding, conflict is treated traditionally as a necessary evil. Liberal democracy is based on the ideal of the independent and autonomous individual with basic rights and responsibilities. Because individuals have different interests, conflict is to be expected, and the political system is designed to handle such conflicts democratically and judicially.

Individuals make their interests and goals known through public declaration. Freedom of speech allows a diversity of interests to be expressed, so that individuals can say what they want, within limits, as long as they do not infringe on other people's right to do the same. Arguments are made by spokespersons and elected representatives, and votes are taken. Through this process, the majority rules, and the minority has the right of persuasion. In certain cases in which disputes cannot be settled through the political system, as in the case of private disputes, the court will listen to respective cases and make a judgment. This is the essence of what Barber (1984) calls "thin democracy."

In his book *Strong Democracy*, Barber (1984) outlines three ways in which conflict has been understood within the American system—the anarchist, the realist, and the minimalist. "Put very briefly, anarchism is conflict-denying, realism is conflict-repressing, and minimalism is conflict-tolerating" (p. 6). He says that Americans are anarchists in their values (privacy, liberty, property); realists in their means (power, law, adjudication); and minimalists in their temper (tolerance, wariness, pluralism). Because of this rather complex combination of attitudes, the three apparently exclusive modes of handling conflict exist side by side in our society:

> The first approach tries to wish conflict away, the second to extirpate it, and the third to live with it. Liberal democracy, the compound and real American form, is conflict-denying in its free-market assumptions about the private sector and its supposed elasticity and egalitarianism; it is conflict-repressing and also conflict-adjusting in its prudential uses of political power to adjudicate the struggle of individuals and groups; and it is conflict-tolerating in its characteristic liberal-skeptical temper. (p. 6)

The anarchistic mode of handling conflict involves a "live and let live" attitude that might be expressed something like this:

> I don't care what you think or do as long as you don't step on my toes. You can do whatever you want, as long as you let me achieve my aims. The last thing we want to do is get entangled with one another, especially if we do not see eye to eye. We are not a community of interconnected groups but a society of autonomous individuals. Individuals should look out for themselves and make their own mark in this world. The only real conflict occurs when you step in front of me as I am moving along.

Anarchism is extremely distrustful of joint participation, especially in the form of government. To give in to the will of the majority or any other ruling institution is to wipe out whatever goods one can achieve by individual effort. Citizenship, which implies allegiance to some larger social power, is to be eschewed. We must pledge allegiance only to a system that makes individual liberty possible. This anarchistic view may seem extreme and obscure, but Barber (1984) says that it is intrinsic in liberal democracy:

> In America anarchism has been a disposition of the system itself, a
> tendency that has in fact guided statesmen and citizens more compul-
> sively than it has motivated dissidents and revolutionaries. It has been
> incorporated into popular political practice and has become an inte-
> gral feature of the political heritage. Wherever privacy, freedom, and
> the absolute rights of the individual are championed, there the anar-
> chist disposition is at work. (p. 9)

The second orientation toward conflict in our society is the realist. In
a realistic world in which obstacles prevent the achievement of individual
interests, power is a valued resource. We can promote our individual aims
only if we have sufficient resources to overcome the obstacles.

The juxtaposition of anarchism and realism is paradoxical. The
freedom to promote one's interest must be won by exercise of power
over others, but the exercise of power subverts individual autonomy.
The paradox is handled in an interesting way: "People are not made to
reformulate private interests in public terms but are encouraged to
reformulate public goods in terms of private advantage" (Barber, 1984,
p. 13). That is why we hear so much about taxes, and the so-called
taxpayers revolt is based on the idea that individuals should not have
to give up their hard-earned pay for government pork.

Because others are viewed as intentionally or unwittingly out to
stifle the achievements of others, conflict to the realist is understood as
something one wins or loses. Many people assume that conflict must
have the structure that we now would describe as a zero-sum game, in
which whatever one party wins must be matched by what is lost by
someone else.

In this way of thinking, only those who are unable to affect the outcome
of the conflict can be neutral; everyone else is either on "our side" or the
"other side." These roles are practically equivalent to those of friends and
enemies. The absence of conflict is seen as a characteristic of friends; the
presence of conflict requires that the other be treated as an enemy, at
least temporarily, making polarization so common in our society.

Constant vigilance, suspicion, and a certain bellicosity are virtues
in the realist world. Security is seen as directly related to our strength,
and whatever strengthens us and/or weakens our enemies is seen as
morally right. This leads to a particular punctuation of events: If our
enemy does not threaten us, it is because we are sufficiently militarily,
morally, or economically strong.

In this concept of conflict, communication has a limited but important function. Communication is the means by which we keep our

enemies under surveillance, the means by which we transmit information and disinformation to them, the means by which we recruit and retain the support of our friends, and a tactical resource for coordinating our movements.

The works of Machiavelli (1513/1976) and Alinsky (1971) provide remarkably compatible examples of clear-eyed, strategic thinking from this perspective, although ironically, they lived in different historical eras and saw their tasks differently. In early 16th-century Italy, Machiavelli was confronted with virtual anarchy in a period of too many competing powers. He was not what we call a liberal democrat, but his teachings were compatible with the realist notion of conflict. Alinsky, of course, was firmly of the liberal tradition, and his views reflect both anarchistic and realist images of the political order.

Machiavelli's writings were in the form of advice to "the prince" who would gain and keep enough power to keep social order. In the mid-20th century in the United States, Alinsky was confronted by what he saw as an overly powerful Establishment. His books for radicals were designed to tell them how to take power from those who have it.

Machiavelli's (1513/1976) advice to the prince was based on two premises: a self-styled realistic assessment of human character and the ethical principle that the end (so long as it is achieved) justifies the means. In an effort to tell "the real truth of a matter [rather] than the imagination of it," he wrote that subjects "are ungrateful, fickle, false, cowardly, covetous, and as long as you succeed they are yours entirely" (p. 22).

Claiming (not quite accurately) that "the Prince was written by Machiavelli for the Haves on how to hold power," Alinsky (1971) asserted that his book *"Rules for Radicals* is written for the Have-Nots on how to take it away" (p. 3). We do not claim that Alinsky was Machiavellian, although he did compare himself with Machiavelli. Indeed, were they living at the same time, Machiavelli and Alinsky would likely wind up on opposite sides of whatever political issues existed. But they would understand each other quite well because their views of conflict have much in common.

According to Alinsky (1971), "The System" is a set of monolithic and wrongheaded institutions that depend on the "apathy, anonymity, and depersonalization" of the people. As a result, "those who are ostensibly citizens participating in self-government become followers, dependent on public authorities" (p. xxvi).

Alinsky (1971) devotes an entire chapter to communication, which he believes is the single quality without which no organizer can be successful. Alinsky's main concern is communication within one's own group as a way of getting ideas across to others, and it includes skills necessary to mobilize supporters.

The third orientation toward conflict outlined by Barber (1984) is the minimalist. Minimalism is aligned more with anarchism than with realism. It suggests that differences will exist and that we must tolerate them. The great mistrust of many U.S. citizens of big government stems from the minimalist tradition. Power is necessary, but individualism is valued. The answer seems to be some sort of golden mean in which government protects individual liberty, nothing more:

> At its best, the minimalist disposition suspects power without condemning it; it respects freedom without idealizing freedom's conditions; and it recognizes that there are no invisible hands to harmonize natural conflict even as it accepts that the visible hands of political man in quest of power will always be dirty. (Barber, 1984, p. 19)

The three traditional orientations toward conflict have different manifestations, but they all have a common center, the "politics of prudence." Barber (1984) likens our system to zoo keeping. Without some form of conflict control, the world would be a jungle of species without order. The alternative is to separate them, to cage them, and to manage their differences: "Like captured leopards, men are to be admired for their proud individuality and for their unshackled freedom, but they must be caged for their untrustworthiness and antisocial orneriness all the same" (p. 21).

According to Barber, this zoo-keeping method of handling conflict leaves much to be desired, as does its foundational philosophy of thin democracy. Later in this book, we return to Barber's analysis and apply it to new ways of managing public discourse and conflict. Such improvements are made possible by certain new orientations toward conflict. In recent years, there has been an unprecedented development in interest and sophistication in understanding conflict and devising innovative ways of resolving it.

▧ The New Sophistication About Conflict

The development of thinking about conflict has been rapid and somewhat uneven. Our discovery of moral conflict is part of this development and is best understood in that context. The new sophistication about conflict can be expressed in four statements:

1. There are different types of conflict.
2. Understanding conflict is more important than knowing how to win.
3. Some ways of managing conflict are better than others.
4. Intervention is an art that can be practiced successfully.

There Are Different Types of Conflict

This new sophistication developed, in part, by focusing on the structure of conflict per se and differentiating among ways of managing conflict. Having achieved this, a new plateau was reached when it was noticed that not all conflicts are alike.

There are important structural differences in types of conflict. Strategies that work well in some conflicts are counterproductive in others. The chance of resolution of some conflicts is much greater than that in others. The opportunities for personal and social growth, empowerment, and recognition are greater in some conflicts than in others.

Two vastly dissimilar intellectual movements produced this insight. One was mathematical game theory; the other was theological dialogue theory.

Game theorists deliberately disregard the "ethics" of conflict. They set themselves to analyze the logic of players' choices and the outcomes of those choices. Careful examination of these logics, and of the way people act when they use them, produces "an entirely new slant on conflict and on the requirement of any discipline which proposes to deal with conflict and with values scientifically" (Rapoport, 1960, p. xiii).

Three types of games have been identified. There are zero-sum games of pure competition, in which whatever one person wins is matched by what another person loses. There are non-zero-sum games, in which all players can either win or lose together. Finally, there are mixed-motive games, in which each participant is confronted by the risky choice to cooperate or compete.

In a mixed-motive game, a player can win a lot or lose only a little, or can win only a little or lose a lot, depending on the choice the other player makes. In the most celebrated version of a mixed-motive, non-zero-sum game, the Prisoner's Dilemma, both players can win a little if they take certain cooperative moves but can win big or lose big if they make other, competitive ones. In mixed-motive games, there are good reasons to choose either cooperation or competition.

Among other things, the discovery that there are different structures of conflict implies that the much vaunted realism of Machiavelli and Alinsky was mistaken. Rather than seeing things "as they are," these flinty-eyed observers perceived that all conflicts were zero-sum games of pure competition.

Machiavelli and Alinsky did not seem to be aware of the constructive nature of language, but because of the power of language, human beings may have the ability to change a conflict from one type to another. In this regard, there is wisdom in Rapoport's (1967) anecdote of the baseball umpires:

> For the strategist's deeply internalized conviction is that he takes the world "as it is." To the critic, however, the world looks somewhat as it does to the wisest of the three umpires. The first umpire, who was a "realist," remarked, "Some is strikes and some is balls, and I calls them as they is." Another, with less faith in the infallibility of the profession, countered with, "Some is strikes and some is balls, and I calls them as I sees them." But the wisest umpire said, "Some is strikes and some is balls, but they ain't nothing till I calls them." (p. 95)

The second approach revealing differences among conflicts is that of Buber (1958), who stressed the strong ties between participants in a conflict. He focused on the quality of their relationship rather than, as in the formal theory of games, on the pattern of choices and outcomes. He emphasized the reflexive effects of that relationship on the participants in the conflict.

Buber's observation subverts the obvious meaning of what *winning* means. If persons become what they are by virtue of the type of relationship they are in, then the prince who keeps his kingdom by acting, as Machiavelli (1513/1976) thought he must, "contrary to faith, friendships, humanity, and religion" (p. 283) may well have lost something more important than his princely entitlements. At the least, this prince has forfeited a variety of other relationships that Fisher and Brown (1988) call "good" relationships; he might also, as a young rabbi once remarked, have gained the world and lost his own soul.

Extending Buber's work, Matson and Montagu (1967) offered an intriguing rereading of the so-called communication revolution in the 20th century. The major revolution, they claimed, did not derive from the advances in technology by which better signals are transmitted faster and farther with less cost. Rather, the most revolutionary advance is a gradual, incomplete, seemingly precarious, but nevertheless pervasive shift from seeing communication as *monologue* (what one person does to another) to seeing it as *dialogue* (what several persons do together).

The moral orders in which monologue and dialogue occur are vastly different. In monologue, the moral imperative is that the end justifies the means and that the best way to participate in conflict is to side with friends against enemies. In dialogue, the moral order is much more complicated because ends as well as means are subject to negotiation and evolution.

This distinction inheres more in the quality of relationships between the communicators than in what specific acts are performed. In monologue, questions are asked to gain a speaking turn or to make a point; in dialogue, questions are asked to invite an answer. In monologue, one speaks to impress or influence others; in dialogue, one speaks to take a turn in an interpersonal process that affects all participants.

Many observers have noted that dialogue is dangerous: One might learn something new that will change what one thinks or who one is. Specific dangers include an increase in self-knowledge, successful challenges to prior conceptions, opportunities for misunderstandings, risks of personal confusion and disruption, the possibility that one's meanings will be "deformed," and the danger of discovering that what seemed a simple misunderstanding is a deep difference (Gunn, 1992, p. 11).

Rapoport described how he changed his mind about conflict. In his early work (*Science and the Goals of Man*, 1950), he assumed that conflicts "were predominantly manifestations of debates, and that violent conflicts, including wars, were . . . continuations of debates by other means" (1960, p. vii). On this basis, he thought that a sufficient solution to conflict was the application of the scientific outlook. This sanguine view of the triumph of the scientific outlook was successfully challenged by critics, who convinced Rapoport "that not all conflicts are the results of clashes between incompatible assertions" (p. vii). In addition to debates, there are at least two other types of struggles. In a fight, according to Rapoport, one may have trouble expressing the positions of the combatants in words. In a game, the players ironically agree to oppose one another. They agree to struggle against one another for incompatible goals, and they agree on the rules by which that will be done.

Like Buber, Rapoport (1960) became convinced that the primary differences among these forms of conflict lay in the relationships among the participants. In a fight, the opponent "is mainly a nuisance. He should not be there, but somehow he is. He must be eliminated, made to disappear, or cut down in size or importance. The object of a fight is to harm, destroy, subdue, or drive away the opponent" (p. 9).

In a game, "the opponent is essential" and must cooperate if the game is to be played well. The opponents must play by the rules and must do their best to win. The goal is to outwit or outperform the opponent. Of the three types of conflict, only games are rational. Rationality exists because there is a community of sorts between the opponents as they share a commitment to follow the rules of the game:

> The opponent speaks the same language; he is seen not as a nuisance but as a mirror image of self, whose interests may be diametrically opposed, but who nevertheless exists as a rational being. His inner thought processes must be taken into account. (Rapoport, 1960, p. 9)

The opponent is essential also in a debate, but rather than providing a standard against which one can measure one's own performance, the opponent is the prize:

> The objective is to convince your opponent, to make him see things as you see them. "Techniques" appropriate in fights (e.g., thrusts and threats) or in games (e.g., stratagems) may be used, but their value is determined only by the final result: is the opponent convinced, really convinced? (Rapoport, 1960, p. 11)

Experience in trying to resolve conflicts has also convinced analysts that conflicts are not all alike. Specifically, they have found that some conflicts respond to attempts to intervene, whereas others do not. For example, Thorson (1989) contrasted *intractable* with *inefficient* conflicts. Intractable conflicts have a structure such that attempts to resolve them fail, and there may be no mutually acceptable resolution. As a result, these conflicts tend to persist for long periods and to transmute the efforts of would-be peacemakers into acts that escalate their intensity. On the other hand, what Thorson called "inefficient disputes" have a mutually satisfactory solution but continue—sometimes as protracted, bloody conflicts—only because the participants fail to discern that solution (p. 1).

To illustrate inefficient disputes, Thorson (1989) cites the familiar situation of two children trying to divide one cake between them. The solution, discovered by parents around the world, consists of having one child cut the cake into two parts and the other child choosing between them. For the children to argue or fight about the cake, or nations to fight about a piece of land, is "inefficient precisely because there does exist a resolution that leaves each such disputant in a better position than it was prior to the resolution" (pp. 1-2).

Understanding Conflict Is More Important Than Knowing How to Win

In contrast to Alinsky's and Machiavelli's idea that a conflict is something to be won, many now view conflict differently. Although it is hard to date the origins of this new perspective, a good case can be made for June 1859.

Shocked by the savagery of the Battle of Solférino in that month, Jean-Henri Dunant organized emergency aid services for wounded soldiers. The unique feature of this project is that it treated the wounded of both sides—the Austrian and French—equally. Dunant saw them all as casualties, not as members of a winning or losing army. In his 1862 book, *Un Souvenir de Solférino* (*A Memory of Solférino*; see "Dunant, Jean-Henri," 1985), he urged the formation of voluntary relief societies in all countries and, after considerable negotiations, the International Red Cross was formed with the signing of the Geneva Convention of 1864. The first version of this convention pledged signatory nations to care for the wounded in war, whether enemy or friend. Later revisions extended the pledges to assist victims of warfare at sea (in 1907), prisoners of war (1929), and civilians in time of war (1949).

The new idea institutionalized by the Red Cross might be stated as declaring that conflict per se is a problem that affects all of us. That is, it transcends the distinctions between "friends" and "enemies" so that medical and other assistance is given to those who need it regardless of which side they are on, and it asserts that the consequences of conflict are so grave that conflict in and of itself, regardless of which side one might be on, becomes the chief issue.

Just a year before the Geneva agreement was signed, Abraham Lincoln expressed a similar perspective, shocking the jingoistic audience gathered on the battlefield of Gettysburg to celebrate a Union victory over the Confederates by paying homage to all those "brave men, living and dead, who fought here." Where Dunant put the human needs of the wounded in the foreground, Lincoln placed a healing patriotism there. Lincoln's patriotism on that occasion did not differentiate among the contending sides in a terrible civil war. The Gettysburg Address became one of the sacred texts of the nation because of its appeal to what Lincoln himself, in his Second Inaugural Address, referred to as "the better angels of our nature."

Like all new ideas, this one was slow in coming, inconsistently applied, and harshly opposed or ignored by those inconvenienced by it. Like some new ideas, it has grown and been applied in other things as well. Many of the contemporary attempts to understand conflict focus on how it can be resolved for the good of all of us, not on how one side can get the better of the other. For example, Burton (1990) said that we must deal with the problems that give rise to conflicts or "finally succumb." He noted the exorbitant costs of conflict and of ways of dealing with conflict that touch only the symptoms rather than the reasons for the conflict.

> In the last few decades we have developed a major and costly industry in security checks, we have spent far less thought and resources on the reasons for robbery and terrorism. We spend more and more on jails, but very little on the sources of deviant behaviors. At great cost we try to make air travel secure, but give little attention to the sources of sabotage. We try to curb drug trafficking and consumption, with little attention being paid to the reasons for drug production and consumption. We use police measures to deal with gang violence, with little consideration of the alienation and identity reasons for gang formation. Greater powers seek to impose their institutions and values on peoples of other nations in the name of democracy and freedom, but there is little analysis and understanding of the oppressive circumstances that have led peoples and nations to their present condition, or of their present felt needs for taking steps toward their independent development.
>
> Meanwhile, the costs of continuing conflict and violence—that is, of treating symptoms by traditional coercive means—are more than societies can afford. The costs of building jails and interning people and then releasing them as less desirable citizens, the costs of ethnic conflict which destroys the economies of nations, the costs and uncertainties of thermonuclear deterrence, are costs never before experienced, and they have grown beyond the capacities of even the wealthiest of nations. Suppression and containment, perhaps possible when societies were smaller and less complex, are no longer practical options either technically or financially. We conclude that there is now

no option but to pay attention to the problems which give rise to conflict, even though this may require altered institutions and policies. (p. 17)[1]

In our judgment, Burton stands on a different side of a paradigm shift from Machiavelli and Alinsky. Burton takes conflict per se as a problem to be dealt with regardless of who wins and loses. That is, his position is compatible with the adage that in the next world war, it will not matter who is right, only who is left.

At the same time, Burton implies that if certain basic structural conditions are eliminated, we will live in peace. That, too, is an over-simplification. Indeed, certain underlying conditions should be addressed, but moral differences should not, and cannot, be eliminated. The problem with conflict is not that it exists but that we often do not handle our differences humanely. One part of the new sophistication about conflict is that the management of difference itself is placed in the foreground.

Alinsky and Machiavelli would judge this new perspective as unrealistic. Burton and others like him counter that their ideas are actually realistic. The problem here is that these two ways of thinking about conflict define realism differently. Their realisms focus on different parts of the social world and lead to different conclusions. Although Machiavelli and Alinsky cite the vulgarity of people and institutions (fickle, false, and cowardly) as a justification for engendering fear and confusion, Burton specifies the social consequences of conflicts based on fear and confusion (an industry of security checks, jails, and police measures). We wonder what would happen if Burton, Machiavelli, and Alinsky were to have a dialogue about the reality of conflict. Interesting thought.

This new way of thinking about conflict is evident in the alternative dispute resolution movement. Some people associated with this movement advocate that methods of conflict resolution be taught in elementary schools as part of the basic curriculum (the so-called Fourth R). Although the Dispute Resolution Act passed by Congress in 1980 has never been funded, more than 20 states have developed alternative dispute resolution programs that follow its structure (Shailor, 1994, p. 5). Currently, there are more than 400 mediation centers in the United States (Bush & Folger, 1994).

Viewed as an alternative to costly litigation, mediation seems to have come of age. Although there are a variety of models for this form of alternative dispute resolution, these share the feature of having a third-party facilitator who assists disputants in reaching agreement. Mediation is often provided as a complement to the court system. Training programs abound, as thousands of volunteer peacemakers prepare to help their neighbors deal with conflicts more gracefully. The yellow pages have entire lists of private mediators specializing in everything from commercial to divorce mediation. Indeed, one of us recently attended a training on international business mediation.

As a movement, mediation professionals are a group of people who recognize each other as insiders and who celebrate what they share. At the same time, however, mediators are also coming to grips with several issues, and the disagreements about what, how, and why mediation should be done are sufficient to maintain a breeze over an otherwise calm ocean.

Whether replacing or complementing legal systems of jurisprudence, the proponents of mediation make sophisticated arguments for the moral and fiscal superiority of their methods of conflict resolution. They identify the values of participatory conflict resolution as empowering the disputants and allowing them to deal with neutral facilitators rather than with adversarial lawyers and judges (Shailor, 1994, p. 5). Indeed, a Society for Professionals in Dispute Resolution (SPIDR), complete with conventions and journals, has been formed.

Other related activities have also achieved some prominence. Congress has established the U.S. Institute of Peace, which sponsors research on conflict resolution, particularly on "Track Two" (citizen-to-citizen) methods. Groups such as the Harvard Negotiation Project have developed procedures (such as the "single text" method) that have been used in such celebrated successes as the Camp David agreements between Israel and Egypt (Fisher & Brown, 1988). Reporting on the stunning successes in at least temporary resolution of long-standing conflicts has become a genre in journalism. These successes include the transition to majority rule in South Africa, the new relationship between Israel and the Palestinians, a halt in the violence in Northern Ireland, the peaceful transition of power in Haiti, cessation of the fighting in Bosnia, and others. Although mind-boggling breakthroughs of seemingly intractable conflicts have occurred, in none of these situations has conflict been eliminated. Rather, it has been changed to a different form. Among other things, this indicates the importance of a sustained engagement with conflict, not a quick fix.

Associated with these initiatives are an unprecedented amount of research and the development of professional skill in understanding the causes, prevention, and resolution of conflict (Burton & Dukes, 1990). Burton (1990) introduced the term *provention* to indicate that his project has loftier objectives than simply containing conflict or settling it after it has started. He focuses on "the transformation of relationships in a particular case by the solution of the problems which led to the conflictual behavior in the first place." This is a problem-solving technique that distinguishes "between resolution, that is, treatment of the problems that are the sources of conflict, and the suppression or settlement of conflict by coercive means, or by bargaining and negotiation in which relative power determines the outcome" (p. 3).

The Red Cross and the counterpart in Islamic countries, the Red Crescent (bless 'em all), are going strong. Further, they have been joined by a wide variety of other human rights organizations such as Amnesty International and Human Rights Watch that insist that people be treated carefully, no matter who is involved in what conflict.

Some Ways of Managing
Conflict Are Better Than Others

A first plateau of sophistication was achieved when analysts focused on conflict per se rather than on the strategies that would give one participant a comparative advantage. A second plateau is reached by what appears to be a contradiction of the first. Some theorists and practitioners deny that conflict is a problem, proposing instead that it provides opportunities for those involved.

> Envisioning an alternative to the problem-solving orientation starts by rejecting its basic premise that conflicts need to be viewed as problems. Instead, disputes that emerge from people's substantive concerns, dissatisfactions, and interpersonal or relational tensions can be seen, not as problems, but as opportunities for human growth and transformation.
>   Specifically, a conflict is seen, in the transformative orientation, as a potential occasion for growth in two critical dimensions of human development: empowerment and recognition. (Bush & Folger, 1994, p. 15)

From this perspective, conflict itself is neither good nor bad but is inevitable. Conflict, however, can be dealt with in many ways, some of which are better than others. Indeed, some—such as the blowing up of a public building and the killing of innocent citizens—are downright evil. When conflicts are handled well, the participants form stronger, more open social bonds; when they handle it badly, they injure each other and diminish themselves.

A long tradition of study of the public management of conflict stresses its potential for positive outcomes. For example, Pythagoras, the so-called Father of Debate, taught that the art of persuasion is both beautiful and just. In the tradition of Pythagoras, the academic study of rhetoric has been the search for "good reasons" for believing what is right, true, and prudent. The genius of this strand of Western culture has been the enfranchisement of conflict itself as the means by which decisions are made (Branham, 1991).

Other strands in Western culture imagine a utopian era when conflict—whether between good and evil or among social classes—will end. This image seems frightfully dull as well as unrealistic. Deliberately running against the grain of this tradition in sociology, Coser (1964) enumerated some of the positive functions of conflict that we would miss if we were to lose them. A more balanced view of the effect of various ways of dealing with conflict was offered by Jandt (1973):

> In situations of social conflict, man has reached to his highest heights and stooped to his lowest depths. Through conflict man has killed millions of his brothers and sisters and has created the United Nations. Though conflict may be expressed in campus and ghetto riots, conflict may also be expressed in action groups. Though conflict may result in divorce, it may also result in loving reconciliation. (p. vii)

There is a newfound confidence in the ability to achieve agreements that resolve conflicts. The search for win-win solutions is advocated regularly in conflict resolution circles. The Harvard Negotiation Project is perhaps best known for this approach.

In *Getting to Yes*, Fisher and Ury (1981) of the Harvard Negotiation Project differentiated three types of approaches to bargaining. The apparent choice, they observed, is which game to play, "hard" or "soft." In a soft game, we treat the other as a friend, seek agreement, make concessions to preserve the relationship, trust the other person, make offers, disclose our bottom line, search for a solution that the other will accept, avoid contest of wills, and yield to pressure. In a hard game, on the other hand, we treat the other as an adversary, seek victory, demand concessions as a condition of continuing the relationship, distrust the other, make threats rather than offers, mislead the other as to our bottom line, search for a solution that we will accept, try to win a context of wills, and apply pressure. Both of these, Fisher and Ury suggest, are variations of *positional bargaining,* in which the process of negotiation is in the background and the positions that the participants take (their wins and losses) are emphasized.

As an alternative, Fisher and Ury (1981) emphasize the process of negotiation itself. That is, rather than playing either hard or soft, they counsel us to negotiate on the merits of the issue. In this approach, we should treat others as problem solvers like ourselves and seek a wise outcome efficiently and amicably. Rather than making or demanding concessions, we are advised to separate the people from the problem. Rather than trusting or distrusting, we should proceed independently of trust and focus on people's interests, not the positions they adopt. Rather than making offers or threats, we should explore our own and the others' interests, avoid having a bottom line, invest energy by inventing options for mutual gain, develop multiple options to choose from rather than focusing on a single outcome, strive to achieve a result based on standards independent of the wills of the participants, use reason and be open to reasons, and yield to principle, not to pressure (p. 13).

Whereas Fisher and Ury (1981) focused on the negotiation of specific agreements, Fisher and Brown (1988) took the development of good relationships as their primary interest. In their view, a good relationship is one that "is able to deal successfully" with differences in "wants, perceptions, and values, and the change in them that takes place over time" (p. 8). They propose an "unconditionally constructive strategy" summarized in the dictum: "Do only those things that are both good for the relationship and good for us, whether or not they reciprocate" (p. 38). This principle is detailed in six areas:

1. *Rationality.* Even if they are acting emotionally, balance emotions with reason.
2. *Understanding.* Even if they misunderstand us, try to understand them.
3. *Communication.* Even if they are not listening, consult them before deciding on matters that affect them.
4. *Reliability.* Even if they are trying to deceive us, neither trust them nor deceive them; be reliable.
5. *Noncoercive modes of influence.* Even if they are tying to coerce us, neither yield to that coercion nor try to coerce them; be open to persuasion and try to persuade them.
6. *Acceptance.* Even if they reject us and our concerns as unworthy of their consideration, accept them as worthy of our consideration, care about them, and be open to learning from them. (p. 38)

Although Machiavelli and Alinsky might find this approach to conflict shockingly unrealistic, Fisher and Brown (1988), too, argue from the base of "realism":

> These guidelines are not advice on how to be "good," but rather on how to be effective. They derive from a selfish, hard-headed concern with what each of us can do, in practical terms, to make a relationship work better. The high moral content of the guidelines is a bonus. I can feel good about improving the way we deal with differences. (p. 38)

Fisher and Brown's (1988) advice fits a growing sensibility among the most hardheaded analysts that good ethics lead to good decisions. This sensibility understands ethics positively, as giving guidelines for what we should do, rather than negatively, as a list of things not to do (Brown, 1990). In this sense, ethics are equated with "the process of deciding what should be done" (p. 2), and *good* ethics are those that periodically reassess their assumptions, are open to new information, take secondary and tertiary aspects of actions into account, and see actions within the context of larger social systems.

One way of understanding this new, still developing, and largely fluid sensibility is to shift from one's own interest to *how* the conflict as a whole is managed. This is nothing mysterious; it is what makes the referee's perspective on a basketball game different from that of a player. From this perspective, there are many more criteria for evaluating conflict management than the question, "Will it help me win?" Other questions assume greater importance: "At what cost does victory come?" "Who pays that cost?" "Is my victory worth what it costs?" "What do I become if I win by using these tactics?"

Intervention Is an Art That Can Be Practiced Successfully

The heading of this section already presupposes something of the new sophistication about conflict. The most naive way of managing conflict does not question how it should be managed; if there is a conflict, then one responds by doing whatever one's moral order dictates. For example, Philipsen's (1975) study of the culture of working-class bars in "Teamsterville" found that there was only one legitimate response to an insult; one must immediately retaliate physically. A slightly more sophisticated method of managing conflict might admit the choices of retaliating immediately or later, physically or economi-cally. A more sophisticated response calls into question the nature of the conflict and one's long-range purposes and might even decide not to retaliate at all but to respond in some more creative way—perhaps by writing an ethnography of the working-class bar!

In addition, the new sophistication about conflict seems to carry with it an ability and willingness to intervene as a third party. Interven-tion assumes that conflicts are malleable (Bush & Folger, 1994, p. 4). It involves a spirit of playfulness, an excitement about transforming what might seem inevitable and interminable conflicts into more tractable and more positive forms of human social activity.

One never just enters and changes the game, however. The efforts of a mediator or negotiator do not have a linear, mechanistic impact on a conflict. Like any other participant, the intervener cannot unilaterally change things. Rather, he or she enters the system of the dispute and becomes one factor among many. All participants in the system have reflexive effects on one another, and the intervener can be affected by the conflict, just as the conflict is affected by the intervener. The effect of this understanding, then, is to see conflict as much more changeable than before, a systemic, continuous process that can be influenced in subtle and sophisticated ways by changing the orientation of the par-ticipants or by adding a third party.

Clearly, there has been a paradigm shift (or series of them) in the way analysts think about conflict, and, just as clearly, a new orthodoxy permitting "normal science" has not yet emerged. We see ourselves in the goodly company of those who are adding to the excitement, not sagacious synthesizers who extract (or impose) order and harmony. In the chapters that follow, we throw yet another log onto the fire rather than try to put out that fire. We offer a conceptualization of a specific type of conflict that has unique characteristics that are of great impor-tance in understanding at least some of the problems with public discourse.

℞ Note

1. Copyright © J. W. Burton. From *Conflict: Practices in Management, Settlement, and Resolution*, by J. W. Burton. Reprinted with permission of St. Martin's Press, Incorporated.

3

The Problem of
Moral Conflict

Back in the mid-1980s, before the current rage over television talk programs, we watched an amazing spectacle. Talk show host David Fenigan pitted a group of conservative Christians against gay and lesbian activists on the topic of gays in the church.

One has to imagine the scene to get the full impact. In a small television studio, three speakers were set up on stage. On the left was the director of the Unitarian Office of Gay and Lesbian Affairs; on the right was the chair of the Massachusetts Moral Majority, a Baptist minister; in the middle was a Reformed Jewish rabbi. We had to believe that the left-to-right arrangement was purposefully metaphoric.

The room was divided by an aisle separating the two audience groups. Perhaps a naive producer had some educational goal in mind, but we think the setup was more appropriate for a fireworks display on the Fourth of July. And fireworks is what we got.

AUTHORS' NOTE: Excerpts from Hunter (1991) are from *Culture Wars*, by J. D. Hunter (New York: HarperCollins Publishers). Copyright © 1991 by HarperCollins Publishers. Reprinted by permission.

Within minutes, the "discussion" degraded to a ruckus. The Moral Majoritarian made articulately degrading and insulting comments about the gay community, while his opponents attacked him for lacking humanity and Christian love. Anger and hurt ran deep, as the Unitarian and Baptist shot salvos across the rabbi. At one point, the Baptist "reported" that the venereal disease rate in San Francisco was 22 times the national average and concluded, "I won't shake your hand."

This television program was but a skirmish in one of the great culture wars of our time. Hunter (1991) describes the situation:

> I define cultural conflict very simply as political and social hostility rooted in different systems of moral understanding. The end to which these hostilities tend is the domination of one cultural and moral ethos over all others. Let it be clear, the principles and ideals that mark these competing systems of moral understanding are by no means trifling but always have a character of ultimacy to them. They are not merely attitudes that can change on a whim but basic commitments and beliefs that provide a source of identity, purpose and togetherness for the people who live by them. It is for precisely this reason that political action rooted in these principles and ideals tends to be so passionate. (p. 42)

The new element in the contemporary culture war, Hunter (1991) notes, is that the "divisions of political consequence" are not, as they were in the past, "theological and ecclesiastical in character" but result from the clash of "differing worldviews . . . our most fundamental and cherished assumptions about how to order our lives—our own lives and our lives together in this society" (p. 42). Culture wars are based on more than value difference; they also involve clashing methods for establishing moral values. At issue, Hunter argues, is

> the matter of moral authority . . . the basis by which people determine whether something is good or bad, right or wrong, acceptable or unacceptable, and so on. . . . It is the commitment to different and opposing bases of moral authority and the world views that derive from them that creates the deep cleavages between antagonists in the contemporary culture war. (pp. 42-43)

▧ Matters of Definition

We call the type of conflict Hunter describes above "moral conflicts." They happen when people deeply enmeshed in incommensurate social worlds come to clash. Because their social worlds are at odds, what they want, believe, and need differs, and the actions of those wants, beliefs, and needs do not fit in the world of the opponent. Because ways of dealing with conflicts are a part of one's social world, when these conflicts do occur, they lack a common procedure for dealing with them. Actions taken by one side to be good, true, or prudent are often perceived by the other as evil, false, or foolish—perhaps even sinister and duplicitous. The intensity of moral conflicts is fueled when such actions are treated as malicious or stupid by the other side.

This description of moral conflict was constructed on the basis of our research and in the writings of others who address similar issues. Our approach, for example, focuses on some of the same features highlighted in Thorson's (1989) notion of intractable conflicts. According to Thorson, in this type of conflict, what someone does as an attempt to resolve the conflict is likely to be perceived by the other participants as a curious or surprising move intended to win the conflict. Rather than resolving the dispute, well-intentioned acts intensify and prolong it.

In the same way, our description of moral conflicts resembles Burton's (1990) notion of real conflicts as opposed to mere disputes. In such conflicts, the basic issues are deeply embedded in the participants' moral orders and are not negotiable.

Although abstract definitions of moral conflicts are useful for certain purposes, they should not be pushed too far. Matters of definition involve a necessary trade-off between abstract terms that are useful for delineating categories and more specific terms that help describe actual events.

The danger of having an overly specific definition is illustrated by Hunter's (1991) analysis of culture wars. His account depends on—and is better because it includes—a specific reading of American history in which the influence of religion is emphasized and the goal of each side in the conflict is to dominate the others. At the same time, Hunter's discussion is relatively silent about the experiences of those outside the Judeo-Christian tradition. Although this degree of specificity serves his purpose well, we must be cautious about applying his definitions to other moral conflicts, such as the political disputes between Hindus and Muslims in India, Jews and Arabs in the Middle East, or Muslims, Chinese, and Indians in Malaysia (e.g., Mess & Pearce, 1986).

So although we believe we have a pretty good definition of moral conflict, we acknowledge the need to be careful with definitions. Somewhere, sometime, someone will show us a moral conflict that has somewhat different features. This chapter is designed to outline our theoretical approach to moral conflicts, with the full recognition that this, like every theory, is partial and may ignore certain aspects of moral conflicts that prove important in the end.

In our writing, we distinguish between moral difference and moral conflict (Littlejohn, 1994a; 1995b). As explained in Chapter 5, moral differences may lie beneath the surface without expression, remaining suppressed and hidden. This is the genesis of oppression. On the other hand, moral differences sometimes are expressed in an open clash, which is the genesis of repression. In Chapter 5, we discuss the difficult choices people make in deciding how and whether to express perceived moral differences. We characterize the set of choices faced by activists, peacemakers, and interested others as a dialectic between expression and suppression, a dialectic that must be managed in every case of moral difference.

ℕ The Heart of the Matter

Moral difference exists when groups have *incommensurate moral orders.* In this section, we look more closely at these two key terms— *incommensurate* and *moral orders.* Moral difference is more than differing opinions about whether one should get an abortion, have homosexual sex, or teach creation science because it lies at a deeper level. Groups that differ morally differ in how they view being, knowledge, and values. Moral differences may tend to be expressed on surface issues such as abortion, sexual orientation, and school curriculum, but the differences that lie deep in the moral order are rarely expressed directly.

A moral order is the theory by which a group understands its experience and makes judgments about proper and improper actions. It is a set of concepts and system of rules and standards for action (Wong, 1984). It is the basis for what most people think of as common sense (Wentworth, 1989). A moral order thus provides a tradition of truth and propriety. Stout (1988) shows that every moral tradition holds certain images of order inviolate. Any action that threatens the concept of order within the tradition will be seen as an abomination, and what is a perfectly acceptable act within one tradition can be an abomination in another.

Moral orders can be understood in a variety of ways. According to Wittgenstein (1972), a moral order is a belief system of "subjective certainty" that consists of the things we do not doubt, or as Johnson (1990) puts it, the "things upon which we can regularly depend" (p. 20). Moral orders are akin to Berger, Berger, and Kellner's (1973) idea of the life plan, which is socially created and includes a sense of the individual's identity. Sennett (1970) sees the moral order as a means for establishing purity in life, "to build an image or identity that coheres, is unified, and filters out threats in social experience" (p. 9).

Knowledge itself is constructed from within a moral tradition (e.g., Harré, 1979, 1984). Reality is social, and the moral order within which it is constructed is a product of a historical process in which stories are told and retold and a moral tradition established. McGee (1984) makes this point clearly with an example:

> People do not simply "have" beliefs. . . . Beliefs are products of interaction with the total environment—which is to say that people think *in groups,* from a particular *perspective* or *mindset,* and with the resources of an *historically-grounded pattern of expectations.* . . . It is sufficient for marketing purposes to know that Elmer Pitt is a 24-year-old steelworker in Gary, Indiana with $2,000 disposable income. . . . It may be more significant to know that Elmer is a deacon in his church and translates every experience into the terms of his Christian faith—a faith he has both inherited from the past as a condition of his life experience and accepted enthusiastically of his own volition. (p. 2)

The moral order cannot be separated from the discourse used to produce it because the two form a loop, each affecting the other. We like to use the term *social reality* as a label for the set of meanings a person uses to interpret and act within a situation. Social realities are learned through communication with others during a lifetime. We are therefore interested in studying the ways in which people understand facts, issues, and conflicts as a function of their communication practices.

A social reality has been described as a production in which a group's "resources," or meanings and assumptions, are tightly intertwined with its practices (Pearce, 1989). Doing and thinking cannot really be separated. Our ways of thinking (our resources) are affected by our practices, and our practices are affected by our ways of thinking. A moral order, then, which is at the root of a group's resources, is constructed and reconstructed in what that group says and does.

The tight knot between the moral order and everyday practice is best illustrated with the twin terms *grammar* and *ability.* Every social situation has a grammar of action, sometimes flexible and sometimes rigid. If the situation is to be coherent, this grammar must be followed. Like the grammar of a sentence, however, there may be many variations of acceptable ways of acting, but it is not the case that "anything goes." If the grammar is not followed, the activity is incoherent. Unlike a sentence, however, most social situations require two or more people to coordinate their actions into a coherent "grammatical" sequence.

We take the metaphor of grammar from Wittgenstein's analysis of language games, in which the meaning of an act or utterance is determined by its place in a rule-governed sequence of events. For Wittgenstein, behavior occurs within structured contexts. He did not mean that games are trivial, such as playing golf as opposed to going to work, or manipulative, such as "games people play" (Berne, 1964). His famous dictum that "meaning is in use" refers to an action being a "move" in a rule-governed sequence of events that has implications far beyond its denotation. For example, "Knight to King's 8" means far more than the movement of a piece of carved wood on a painted square; it might be utter foolishness or an astonishingly brilliant play that guarantees the fame of the player, depending on its use in the game.

In addition, Wittgenstein argued that language games have a family resemblance and are themselves "moves" in a "form of life." When Martin Luther refused to recant his theological writings, his statement, "Here I stand; I can do no other," was not just an expression of some intrapsychic state. It was a strategic move at the juncture of different grammars of epistemology, morality, and authority. It changed history by setting off a sequence of events that reconstructed the dominant "form of life" in Europe.

The term *grammar* describes the structure of these games and that which connects them to each other within forms of life. But what is the relationship among different grammars? Is it possible to understand a grammar incommensurate with one's own? Although he did not use the term, Winch (1958) suggested that each grammar is a *particular* way of being human and that all grammars are *various* ways of being human. By exploring other grammars and forms of life, we can move in other social worlds.

> Ways of speaking are not insulated from each other in mutually exclusive systems of rules. What can be said in one context by the use of a certain expression depends for its sense on the uses of that expression in other contexts (different language games). Language games are played by men who have lives to live—lives involving a wide variety of

different interests, which have all kinds of different bearings on each other. Because of this, what a man says or does may make a difference not merely to the performance of the activity upon which he is at present engaged, but to his life and to the lives of other people.

What we may learn by studying other cultures are not merely possibilities of different ways of doing things, other techniques. More importantly we may learn different possibilities of making sense of human life, different ideas about the possible importance that the carrying out of certain activities may take on for a man, trying to contemplate his life as a whole. (p. 318)

We understand people to be "powerful particulars" (Harré, 1984) who have abilities to act into such situations. By using the metaphor of abilities, we deliberately frame individuals' social performance as learned, variable, and open to critique, just as the ability to perform a musical instrument or play football is. We are specifically interested in people's abilities to perform within the grammars of specific situations, to relate to persons who live within other grammars, and to move among language games.

As we use the term, moral orders have (on the *moral* side) little to do with codes of sins and virtues and (on the *order* side) little to do with orderliness. We chose the term *moral* because we want to emphasize that people's actions are based in what seems good and right. We chose the term *order* because we want to emphasize that in a specific situation, there are always constraints on our actions in the form of ideas about truth and right. These ideas are not abstract but are products of the interaction we have with other people in our social groups. Actions and ideas are closely tied together; our actions create ideas, and ideas constrain actions. The term *moral order,* then, denotes the pattern of one's compulsions and permissions to act in certain ways and one's prohibitions against acting in other ways.

In a sense, then, moral orders create the boundaries of what a person is able to do. But the notion of abilities does not lend itself to the categorization of people or prediction of their behaviors. An ability is always contingent on circumstances. Such unpredictability is a crucial ingredient of social life. We like anthropologist Frake's (1980) warning that "culture" is not "a script for the production of social occasions" but "a set of principles for creating dramas, for writing scripts, and, of course, for recruiting players and audiences."

Culture is not simply a cognitive map that people acquire, in whole or in part, more or less accurately, and then learn to read. People are not just map-readers; they are map-makers. People are cast out into the imperfectly charted, continually shifting seas of everyday life. Mapping them out is a constant process resulting not in an individual cognitive map, but in a whole chart case of rough, improvised, continually revised sketch maps. . . . Different cultures are like different schools of navigation designed to cope with different terrains and seas. In this school, one must learn not only how to map out everyday life, but also how to fix one's position, determine a destination, and plot a course. And because people do not voyage alone, one must recruit a crew. Maps, positions, and courses must be communicated and sold. The last time—on a real boat in a real sea—I tried to sell a position and course to my crew . . . , I won the argument but promptly ran the boat aground. That's the way life is. (pp. 6-7)

In our work, then, we wish to describe ways in which people together follow grammars, or logics, in episodes and how social worlds are created in this process. Most forms of conflict are played out within some frame, a grammar that provides options and moves from which to choose. One person's moves are governed by rules, but they are also governed in part by the contingent responses of the other person.

Moral conflict occurs when disputants are acting within incommensurate grammars. Because they (*plural*) are trying to play different games simultaneously, each (*singular*) finds his or her own abilities to act, to think, to feel, and to relate to others reduced by the actions of the other. In moral conflicts, new types of abilities are required—not just the ability to act skillfully within the context of one's own grammar but the ability to transcend one's own grammar, to join the grammars of others, and to weave these grammars together.

Moral conflicts mark the sites in our society in which incommensurate forms of life overlap. As we unwrap this text, we hope to show that new grammars and hence new games, even new forms of life, may become possible.

Our analysis takes the perspective that particular beliefs, sayings, or doings are not well understood if taken in isolation from everything else that the person involved believes, says, and does. Each utterance is the tip of a semantic iceberg; each action is part of an ecology of significations in which the relations among the acts define the meaning of the acts themselves. Each thing that we do or say is a move in a language game, and this language game, in turn, is part of a cluster of such games that compose a form of life. We are confronted at every moment with the question "What shall we do?" and that question is embedded within a matrix of obligations, prohibitions, duties, rights, and aspirations. These overlapping webs constitute what logicians call a deontic logic of "oughtness," which, we believe, is the substance of our positions as persons in conversations with others (Pearce, 1994; Pearce & Cronen, 1980).

Although the concept of deontic logic may seem a little stuffy, it is not removed from mundane experience. Indeed, it calls into relief those things that connect one person's acts to those of other people. The conclusion we reach when we use deontic logic is not just a proposition about a state of affairs—such as Socrates's man being mortal—but a sense that one ought to act in a particular way.

This deontic logic is sometimes powerfully felt as the compulsion to act in certain ways and refrain from acting in others. People often report that they have no alternative, that they simply have to (or cannot) act. Sometimes, this deontic logic is more subtle and not prescriptive. It may permit a range of actions or allow choice. In general, here is how we reason deontically:

> When people like them do that kind of thing, in a situation like this, someone like me "must," "should," "may," or "must not" respond by taking this action, because that will make them do what they should, and I can confirm my concept of self and transform my relationship with them.

If, for example, the members of a militia believe that (a) there is an international conspiracy to take over the United States and form a one-world government, (b) this will mean an end of our cherished liberties, and (c) the only way to prevent this is to prepare to resist, then they will conclude that right-minded people should form an armed organization, go to boot camp, and have weekend drills.

People give ordinary descriptions of this deontic logic when they account for their actions or talk about their motives and intentions. Our vocabulary of passion, interest, and fear consists of various ways of connecting our actions to those of others and the world around us. One of the reasons groups in conflict have trouble breaking the pattern of interaction between them is that each is sealed into its own deontic logic, caught in the loop of its moral order.

As a case in point, consider the "beautiful choice" television commercials of the early 1990s (Littlejohn, 1993). The campaign consisted of a number of "gentle" television commercials opposing abortion. It was put together by the Arthur S. DeMoss Foundation, a Christian organization that gives money to conservative causes such as Campus

Crusade for Christ, Walk Thru the Bible Ministries, the Pat Boone Foundation, and the Fellowship of Christian Athletes.

The commercials are highly professional 30-second spots. Most feature the celebration of the birth and life of children who might otherwise have been aborted. (One expresses the regrets of a mother who did choose abortion; another features a child who survived an abortion attempt.) All the commercials end with the slogan "Life. What a Beautiful Choice."

The content of the advertisements is highly emotive and features attractive people usually in happy scenes with lovely background music. They are, as one observer noted, reminiscent of Hallmark card ads (Ames, Leonard, Lewis, & Annin, 1992). We know of seven commercials in the campaign. The discourse, linguistic and visual, of the entire series of commercials provides an idea of the elements of the moral order tied to it. The moral order reflected in the DeMoss commercials is consistent with that of religious antiabortion rhetoric in general. A substantial overlap seems to exist between the moral categories in the DeMoss commercials and those found in our earlier studies of the Religious Right (Pearce, Littlejohn, & Alexander, 1987, 1989), including the dimensions of simplism, moralism, monism, and preservationism, categories defined earlier by Lipset and Raab (1970).

Simplism is the notion that life's situations are not really complex. They may be problematic, but the available lines of action are few in number and easy to separate. The essential ingredients of the problem are always the same, and particular individuals and context have little to do with it. In all cases, one can and should make a clear decision in favor of one course of action over the other.

In antiabortion rhetoric, simplism requires that we view the unplanned pregnancy as a simple, if anxiety-provoking, situation. One's unique circumstances do not change the nature of the situation. There are two choices, abort or give birth, as the DeMoss commercials clearly express.

This moral tenet differs substantially from the idea commonly found in proabortion discourse that problematic situations are complex and that their solutions are not simple. In deciding what to do about an unwanted pregnancy, a woman must weigh several factors. The right thing to do in one set of circumstances is not the same as that in another. Furthermore, the options are several, and they are not simple. From a pro-choice perspective, any decision a woman might make entails consideration of a large number of other possibilities.

The second dimension of this system of thought is *moralism.* Moralism defines all action in moral terms. In other words, one's actions can always be defined as good or bad, right or wrong. This premise allows one to choose among the few possible responses to a problem on the basis of which is best. Good decisions follow the path that is morally clear and leads to the prescribed state, whereas bad decisions prevent the achievement of this goal. The DeMoss spots clearly express this tenet. One choice, birth, is good; the other, abortion, is bad. Giving birth will lead to desired ends, whereas having an abortion will lead to undesirable ones. There is no middle ground.

In contrast, pro-choice advocates are less able to judge individual choices as good or bad. A choice may be considered good and bad, involving both advantages and disadvantages. Pro-choice advocates are less able to define a single desired moral state. Instead, moral outcomes are considered highly relativistic and individual.

Moralism requires the presence of another dimension, *monism,* or the use of a clear set of standards for right and wrong. It is the adoption of a doctrine to guide moral choice. The standard of good and evil, usually prescribed by an authority, is clearly stated and can be applied in all situations. For the Religious Right, this standard is usually scriptural, and the states to which we aspire are defined by God. In conservative Judeo-Christian thought, only God can give and take life, making clear the conservative religious stand on abortion and euthanasia.

The pro-choice movement, of course, is based on a moral premise quite at odds with monism. People become pro-choice advocates in part because they do not believe single moral authorities can be trusted. Their rhetoric expresses a much more situational ethic, in which courses of action are decided on the basis of individual needs and situational circumstances.

The fourth dimension of the religious antiabortion moral order is *preservationism,* a quality of most conservative thought. Values that are perceived to be maintained through time are considered good and to be protected. Such ideas are sustained by consensus within the community because they protect the community. They are usually based on time-tested virtues or expectations for how individuals should behave (MacIntyre, 1981).

The contrast between the preservationism in antiabortion rhetoric and the individualism of pro-choice rhetoric is striking. For pro-choice advocates, *Roe v. Wade* (1973) was a moral victory because it departed from traditional arrangements that were viewed as oppressive to women.

Our analysis of the "beautiful choice" campaign shows that it is possible to learn something about a moral order by looking carefully at the discourse produced as part of it. Moral orders, however, resist precise description because they are not objects standing still for our inspection, and we do not occupy a pristine position from which to describe them.

> In every instance . . . we are partly insiders with immediate awareness of what it is to be, and partly outsiders looking at surfaces. The dual role, the in-and-out movement of the mind seeking to penetrate its object, frames every experience with the irony of its own finitude. In the distractions of practical life and in the security of theorizing alike we may lose sight of that irony. (Wheelwright, 1954, p. 13)

To understand and work with a particular moral order, however, we will need to develop a language that permits us to understand it and, as we will see later, to compare it with others. Some useful concepts for making perspicuous contrasts are found in the scholarly literature.

For example, Cooper (1981) differentiated individual, social, and anchored moralities, each of which may be either monolithic (based on single premises) or polylithic (based on multiple premises). In monolithic moral orders, everything is seen as related to simple moral principles, whereas in polylithic ones, issues are seen as separated and context bound. This distinction helps to clarify one difference between the pro-life and pro-choice positions described above.

Nisbett (1966) made a distinction between moral orders built on rights and those built on virtues. A rights-oriented order is based on the individual as the independent unit of action. It assumes individual differences, and moral actions promote the dignity and choice of persons. A virtues-oriented order is based on the community as the unit of action. Individual differences are insignificant, whereas group differences are important. Proper actions conform to social expectations, promote the welfare of the community, and thereby award honor. Many of the most vexing social issues in contemporary society seem to reflect these distinctions, but in interesting ways. For example, a claim of a woman's right to control her own body leads to actions that make great sense within a rights-oriented moral order but that are incomprehensible within a virtues-oriented one.

A historian or anthropologist exploring the sediments of history in the rights- and virtues-oriented moral orders will uncover particular forms of society and ways of being human associated with each. As a structuring concept, individual rights emerge from the particular historical context of the Enlightenment and modernity; a virtues-based approach emerges from traditional society. As detailed elsewhere (Pearce, 1989), part of these moral orders have to do with ways of conducting conflict. When modernists act in ways that seem obligated and good within their moral order, these very acts offend traditionalists and "prove" the perfidy of the modernists. At the same time, when traditionalists act in ways that seem obligated and good within their own moral order, they "prove" their ignorance and intransigence to the modernists. As such, the ways in which the various sides act in the conflict themselves become the issue in the conflict.

In sum, then, moral difference is defined by differing moral orders, each constructed within a tradition of communication. But these differences are never simple. A moral difference is characterized by another term we find ourselves using frequently—*incommensurate*. Differing moral orders are incommensurate.

The idea of incommensurate differences is probably most commonly attributable to Kuhn, who used the term to describe different scientific paradigms. In *The Structure of Scientific Revolutions* (1970), he wrote,

> The proponents of competing paradigms practice their trades in different worlds. . . . One is embedded in a flat, the other in a curved, matrix of space. Practicing in different worlds, the two groups of scientists see different things when they look from the same point in the same direction. Again, that is not to say that they can see anything they please. Both are looking at the world, and what they look at has not changed. But in some areas they see different things, and they see them in different relations one to the other. That is why a law that cannot even be demonstrated to one group of scientists may occasionally seem intuitively obvious to another. Equally it is why, before they can hope to communicate fully, one group or the other must experience the conversion that we have been calling a paradigm shift. Just because it is a transition between incommensurables, the transition between competing paradigms cannot be made a step at a time, forced by logic and neutral experience. Like the gestalt switch, it must occur all at once [though not necessarily in an instant] or not at all. (p. 150)

Scientists from incommensurate traditions may have trouble talking to one another because they use a different vocabulary and logic, but this does not mean that they cannot talk to one another at all.

Incommensurate systems of thought cannot be mapped point by point onto one another, but they can be compared. Bernstein (1985) made incommensurability a key concept in his analysis of contemporary philosophy and social theory, and he focused on a type of openness that permits comparison:

> What is sound in the incommensurability thesis is the clarification of just what we are doing when we do compare paradigms, theories, language games. We can compare them in multiple ways. We can recognize losses and gains. We can even see how some of our standards for comparing them conflict with each other. We can recognize—especially in cases of incommensurability in science—that our arguments and counter-arguments in support of rival paradigm theories may not be conclusive. We can appreciate how much skill, art, and imagination are required to do justice to what is distinctive about different ways of practicing science and how "in some areas" scientists "see different things." In underscoring these features, we are not showing or suggesting that such comparison is irrational but opening up the types and varieties of practical reason involved in making such rational comparisons. (pp. 92-93)

Comparing incommensurate worldviews of any sort, whether scientific theories or the moral orders of antiabortion and pro-choice activists, is not easy. It is an art and, like any art, can be learned and evaluated. Bernstein (1985) wrote,

> The skill or the art here (and it is a rare art) is to do this in a manner that avoids two extremes—the extreme of mutely contemplating something without any understanding, and the extreme of too easily and facilely projecting our own well-entrenched beliefs, attitudes, classifications, and symbolic forms onto the alien phenomenon. While this is an art that requires patience, imagination, attention to detail, and insight—and cannot be completely captured by the specification of rules of procedure—it is certainly a rational activity in which we can discriminate better and worse understandings and interpretations of the phenomenon. (p. 91)

As an abstract term, *incommensurate moral orders* is somewhat vague but, we think, useful. These terms sensitize us to the form of conflict that seems most difficult to manage well. Our perspective as communication theorists orients us away from propositions about moral conflict and toward the real world of actions and meanings. We take as the primary data what real people in real situations actually say and do to and with each other, and our interest, ultimately, is to do something in moral conflicts that will help manage them better. By being sensitized to the moral orders in which specific acts occur and their differences, we are challenged to intervene in ways that do not oversimplify the situation.

▧ Special Issues in Moral Difference

As we study the dimensions of moral orders, we are struck by the importance of certain issues that have not yet been addressed in this book. We think these are important enough to bring out early on, so we address them now. Specifically, we are talking about culture, empowerment, and emotion.

Cultural Issues

Precisely because realities are socially constructed, culture is a powerful influence on the moral order. Persons are always cultural because they are always born into and live in a culture, but persons are also individuals because no two people have identical socialization histories. Some people are more or less monocultural, even traditional, and possess a rather unified worldview shared with many other members of the culture. Others are multicultural and have a more diverse, sometimes even contradictory, worldview. So we never know exactly how other people will respond, although we can always bet that the response will be in some way or another cultural.

In the natural course of events, we usually assume that the other people with whom we are engaged share a common cultural view. Often, however, this is not the case. Cultural divergence becomes painful in conflict situations when others challenge our common expectations about how to proceed (e.g., Donohue & Bresnahan, 1994). Problems arise when one party in essence says to the other, "People like us don't do it that way." Behind this feeling is a more fundamental fact: "People like us don't think about things that way." Thus, thinking itself differs from one culture to another, making cultural forms fundamentally moral.

A number of writers have reflected on the moral basis of cultural difference. Carbaugh (1985), for example, describes cultural differences as the dominant and oppositional symbols that are important to members of a group. Many Americans, for example, treat symbols of the nation such as the flag as significant and contrast these with symbols of internationalism and world government such as the United Nations. For other cultures, this national-international distinction is meaningless. Some cultures hold up symbols of the family as significant and look at symbols of individual autonomy as antithetical to that. Some cultures revere religious symbols and consider profane ones in opposition; for others, the sacred-profane distinction is not part of the moral order. For any set of symbols and oppositions that frame a culture's moral order, some other group will find the distinction insignificant.

The many ways in which cultural ideas vary are well documented (Triandis & Albert, 1987). These include, among others, broad versus narrow, abstract versus concrete, personal versus nonpersonal, and process versus product. Often these differences correspond with varying beliefs about what constitutes moral action. Different cultures have different ideas about what is appropriate and inappropriate, desirable and undesirable, behavior.

Especially important are ideas about how conflict should be handled. For example, men in "Teamsterville" (the working class in South Side Chicago) handle their differences by insults, threats, and fighting (Philipsen, 1975). In the Navajo Peacemaking Court, by contrast, a dispute is never considered an isolated incident between two individuals and is not handled by trading insults or blows. For the Navajo, the dispute always affects the families and the larger community. The peacemaker meets with the entire family, provides structure, makes suggestions, asserts Navajo values, and teaches the parties how to restore community (Fagre, 1995).

Like Teamsterville and the Navajo Nation, most cultures of the world have some form of third-party intervention in disputes (Merry, 1989). Our colleague Jonathan Shailor (1988) reviews 15 case studies of conflict resolution across cultures from the ethnographic literature, ranging from the Assadi of Iran to the Baptists of Hopewell, Georgia. Shailor notes many differences in how the peoples of the earth think about, express, and resolve their differences. As an example, consider the role of talk in conflict resolution:

> Some theorists assume that maximizing the exchange of information between disputants is an important means of developing a satisfactory compromise. In other words, "the more communication, the better." Five cases from the current corpus directly contradict this assumption.

> In "Teamsterville" [South Side Chicago], talk geared toward produc-
> ing mutual understanding is often considered an invitation to vio-
> lence. . . . In some cases of mediation in Iran, mutual *mis*understanding
> between disputants is the goal of the mediator. In separate private
> sessions, the mediator attempts to convince each disputant that he/she
> has successfully "rubbed the nose of the opponent in the dirt." Clearly,
> in both Teamsterville and Iran, "mutual understanding" through
> "more" or "better" communication is not a culturally valued goal.
> Neither is it among the "Yanuyanu" or the Ilongot, or on the island of
> Kiriwina. (pp. 197-198)

The use of silence also varies across cultures. Fagre (1995) compared
the place of silence in the Navajo Peacemaking Court on the reservation
and non-Navajo mediations in the Albuquerque Metropolitan Court. The
Navajos generally saw words as powerful. For them, silence was a way to
protect against harming others or damaging interpersonal harmony. For
the non-Navajos, silence was uncomfortable and signaled something wrong.

We live in a world in which numerous cultural groups, not all
ethnic, regularly bump against one another. This is certainly the case in
many communities in the United States. In the Southwest, for example,
Native American, Hispanic, and Anglo cultures frequently interact, and
intercultural mediations are common. One of us recently heard a Hispanic mediator say that he feels quite comfortable mediating disputes
within his own group of "native" Spanish in northern New Mexico but
is at a loss in handling disputes among Mexican Americans in the
southern part of the state. With comments such as this, it is no wonder
that mediation administrators in the Southwest, like those in many
other parts of the country, are increasingly concerned about the intercultural problem.

Empowerment Issues

Another source of moral difference consists of ideas about empowerment. What does it mean to have power? A woman once declined a
friend's invitation to an event because, as she said, "My husband won't
let me do that." From the friend's feminist perspective, that looked like
pure submission. The feminist did not realize, however, that this woman's
husband got liver for dinner that night.

We cannot tell the power arrangements between two people by
watching them interact for a short time because we do not know what
their actions mean to them from the perspective of their own system.

What may appear to be aggressive behavior by a spouse may be quite submissive when we better understand what the interaction means to the couple itself.

Empowerment can never be divorced from the context of meaning and action in which persons are operating. Before we can ask how to empower someone, we must ask other questions first: Empowerment toward what end? What counts as empowerment within the moral community? For people with communitarian ideals, empowerment does not mean learning to act in a self-determined way. For people with an expressive-emotive notion of the word, empowerment means being able to say (verbally or nonverbally) what they feel. For those whose reality is based on hierarchy, empowerment means perpetuating the system and maintaining their place of honor within it. Only in the most utilitarian and individualistic moral orders does empowerment mean the ability to maximize personal interest.

Empowerment is often important in conflict resolution settings. Most American mediators, for example, consider empowerment to mean creating a set of conditions in which each disputant can achieve self-determination (Shailor, 1994). This is a thoroughly monocultural view. To the extent that good outcomes are beneficial to both parties, this view of empowerment means that disputants are enabled to cooperate in achieving a joint solution that meets both of their interests.

Bush and Folger (1994) see this condition as a dual process in which empowerment is the twin of recognition. *Empowerment* occurs "when disputing parties experience a strengthened awareness of their own self-worth and their own ability to deal with whatever difficulties they face, regardless of external restraints" (p. 84), and *recognition* occurs when they "experience an expanded willingness to acknowledge and be responsive to other parties' situations and common human qualities" (p. 85). This idea of empowerment is appropriate in certain moral orders but not in all. Critics (e.g., Harrington, 1986; Littlejohn, 1995a) are quick to point out that ideas of power based on individualism and neutrality may actually disempower individuals from cultures that do not share this reality.

Emotional Issues

No discussion of conflict would be complete without addressing the role of emotion. People come to clash because of their passions. Parties engaged in significant conflicts "feel" strongly and experience emotion. Some say that extreme reactions in conflict situations are primarily emotional.

People normally experience emotions as raw and real. Anger, joy, and sadness are nothing more than what they are—anger, joy, and sadness. Experiencing emotions as pure and universal, disconnected from the moral order, is perfectly understandable because emotions seem to come on us as a natural state, and we feel them physiologically.

But those feelings are labeled, understood, and acted on in ways that are socially constructed. The meaning of emotions and how they should be handled, like all aspects of human action, arise in moral orders. According to Averill (1986), emotional concepts consist of rules and norms that define what certain feelings should be taken to mean, whether they should be considered positive or negative, and how they should be played out. What do anger, grief, elation, and envy look like? These emotions are "performed" and identified differently in different cultures. And they may not even exist in some cultures.

Consider, for example, what we have to presume to feel jealous. First, we must believe that individuals engage one another in relationships. Second, we must have a concept such as loyalty or exclusivity in relationships. Third, we must see ourselves as separate from others but in need of others. Many cultures of the world do not have concepts for separateness, relational loyalty, individual autonomy, or dependence, and in such cultures, jealousy would be a foreign emotion.

Some emotions are now obsolete because we no longer have the beliefs that make them possible (Harré, 1984). An example is *accidie*, which was commonly suffered in the Middle Ages. We have no way today accurately to define this term, but it is something like guilt arising from not having fulfilled one's spiritual obligations. *Melancholy* is another term we no longer use today. It was something like a state of depression, but not exactly that. It had a good dose of wistful nostalgia connected with it.

So it is not inconceivable that individuals embroiled in a conflict may understand and act on their emotions somewhat differently. Many North Americans see emotions as contained within them (Carbaugh, 1988). We hear expressions such as "bursting with joy," "full of anger," "boiling over," "letting off steam," "brimming with pride," and "holding it in." The container idea of emotion is a socially constructed one, and not all groups experience emotion in this way. For example, some people talk about emotion as "being possessed."

Some therapists and mediators encourage clients to engage in emotional *venting*. Virtually every mediation training in the United

States teaches that disputants should be given an opportunity to vent their pent-up emotions if necessary. The idea here is that emotions will get in the way of rational negotiation and must be reduced by letting the emotions out.

Have you ever talked to emotional persons who seemed to get more and more worked up as they spoke? They don't seem to calm down with venting. With this type of person, expressing feelings is more like "rehearsing" than venting. For others, expressing feeling is more like getting the other person's attention than letting out tension. Still other people come from a tradition in which emotions are not something to be let out but something to be controlled.

As a consequence of these different ideas about different emotions, some people find venting alienating, embarrassing, or just plain inappropriate. There are people who see the expression of emotions as a private and personal thing that is never done in the presence of others, certainly not around a stranger such as a mediator. Others see the expression of feeling as a way of showing affection, concern, and caring, not venting. And some use emotional expression as a way to tell others that they really mean what they are saying.

Ideas about emotions—what they are, where they are located, and what to do about them—are deeply embedded in the moral order. For some people, "telling it like it is" is the best way to communicate with others. For other people, "controlling your emotions" is an act of adult responsibility. For still others, emotion is a resource to be used strategically to gain power and change things. Each of these modes of response is appropriate, right, and good from the perspective of the communicator's moral order, but it is appropriate, right, and good only in the context of many other related ideas that constitute the communicator's moral order. One cannot divorce the construction of emotion from the totality of a person's belief system.

Moral difference is part of the human condition. Let us turn now to a more careful examination of what happens when social worlds come to clash.

▨ From Difference to Clash

How do you know a moral conflict when you see one? There is no formula, but certain markers (we hate to use the term "red flags") will be apparent:

1. The participants use the same vocabulary but mean different things by it. For example, *honor* for one means martial excellence, but for the other, economic success.

2. The participants use different vocabularies for comparable functions. For example, one uses a vocabulary of *rights* and the other a vocabulary of *virtues* to discuss morality.

3. The participants describe themselves as locked into opposition with each other. For example, they deny that they have any choices and claim that "in a situation such as this, when they do what they did, a person like me has no alternative, I must . . ."

4. Actions that one side thinks will defuse the situation or even resolve the conflict are perceived by those on the other side as demonstrating the perfidy of the first and obligating them to respond by continuing or intensifying the conflict.

5. Participants are unable to articulate the logic of the other side's social world in ways that the other side will accept.

6. The discourse between the conflicted groups contains a large number of statements about what is wrong with the other group.

7. If asked to imagine a resolution to the conflict, the participants can think only of capitulation and elimination of the other group.

Our studies have led us to expect moral conflicts to have four general characteristics. They are (1) intractable, (2) interminable, (3) morally attenuated, and (4) rhetorically attenuated.

Moral Conflicts Are Intractable

Moral conflicts tend to be intractable in two senses. They are intractable, first, because they are self-sustaining. The original issue becomes irrelevant, and new causes for conflict are generated by the actions within the conflict itself. The means by which the conflicted parties seek resolution become the provocation of continued conflict.

How do we resolve a conflict about a matter of theology when one person appeals to the definitive interpretation by a religious leader and another denies the legitimacy of that leader? How do we resolve a question of political legitimacy when one side appeals to the constitutionality of its position and the other intends to set aside or rewrite the constitution? In contemporary society, the question of how to deal with others who do not think and act like us is a difficult challenge (Pearce, 1993).

Traditional ways of dealing with conflicts assume that there should be an agreed-on way of dealing with conflicts. This agreed-on procedure may specify duels to the death, impartial judicial proceedings, or the decree of the king, but whatever their content, they provide an agreed-on context or frame within which conflicting parties may manage their conflict. In contemporary society, however, this common frame is not always present. In moral conflicts, the conflicting parties not only find themselves at loggerheads about some issue but also disagree about how to go about resolving their conflict. In many cases, each is morally repulsed by actions that the other takes as the appropriate means of resolving the conflict.

Social worlds collide when attempts to resolve even the most ordinary conflicts of mundane life (the problem of garbage removal and disposal?) reveal that we (whoever *we* might be) disagree with them (whoever *they* might be) not only about garbage but also about what means of resolving our differences are morally right, aesthetically preferred, and politically prudent. The question of which one of us is right has produced many a quarrel, but this question is much more tractable than the question of how we should go about determining which one of us is right. Should we resolve our conflict by ballot, bullet, or Bible? Should we persuade each other with good reasons, consult the entrails of a chicken, or conduct a media campaign to convince a plurality of the voters to support our side of the controversy? Should we employ the services of third-party intervention agents, or should we kill or disempower those who disagree with us (including those pesky third-party intervention agents)?

Whatever the issue or cause of conflict in contemporary society, it risks mobilizing groups with incommensurate traditions. In moral conflicts, when each group tries to act consistently with what they perceive is morally good, ethically just, and politically expedient, they "prove" to the other side that they are fools or villains. As the conflict continues, the originating issue is lost and the other side's means of dealing with the conflict is itself the force that drives the interactions among the various conflicted parties.

The originating cause of moral conflicts quickly disappears from the public discourse or is cited more as a club with which to beat one's opponent than an issue to be resolved. Public discourse often focuses on the ways in which the other side's methods of handling conflict are morally depraved.

So moral conflicts are intractable because they are self-sustaining. They are intractable, too, because, ironically, perpetuating the conflict is seen as virtuous by those involved. These individuals are not always—or even usually—oriented toward finding a solution; instead, they may derive important aspects of their identity from being warriors or opponents of their enemy (Northrup, 1989). Conflicts are often treated as if they are disagreements between people who want to settle, but the continuation of conflicts offers highly desirable roles to some participants. Some moral orders even sanctify the role of combatant. If the conflict were to disappear, those most deeply enmeshed in it would miss it most. Coser (1964) noted that conflict is not just a matter of clashing ideas but "a struggle over values or claims to status, power, and scarce resources, in which the aims of the conflicting parties are not only to gain the desired values but also to neutralize, injure, or eliminate their rivals" (p. 232).

On some occasions, the continuation of a conflict is preferable to what would have to be given up if an accommodation with the other side were reached. Azar (1990) suggests that moral conflicts originate in basic human needs, such as "security, distinctive identity, social recognition of identity, and effective participation in the processes that determine conditions of security and identity, and other such developmental requirements" (p. 146). The costs of prolonged conflict might seem easily bearable if these matters were at stake. Those deeply enmeshed in a moral conflict may be unable to discern the effects of the conflict itself, even if those effects themselves threaten the basic human needs that compel the conflicted parties to continue their conflict.

Public discourse in moral conflicts contains the "power words" of the participants. Because the actions of the other side are seen as alien, the discourse seldom stays focused on specifics; it quickly moves to sweeping generalizations, oracular pronouncements, and abstract principles.

Hunter (1991) notes that the conflict between the "progressives" and the "orthodox" is "not just an expression of different 'opinions' or 'attitudes' on this or that issue, like abortion." Rather, "the culture war emerges over fundamentally different conceptions of moral authority, over different ideas and beliefs about truth, the good, obligation to one another, the nature of community, and so on" (p. 49). As a result, the proponents cite God, patriotism, sanity, freedom, the Founding Fathers, or whatever else constitutes their foundational authority.

This excerpt from an argument (quoted by Hunter, 1991) between Randall Terry, a spokesperson for the pro-life organization Operation Rescue, and Faye Wattleton, then president of Planned Parenthood, shows how the issue is fought not on specific issues of policy but on the larger issues of how one's moral order is structured.

Terry: The bottom line is that killing children is not what America is all about. We are not here to destroy our offspring.

Wattleton: Well, we are also not here to have the government use women's bodies as the instrument of the state, to force women into involuntary servitude.

Terry: (laughing) Oh, come on, Faye.

Wattleton: I think that as Americans celebrate the Fourth of July, our independence, and when we reflect on our personal liberties, this is a very, very somber time, in which the courts have said that the most private aspects of our lives are now . . . not protected by the Bill of Rights and the Constitution. And I believe that this is a time for Americans to reflect on the need to return to the fundamentals, and the fundamentals of personal privacy are really the corner-stones upon which our democracy is built.

Terry: I think that to assume or even suggest that the founding fathers of this country risked their lives and many of them died so that we can kill our offspring is pathetic. (p. 49)

Note the power words. Terry introduces the phrase "what America is all about." Wattleton offers some portion of her understanding of the term, identifying "personal liberties" as the key, equating control over "women's bodies" with "involuntary servitude," and citing "personal privacy" as a "cornerstone" of the Constitutional guarantees of liberties. Terry does not refute her attempt to articulate "what America is all about" but pronounces it "pathetic," and the by now familiar pattern of public discourse in moral conflict continues.

Moral Conflicts Are Interminable

Moral conflicts are interminable because they are intractable, but they are interminable for other reasons as well. In moral conflicts, the issues cannot be adequately described in the terms that any of the participants would supply. Because their moral orders differ, they disagree about the meaning and significance of the issues, tactics, or potential resolution. As Wittgenstein (1969) said, "When language-games change, then there is a change in concepts, and with the concepts the meanings of words change" (p. 65).

We have been told of the failure of a well-meaning negotiator who urged both sides of an international conflict to be willing to compromise. One side, valuing compromise as a necessary and virtuous means of democratic politics, readily agreed; the other, for whom compromise meant an irresponsible and immoral surrender of one's principles, was offended and broke off negotiations.

MacIntyre (1981) believes that moral conflicts have "no terminus" and thus "go on and on and on" (p. 6) because the contemporary language of morality is disordered. We inhabit, he suggests, fragments of various intellectual traditions and put them together in incompatible ways. Thus the debate about U.S. military intervention in the next Third World country selected for this honor cannot come to resolution because the disputants are, unknown to themselves, arguing from different moral positions. Even if we can get back to the original positions, we have no basis for choosing among them; thus the conflicts continue unabated.

> It is precisely because there is in our society no established way of deciding between these claims that moral argument appears to be necessarily interminable. From our rival conclusions we can argue back to our rival premises; but when we do arrive at our premises argument ceases and the invocation of one premise against another becomes a matter of pure assertion and counter-assertion. Hence perhaps the slightly shrill tone of so much moral debate. (MacIntyre, 1981, p. 8)

There is relatively little extension of arguments in moral conflict. Each side understandably becomes reticent about offering its cherished beliefs when the other side criticizes those beliefs and/or uses them as "proof" of the other's mistakes. Arguments are not extended because they go past each other by using incommensurate terms and meanings. Even if the participants in a moral conflict wanted to extend their argument, they would be frustrated.

Public discourse in moral conflict is filled with predictable misunderstandings and erroneous perceptions of the other. Key terms for one side are passed over as unimportant by the other or are defined and used differently. For example, in his analysis of culture wars, Hunter (1991) noted that both sides use the same terms—*freedom* and *justice*—but with "almost precisely inverted" meanings. "Where cultural conservatives tend to define freedom economically (as individual economic initiative) and justice socially (as righteous living), progressives tend to define freedom socially (as individual rights) and justice economically (as equity)" (p. 115).

A common pattern in moral conflict is the juxtaposition of incommensurate assertions, followed by a stunned silence or pause after which each side acts as its own moral order suggests. Each participant is surprised and offended by the other's actions and denounces it. Each takes offense at being denounced and protests its own virtue . . . and so it goes.

Public Discourse in Moral
Conflicts Is Morally Attenuated

Participants in moral conflict often abandon what their own moral order values as the "best" forms of behavior. During the Cold War, for example, the West engaged in many undemocratic practices because it was "forced" to do so by the actions of its enemy, the international communist bloc.

Those who engage in conflict always run the risk of coming to resemble the other—their "enemy"—with whom they are locked in the most intimate of embraces. Gay rights activists sometimes sound awfully hateful when they accuse their opponents of being hatemongers. We can delude ourselves into thinking that "our" new weapons are good but that "their" new weapons are threats to peace. The dreadful irony is that in the very process of combating that which we despise, we become it.

Less metaphysically, conflict always privileges some tactics over others, and there is no reason to assume that the values of one's moral order fit perfectly with the winning tactics in a particular conflict. Given a discrepancy, will the ideal or pragmatic prevail? Those who prize integrity over success may preserve their integrity but lose the contest; those who prize success may win the contest but not recognize themselves when they ascend to the victor's platform.

In moral conflict, demonization of the opponent is a particularly seductive strategy. Once demonized, any other dirty trick, from simply excluding them from polite conversation to wars of extermination, seems appropriate.

Our capacity to live peaceably with each other depends upon our ability to converse intelligibly and reason coherently. But this ability is weakened by the very differences that make it necessary. The more

we need it, the weaker it becomes, and we need it very badly indeed.
(Stout, 1988, p. 3)

Public Discourse in Moral
Conflicts Is Rhetorically Attenuated

The rhetoric of moral clash contributes to a state of disarray in public discourse. We do not wish to blame anyone for this problem. We believe that the poor quality of much of contemporary public discourse is the unintended outcome of well-meaning spokespersons who are doing their best to handle difficult conflicts. As Burgess (1970) noted, however, the times are out of joint, and normal ways of dealing with conflict do not work (p. 125). Said differently: Not all conflict is alike, and the ways of managing conflict that are effective and positive in some situations may be ineffective or counterproductive in others.

Many genres of talk are possible in moral conflict. These include dialogue, interviews, appeals to precedents or maxims, elaborations of particular visions or the good and beautiful, exhortations to do good and resist evil, condemnations of the other, and research into the pragmatic effects of various policies. Given so rich an array of possibilities, MacIntyre (1981) was struck by the frequency with which statements that express disagreement are used in moral conflict and the infrequency of the other types of statements (p. 6). Perhaps MacIntyre's observations focused on more restrained people than ours; we are struck by the extent to which people in moral conflicts invidiously categorize and descriptively denounce the personalities, intelligence, social manners, personal ancestries, prospects for eternal abode, and reasoning of those with whom they disagree.

Of course, to say that a discourse is *attenuated* means "compared with something else." We are particularly struck by the contrast, noted in our report of the anti-CIA demonstration in Chapter 1 of this volume, between the discourse that takes place when opposing sides converse with or at each other in public and that which takes place when they speak in more friendly situations, whether among themselves or to a good listener not identified with the other side. The discourse between groups is coarse, brutish, shallow, and brittle compared with that within groups. To the extent that the content of public discourse resembles this between-group rhetoric, it cannot function as the site of democratic processes.

Sophisticated rhetoric consists of a shared quest for "good reasons" for believing or acting in certain ways. In moral conflict, the patterns of communication that occur more typically include ad hominem attacks, denunciations, and curses. Slogans and chants replace arguments intended to persuade and inform; various forms of denunciations and diatribes squeeze out scarcely noticed opportunities for dialogue.

In our experience, deeply enmeshed members of conflicting groups usually cannot give rich accounts of the moral orders of the other group. When they are urged to do so, their accounts end rather quickly in offensive descriptions ("they are just stupid!") or attributions ("they are evil and can't be trusted"). They are able to give rich accounts of their own moral orders, however—if we can hear them in their own terms.

Hearing another person's moral language, if that differs from our own, is difficult. In a major study of contemporary American society, Bellah, Madsen, Sullivan, Swidler, and Tipton (1985) sought to identify the moral languages of "ordinary Americans" (pp. 20, 161-163). The researchers "did not seek to impose our ideas on those with whom we talked"; however, they "did attempt to uncover assumptions, to make explicit what the person we were talking to might rather have left implicit. The interview as we employed it was active, Socratic" (p. 304).

A respondent in one of these interviews said that "lying is one of things I want to regulate." The interviewer, Ann Swidler, asked, "Why?"

> Well, it's a kind of thing that is a habit you get into. Kind of self-perpetuating. It's like digging a hole. You just keep digging and digging. . . It's just so basic. I don't want to be bothered with challenging that. It's part of me. I don't know where it came from, but it's very important. . . . . Well, some things are bad because . . . I guess I feel like everybody on this planet is entitled to have a little bit of space, and things that detract from other people's space are kind of bad. (Bellah et al., 1985, pp. 304-305)

Swidler and the others interpreted this conversation as showing that this respondent lacked a sufficiently powerful moral language. When confronted by a persistent Socratic interviewer, he was quickly reduced to incoherent babbling about everybody having space and so forth. Noting that he is a middle-aged man who is successful in business, whose first marriage failed but who has remarried and is thoughtfully restructuring his life to make sure that this marriage succeeds, Bellah and his colleagues concluded,

> His description of his reasons for changing his life and of his current happiness seems to come down mainly to a shift in his notions of what

would make him happy. His new goal—devotion to marriage and children—seems as arbitrary and unexamined as his earlier pursuit of material success. Both are justified as idiosyncratic preference rather than as representing a larger sense of the purpose of life. (p. 6)

In his commentary on this research, Stout (1988) suggested that Palmer spoke an eloquent moral language, just not the one that Swidler was prepared to hear. Palmer grounded his moral judgments in a narrative of his own life rather than attempting (until Swidler kept prompting him) to make categorical ethical pronouncements. When describing his own experience, Palmer used a moral vocabulary of reciprocity, involvement, shared goals, and mutual respect; his lame individualism was not his "first moral language" but his language of "last resort" when talking with a relentless (and relentlessly academic) interviewer (pp. 195-196). In his analysis of the interview, Stout warned that

there are many propositions that we are justified in believing but wouldn't know how to justify. Anything we could say on behalf of such a proposition seems less certain than the proposition itself. By now it is hard to debate with flat-earthers. What real doubt do they have that can be addressed with justifying reasons? . . . We ought to be suspicious of people who want reasons even when they can't supply reasonable doubts. (pp. 35-36)

When Brian Palmer said that the wrongness of lying is basic, Stout (1988) argued that what he means is that "he can't think of anything more certain than the wrongness of lying that might be introduced to support the idea that lying is wrong. He'd rather not be bothered with the sort of challenge that the question implies" (p. 195).

Palmer's rich moral language became rhetorically attenuated in his attempt to respond to his interviewer, and his interviewer was unable to give a well-developed analysis of his moral order because she was not attuned to hear what he said as an answer to her questions. In this way, the discourse among people with different moral orders often become rhetorically attenuated.

✺ Is There a Better Way?

The more important issue, of course, is not whether we can recognize or even understand moral conflicts. It is whether we can do something about them. Fortunately, we do not have to hope or imagine that there are effective ways of improving the quality of public discourse in moral conflict. Part III of this book describes several projects that demonstrate both that it can be done and some of the ways in which it can be done.

Moral conflicts can be viewed from many perspectives, of course. However else they may be seen, they may be understood as a particular form of communication. This perspective is useful in understanding how moral conflict can be managed more effectively.

Conflict Is a Precarious Pattern of Interaction

The heading of this section is deliberately designed to be provocative. If one's interest in moral conflict starts, as ours did, by observing fully grown, passionate struggles, patterns of communication seem remarkably persistent and impervious to change. But if one looks more closely at their etiology, these patterns appear far more unnecessary and fragile. Indeed, asking how conflicts begin and how they develop can be useful questions.

If we ask how people get from "here" to "there" in a conflict, then we begin to wonder, "Aren't there a number of points at which people could have handled their conflict differently?" And then the next question becomes, "What did they do to get into this sorry state of affairs?" When we address this question, we are guided by three principles of communication.

First, communication is a process of *making* and *doing*. If we want to understand communication, we must ask what is "made" and what is "done" when it occurs. So, for example, when Bob and Ellen argue about money, they may be *making* a personal world in which money is a defining quality of their relationship. And, depending on their own sense of what is going on, they may be *doing* any number of things— fighting, arguing, bantering, kidding, filling time, establishing power, or something we cannot even imagine.

Likewise, when anti-gay moralists and pro-gay advocates fight in the street, they are doing something they might call "returning to basic values," "protecting human rights," "fighting hate," "resisting oppression," "establishing moral action," and so on. And in the process, they are making what we call moral conflict.

We can never know exactly what is being made or done in the abstract because the meanings of communication depend on its context.

And that is our second principle: Communication is contextual. Just about everybody takes this general idea as a truism, but we mean something more muscular than the common idea that meanings are determined by context. For us, the context affects meaning, but meaning in turn establishes context.

Any act of communication, such as Bob and Ellen's argument or a gay rights battle, is connected to what has gone before and what will happen next. Each act we perform is both "out of" and "into" a context. What Bob and Ellen are doing and what they are making are determined in part by what they did and made before, and that in turn establishes a basis for understanding what they will do and make next.

Furthermore, we assume that there is never only one context. We are always acting out of and into contexts structured by stories of who we are, of our relations to other people (whether present or not), of what we are doing, and of what is going on around us. There is no fixed limit to the contexts of any action.

We assume further that contexts are made by the communicative acts that occur in them, just as actions themselves are formed by the contexts in which they occur. Both the text and context are aspects of unfinished, continuous patterns of communication. If one asks activists to interpret something they said during a gay rights campaign, they will answer differently, depending on the outcome. If the gay rights measure passes, proponents will describe their actions as skillful campaign practice, and opponents will say that they fought the good battle for morality. If the measure fails, proponents will say that they stood up for individual rights in the face of great adversity, and the opponents will say that they were merely expressing the moral sense of the majority. What is made and done depends on the past, but it depends on the future, too.

The third principle that guides our analysis is this: Communication is a process of coordination. Although awkward to express, the point is that an act is never completed by one party alone. A request requires the presence and response of someone who can grant the request. A promise requires another person to hear and respond favorably to an intention. A child is always disciplined by another person, and an audience does not exist without a performer. How can there be a war with only one side? How can there be a debate with only one advocate? The meaning of an act, then—what is made and done—depends in large measure on the responses it elicits. And the response elicits a response, which leads to another response, and another, and another. Communication, then, is not merely a process of transmitting information to another person; it is always a continuing process of coordinating actions.

Hope for Change

The three principles outlined in the previous section provide real hope that negative and intractable patterns can change. Because communication is contextual, people can change the pattern of conflict by telling different stories about what they are doing and making. Mediators are often successful because they do offer opportunities for changing the context of the dispute by suggesting new frames for defining what is going on.

Looking at the pattern of interaction in a new way is nothing more than restructuring the context. There are a number of practical ways in which this is done. One is to change the number of participants and the roles they play. Staub (1989), for example, notes the effect of bystanders or observers in inhibiting the worst excesses of violent behavior. Just by having others there and bearing witness to some other group, the context changes.

The context can be changed by addressing a different audience. For example, when Reagan and Gorbachev met at their first summit meeting, they found that the discourse they had previously used became strikingly inappropriate when they were in one another's presence (Pearce, Johnson, & Branham, 1992). The same thing happens when people who are accustomed to yelling at each other at public rallies and street confrontations are put into a private setting. People can restructure the context too by establishing special forms of communication requiring new types of responses. Some of these are discussed in detail in Part III of this book.

If communication is created by people together as an act of coordination, then third parties can skillfully participate in making new, more productive patterns. Without a mediator, for example, a gang member's demand to meet with the mayor might well be judged as a ploy and rejected out of hand by the mayor's staff. A mediator, on the other hand, might ask just the right question to elicit a different response: "If the mayor agreed to meet with you, how would that make things different?" Here a "demand" is changed to a "prediction."

Without a third party present, a spokesperson's accusation that opponents are fools would likely be greeted with a counterinsult. A mediator, on the other hand, might reframe the comment in a way that transforms the context: "It sounds as if you would really like to discuss this issue on an intellectual level." Here a dirty "insult" is changed to a positive "challenge." These types of intervention moves can open up the opportunity for different patterns of communication to develop.

◙ From Theory to Practice

The only (!) problem with the ways of improving the quality of public discourse outlined above is that they require us to act skillfully in ways that are not anticipated in the natural course of events. They require the development of new forms of communication and new skills, and that is hard work.

These skills do not require inordinate motor reflexes or even unusual intelligence. They do require certain unlearnings. One cannot practice these skills well if one shares Plato's distrust of the people, which leads to a single-minded reliance on expert opinion. Such a preference for expertise, coupled with the facts that experts differ in their opinions and that some of these differences are incommensurate, constitutes a recipe for moral conflict. The opposite of this preference for expertise is not the absurd belief that ignorance is best but the recognition of the difference between technical expertise and knowledge of other sorts. It is the difference between a single-minded subordination of all human interests to the technical and the enlightened recognition that even folks who do not know how to build a bridge have interests that might be best served if the bridge is not built.

In the same way, these skills in managing moral conflict cannot be practiced well by those who think of conflict as do Machiavelli and Alinsky. As Fisher and Ury (1981) taught us, the dichotomy between a hard and soft style of bargaining does not exhaust the available alternatives. If it did, there would be no difference between giving in and transforming the conflict; there would be no difference between the sensibilities of Jean-Henri Dunant, who saw something more fundamental than the question of who won and who lost, and the sensibilities of a coward with no physical courage. Yet these differences are regularly occluded in the editorial pages of our newspapers and on radio talk shows, where self-appointed savants equate openness to new solutions with a failure of nerve, inconsistency, and a backing down from one's position.

Finally, these skills cannot be practiced well by those who cannot see what is said and done in a conflict as a move in a game that is incomplete and framed within many contexts. The ability that needs to be developed is that of focusing on what one wants to create rather than responding to what other people have done. For example, several nations—including Germany, Cambodia, Japan, Argentina, Uruguay, Chile, El Salvador, Nicaragua, and Haiti—have recently been confronted with the problem of dealing with people who committed atrocities. If the issue is posed as a choice between justice or mercy, then it seems that one must decide to punish them or to grant them amnesty, and both have significant negative implications. The decision to punish them continues the cycle of state-sponsored violence; the decision to grant them amnesty undercuts the sense of justice.

Several countries have hit on a strategy that recognizes the atrocities and holds the perpetrators to account but does not punish them. The decision is to frame the issue as "truth." For example, in Argentina, a blue-ribbon committee published an exhaustive account, naming names and showing pictures, of the atrocities of the "dirty war" and presented it in a formal ceremony to the president. It was titled *Nunca Más*, or "Never Again." There is a sensibility here that is hard to describe. It involves taking responsibility for perpetuating patterns of social interaction, whether of war, abuse, oppression, or simply a devalued public discourse, and, without exonerating the guilty, simply declares that the pattern stops here and acts accordingly.

We can respond to moral conflicts in a number of ways. In the following section of the book, we explore several communication patterns that collectively form a response to the difficult character of contemporary times.

PART II

Communication and the Expression of Difference

4

The Quality of
Public Discourse

In August 1994, Congress was battling over the Omnibus Crime Bill. President Clinton, knowing that crime was a pivotal issue among voters, had a lot at stake politically, and congressional Democrats too saw the bill as a way to gain votes. But alas, the bill included more than money for law enforcement and prisons. It included substantial funding for social prevention programs such as Midnight Basketball. There the Republicans joined the issue and prevented passage of the bill. This was a significant defeat for the president and a precursor of the Republican sweep just three months later.

The debate on this bill, like that on all major legislation, should have modeled the finest and most eloquent discourse of our society. It should have been a time in which keen argument and incisive analysis were

AUTHORS' NOTE: Excerpts in this chapter quoted from Carey (1993) are from P. Gaunt, ed., *Beyond Agendas* (Greenwood Press, Westport, CT, 1993), pp. 177, 181, and 183. Copyright © 1993 by Philip Gaunt. Reprinted with permission. The story "Warrior of God on Terrorist," by Rob Hampson, is reprinted here by permission of the author.

presented for public scrutiny. But instead, political argument in the United States often models the worst rhetoric. What seems to secure votes and what enlightens the citizenry appear to be two different things.

During the Senate deliberation on this legislation, Senator Alfonse D'Amato displayed a picture of a pig and unabashedly sang, to the tune of "Old MacDonald," lyrics that described the bill as having "some pork here; some pork there; here pork; there pork, everywhere pork pork." Although Senator D'Amato's doggerel is not the first bit of nonsense introduced in congressional deliberations and the "speech" was perhaps not exactly typical, it does show the levels to which major politicians can stoop to get a vote or two (Lev, 1994, p. 4).

In criticizing the state of public discourse, we are imagining the possibility of a public sphere in which democracy can take place. The issue turns on whether the public sphere is something we have lost or whether it never existed except as a convenient fiction. Robbins (1993) compiles an impressive array of arguments that "the public" in modern capitalistic nation-states never has and never will exist (pp. ix-xiii). In our view, there are many publics, all of which have multiple agendas and overlapping memberships, and public discourse is far too richly textured to constitute consensus:

> The languages of morals in our discourse are many, and they have remarkably diverse historical origins, but they do not float in free air, and their name is not chaos. They are embedded in specific social practices and institutions religious, political, artistic, scientific, athletic, economic, and so on. We need many different moral concepts because there are many different linguistic threads woven into any fabric of practices and institutions as rich as ours. It is a motley: not a building in need of new foundations but a coat of many colors, one constantly in need of mending and patching, sometimes even recutting and restyling. (Stout, 1988, pp. 291-292)

The lack of a political consensus or the plurality of moral languages, then, does not prohibit good public discourse or democratic process. Rather, it simply requires the development of the skills in and the establishment of better forms of communication. Such forms of communication exist; they do not have to be invented. They do need to be institutionalized as a regular part of our public life.

Given the possibilities in these forms of communication in light of Bakhtin's (1986) description of how the heteroglossic "carnival" is a defense against tyranny, who would want a public sphere? Who would seek consensus or an official language of culture or morals? That is not our aim in this book because to achieve such a consensus, even if it were possible, would be to stifle inherent moral diversity that needs to be expressed in the full light of day—but expressed in new ways. In this chapter, we are concerned with four questions:

1. How should the quality of public discourse about public issues be evaluated?
2. How important is the quality of public discourse about public issues?
3. What explanations can be offered for the poor quality of public discourse?
4. Can anything be done to improve the quality of public discourse about public issues?

Our answers to these questions are straightforward. We judge the quality of public discourse about the public's issues as poor and take this as important. We believe that public discourse of a sufficient quality is essential for any government that claims to be, in Abraham Lincoln's terms, of and by as well as for the people and for those who define themselves as citizens rather than subjects or consumers.

The poor quality of public discourse stems from several factors, of course. In this book, we describe one that has received relatively little attention: the prevalence of and difficulty in managing moral conflicts. Moral conflicts differ structurally from other forms of conflict and require unusual patterns of social communication to be managed well. Because of their unique characteristics, application of "normal" ways of managing conflicts only exacerbates moral conflicts and erodes the quality of public life.

Finally, we show that public discourse, even discourse within moral conflicts, can be improved. This claim is not simply idealistic. In Part III of this book, we cite several existing projects that succeed in creating the conditions for better public discourse.

☙ What Is the Quality of Public Discourse?

Discourse in the United States is in an alarming state of deterioration; it sorely needs critical analysis and reconstruction. Communication has become increasingly ill tempered, abusive, and dogmatic; the agencies responsible for nonpartisan inquiry and reporting are too readily engaged in distortion and special pleading. The intellectual class is smug and intolerant; its members speak with contempt not only for the opinions of the general public, but for those of each other as well. (Gouinlock, 1986, p. 5)

Not everyone agrees with Gouinlock's assessment that the quality of public discourse displays "an alarming state of deterioration." Some who disagree focus on the amount of information available within U.S. society. They point to the four freedoms of the First Amendment to the Constitution and recent Freedom of Information legislation. They remind us of the sheer impossibility of restricting access to information in an era in which photocopiers, e-mail, computer disks, telephones, and the Internet are available. The most common problem with information is that of indexing and processing rather than not having enough of it.

Others who disagree focus on the strategic use of information. Our dismay at Senator D'Amato's song will seem naive to those who are primarily interested in achieving their own purposes through strategic use of public messages. For those with a campaign manager's or advertiser's ear, D'Amato is likely to be praised. His performance got him ample media attention (this was the substance of most newscasts' treatment of the crime bill on that day), and he expressed his position on the bill in a manner that was powerful and memorable. From this perspective, that we opened this chapter with a reference to D'Amato's song proves their point: D'Amato acted skillfully and effectively within the context of contemporary public discourse by getting us to remember and repeat his message years later in a new context.

Still others who disagree with Gouinlock's assessment focus on access to the media. We are in an era of unprecedented access to the means of producing messages. Just as the typewriter and printing press made it possible to publish books without having to pay for a roomful of scribes, so the development of the computer, modem, fax machine, photocopier, direct mail technology, and audio and videotape recorders has enfranchised ever larger groups within society as potential rhetors.

Yet others who disagree with Gouinlock's judgment that the quality of public discourse is poor cite the extent to which elected officials confer with "the public" and respond to their constituents. But these appearances are deceiving, as veteran pollster Daniel Yankelovich (1991) argues:

Paradoxically, the more "democratic" the formal side of American political life has become, the less real voice the American public has in shaping national policies. . . . Talk to members of Congress and they will tell you that they spend most of their time being responsive to their constituents. But if you ask them who these constituents are, they turn out to be lobbyists and special interests, not individual citizens— or at least not those with average incomes. (p. 2)

We are sympathetic to Yankelovich's suggestion that the "deep structure" of public discourse excludes certain voices. It also lacks argumentation in which assumptions are challenged, in which the challenge is heard and responded to, and in which the response itself is understood and taken into account. Lacking extended and developed rounds of rebuttal, public discourse is poor in comparison with what a good argument should look like.

We take public discourse to be the place in which people who disagree with each other should and can come to understand each other's reasons for their beliefs and together make judgments about what is right, true, and prudent; we have in mind discourse that serves the interests of the public good. We are dismayed by the extent that the term *public discourse* is often identified with "the news," with "horse-race reporting" about who is winning and losing a political contest, with sound bites and slogans of partisan wrangling, and with the reciprocated diatribe of those who wage verbal warfare.

The quality of public discourse about the public's business has been routinely criticized in recent years, and with good reason. Important issues are avoided or ensnared in hostile, partisan charge and counter-charge. As a result, the public's ability to form judgments about the common good is often paralyzed among "competing systems of moral demand" (Burgess, 1970, p. 125) that leave the public without a clue as to what to believe and how to act.

Some blame the poor quality of public discourse on public apathy, but those who talk with ordinary people about public issues challenge this description. "Decades of public opinion poll data . . . show that this charge of voter apathy is a bum rap. Average Americans, including those who do not vote, hold deep and passionate convictions on many issues of public concern" (Yankelovich, 1991, p. 3). Yankelovich adopts the metaphor of the "glass ceiling" to describe the condition of the public:

Beneath the surface of formal arrangements to ensure citizen participation, the political reality is that an intangible something separates the general public from the thin layer of elites—officials, experts, and leaders who hold the real power and make the important decisions. (p. 3)

At least part of this intangible barrier is a pattern of discourse so fractured that citizens are frustrated in their attempts to take a turn in the public conversation.

The quality of public discourse, not the quantity of opportunities to exchange messages, drives the people out of politics. Studies by the Harwood Group (1991) show that citizens see public discussions, letters from congresspersons, and the like as a waste of time because there is far too much lecturing, posturing, and evasion and not enough listening and responding to their concerns.

> People report, "I have been to too many public meetings wondering if I'm wasting my time." Or they confess, "When I come home from work I think, 'Why should I attend a public meeting since it won't change anything?'" Comments like these are common. People think that hearings don't work because little hearing goes on. Officials usually make presentations or get lectured to by some outraged individual. Little two-way communication occurs. And with no feedback, people don't think they have been heard. The prevailing sense is that a decision was reached long before the hearing was scheduled.
>
> Rather than answer questions, citizens feel that officials will dance around them by answering a question that was never asked or by attacking the individual who posed a question originally. A woman described the experience that led her to this conclusion: "In a recent debate, I hoped that the candidates would say something that would be really clear. But it turned out to be mudslinging at the other candidate. I feel like making them answer the question." So Americans get the impression that officials "give the public lip service and go their merry way." (Mathews, 1994, p. 23)

We believe that thorough, balanced, empowered, egalitarian public discussion is the driving force of democracy. The most common forms of public discourse in contemporary society, however, are simplistic and shallow. Much of the talk by public figures seeks to influence and persuade, not to invite dialogue, to subvert the messages of others rather than to engage them. People tend to blame and demean those who disagree with them rather than to find opportunities to discover why it is that equally intelligent and well-meaning people can come to opposing sides on an issue.

Our "leaders" employ the sophisticated tactics of advertising to control the national agenda, even though this means reducing public issues to slogans and sound bites and treating "we, the people" as consumers of political products rather than as citizens active in the process of self-government. Consider Michael Deaver, who served in the Reagan administration as a public relations adviser. At least in the early days of the administration, he was reputed to have equal policy-making influence with Attorney General Edwin Meese and White House Chief of Staff James Baker. Deaver described his work at the White House as "a Hollywood producer" and boasted of his ability to get the television news media to present candidate (and later President) Reagan in a manner that fit his strategy. He deliberately used pictures rather than words and simplistic slogans rather than more fully developed arguments. Asked if he were proud of his effect on public discourse, he described himself as regretfully adapting to the sorry state of the public (Moyers & Flowers, 1989).

We believe that Deaver's derogation of the American public is common among those who shape public discourse and that it has two deleterious effects. First, it impoverishes the public sphere by excluding "moments of moral doubt and strategic indecision. . . . There can be no room for qualification, no allowance for unforeseen contingency. Since real social problems cannot be solved this way, ceremonial public discourse must become increasingly detached from political reality" (Weiler & Pearce, 1992, p. 13). Second, "It creates what it portrays itself as responding to: an apathetic electorate, uninterested in the campaign, uninformed about the issues, and increasingly alienated from the practice of national political power" (p. 14).

There is no shortage of public discourse, but there is, in our opinion, a great shortage of quality discourse in which good questions are more important than assertions of moral privilege or the exercise of power. Conspicuously missing is discourse in which we discover the values and ideals that underlie our differences rather than shouting down or overpowering those who disagree. MacIntyre (1981) quite rightly refers to the "shrill" nature of moral conflict (p. 8), and Goldfarb (1991) noted that although "serious intellectual reflection continues to exist . . . it is becoming a specialized market, along with surfing, skiing, and gourmet cooking, consistently not reaching the general public. Shouting, partisan, talking heads are replacing the pluralistic search for the common good" (p. 63). There is a sad shortage of what Evans and Boyte (1992) call "free spaces" (p. 15) in which "people are able to learn a new self-respect, a deeper and more assertive group identity, public skills, and values of cooperation and civic virtue" (p. 63).

❦ Is the Poor Quality of
Public Discourse Important?

People disagree not only in their assessment of the quality of public discourse but in their judgment of the importance of public discourse itself. At issue is one's theory of communication, including a notion of how communication works and what it does. Those who think that communication is a secondary process of publicizing a plan will not treat the quality of public discourse as important unless it hinders the plan.

On the other hand, those who consider communication a form of action that constitutes the events and objects of our social world treat public discourse as inherently significant. Here, communication is the "stuff" that composes the public's business, the process in which our social worlds are made (Pearce, 1989).

The relation between communication and the other aspects of our social worlds—such as truth, reality, knowledge, and morality—has been a source of conflict throughout the history of Western civilization, and the position one takes on this issue determines much of the rest of one's political or intellectual project. Twenty-five hundred years ago, the issue was contested by the Sophists on one side and Plato on the other (Pearce & Foss, 1990). Plato treated communication as a secondary social process. He believed that whatever is "real" must be eternal and immutable. As a result, communication worked best as a means of discovering already existing truth (through a discursive form known as the dialectic) or by making already known truth more persuasive through rhetoric. Because of what Plato described as the sorry state of the audience, politicians or educators might have to embellish truth with rhetorical devices (such as singing to the Senate and the television cameras about pork in the crime bill) to persuade them of what the enlightened leaders already knew.

Plato scolded his contemporaries, the Sophists, for making these rhetorical tricks available to people who had not gained philosophic insight. As a result, Plato thought, uneducated people would use communication irresponsibly, to make the worse appear to be the better and to sway "mere" opinion rather than help people discover truth. According to Plato, dealing with communication in itself, rather than as a means of expressing "knowledge" gained through philosophic insight, was an unworthy enterprise; at best, it produced a knack like cooking rather than wisdom.

Plato's influence established an undemocratic tradition. Among other things, it set up a bias against public opinion, viewing it as fickle, inconsistent, and with no solid foundation in unassailable knowledge. As a result, communication with "the people" is seen as a way of generating consent for policies chosen by their betters. Plato would see no problem with the state of affairs that so many contemporary commentators worry about, the inability of the public "to participate in the political decisions that affect their lives."

> The fateful decisions are made in Washington, in corporate boardrooms, on Wall Street, in state legislatures, and in city halls. They are shaped by economic experts, military experts, scientific experts, trade experts, PR experts, media experts. Less and less are they shaped by the public. (Yankelovich, 1991, pp. 1-2)

Plato's foil, the Sophists, treated communication as the primary social process. They believed that the use of language creates and destroys reality as well as revealing and concealing it. This view has had new life in the 20th century. For example, Dewey (1922) said, "Apart from conversation, from discourse and communication, there is no thought and no meaning, only just events, dumb, preposterous, destructive" (p. 280). Rorty (1979) articulated an increasingly popular direction in current social theory—the idea that what we know is created by conversation, "the ultimate context within which knowledge is to be understood" (p. 389).

Those who treat communication as the primary social process—and we count ourselves among them—have deep affinities for democracy. We are not blind to the often cited problems with public discourse, but they are convinced that public discourse is the only way by which good decisions can get made. This commitment to public discourse is a commitment to what Barber (1984) calls "strong democracy." He describes the discourse necessary for this type of public deliberation as involving "receiving as well as expressing, hearing as well as speaking, and empathizing as well as uttering" (p. 174). He elaborates further that

> "I will listen" means to the strong democrat not that I will scan my adversary's position for weaknesses and potential trade-offs, nor even . . . that I will tolerantly permit him to say whatever he chooses. It means, rather, "I will put myself in his place, I will try to understand, I will strain to hear what makes us alike, I will listen for a common rhetoric evocative of a common purpose or a common good." (p. 175)

This way of thinking opposes any absolutist theory held by partisans who cannot or will not engage in dialogue when their most cherished commitments are potentially subject to question and revision. Such partisans fail to realize that their own commitments are themselves made up of particular patterns of communication, and their sense of loyalty, integrity, and sometimes even fanaticism are deeply rooted in their own form of discourse. Consider the following, all-too-familiar scenario.

Committed to a progressive style of government, a city council holds public hearings on a proposed city ordinance. The council chambers fill up with perhaps a hundred concerned citizens. Each is allocated three minutes to speak. Virtually all use their time to demand, persuade, or advise the council to vote for or against the policy. After the marathon session, council members are dazed and numbed, but they receive little help in weighing the choices they face or in assessing the relative merits of the arguments for and against the ordinance. Afterward, they note that all the citizens talked to the council, not to each other, and that all left even more convinced of the rightness of their own position. As a result, anything that the council decides to do will infuriate those citizens who took the time to come to the council and now feel that their voices were not heard.

This problem is not limited to the United States, of course. Local authorities in some European countries are concerned about the low level of public support for their policies. No matter how carefully they research the various possibilities, and no matter how confident they are that they have made the right decision, they find that the residents in their towns are suspicious of them and do not support the choices they have made. This is often more than just a cause for regret. Lack of consensus sometimes translates into an inability to implement the decisions and sometimes means that they lose their jobs during the next elections. Some communities in Germany and some other countries are experimenting with "citizen juries." In the same way that juries are selected for a criminal trial, a panel of citizens is chosen to listen to advocates argue for and against the policy. The decision of the jury advises the authorities and is seen as a way of saying, credibly, that the authorities involved citizens in the decision.

One criticism of the citizen jury system is that although it does involve a sample of citizens, it maintains the adversarial forms of communication that have become the model in much of public discourse. This adversarial model has virtues, of course, but increasingly its limitations are being recognized. Among these limitations is the treatment of the issue as a dichotomy; the type of argumentation that citizens hear freezes them as well as the advocates into totalizing defense of particular positions. Left unsaid—and which become virtually unsayable in these forms of communication—are all the moves that might introduce additional options or more moderate positions.

As these examples show, a concern with the quality of public communication is not limited to idealistic professors insulated from the hurly-burly of political realities. Increasingly, those in the trenches of political offices, campaigns, and journalism are expressing deep concerns about what is done and not done in public communication. They note that there are few models of public deliberation and that campaigns have become competitive contests in image building and sloganeering in ways that treat candidates as commodities to be packaged and sold rather than avenues for the intelligent discussion of issues.

The technology of mass communication, the professional conventions of journalists, and some robust characteristics of group dynamics combine in a way that make extremism a winning strategy of personal aggrandizement and social power. The most extreme voices are the ones that make news; shrill voices denouncing enemies become identified as the spokespersons of the group. Important issues such as a national health care program or balancing the budget are either displaced in the public sphere by recriminations about family values (as if anyone were actually opposed to them) or transformed into bargaining chips in a competitive campaign for partisan advantage.

From our perspective, it makes sense to inquire about the affordances and constraints of any form of discourse, to explore fully the powers and limits of each. Our position is a shift from an emphasis on the "truthfulness" or "correctness" of a principle or decision to an emphasis on the continual process of communication in which that principle or decision is a part. Rather than be "right" (whatever that might mean), we prefer to have what Aristotle called practical wisdom and Dewey (1929) social intelligence.

As Wittgenstein (1969), Dewey (1929), and Bernstein (1992) have shown, this is a radical innovation in Western intellectual history; its counterpart in public discourse is correspondingly radical. Among other things, it leads to an uncompromising commitment to the importance of the quality of public discourse and to the institutionalization of new ways of dealing with moral conflicts.

▧ Why Is the Quality of
Public Discourse So Poor?

> Our capacity to live peaceably with each other depends upon our
> ability to converse intelligibly and reason coherently. But this ability
> is weakened by the very differences that make it necessary. The more
> we need it, the weaker it becomes, and we need it very badly indeed.
> (Stout, 1988, p. 3)

There are many strains on the quality of public discourse. Among
the most frequently cited are these:

- The hegemony of "experts" and an increasing gap between expert/technical discourse and the discourse of the electorate
- Public apathy and the triumph of advertising over deliberation as the preferred genre of campaigning
- The structure and function of the media, which favor short, shallow, photogenic messages and which have an insatiable need for "news," particularly the sordid and the sensational
- The incommensurate demands between the goals of late capitalism and democratic processes, particularly the commoditization of politicians, political principles, and the arenas for public discourse
- The transformation of the public into consumers that results when politics becomes a subset of marketing
- The de-evolution of the polity into multiple special interest groups and the evolution of lobbyists and political action groups (PACs) as the primary rhetors in public discourse
- (Of course) Greed, arrogance, and immorality of politicians

Without commenting on these and other factors, we hope to create an
awareness of another: the prevalence of and inadequate ways of dealing
with moral conflicts.

Moral conflicts degrade the quality of public discourse in at least
three ways. First, unless they are handled well, the patterns of communication produced in moral conflict do not facilitate democratic processes or enhance the quality of public discourse. As we showed in
Chapter 3, "normal" ways of handling conflicts, when applied to moral
conflicts, result in communication patterns that are intractable, interminable, morally attenuated, and rhetorically attenuated. They fit Mathews's
(1994) description of many Americans' perception of politics: " 'Politics'
makes them think about what they see on television and read in the
newspaper: massive and indifferent bureaucracies, corrupt officials,

pressure tactics, negative campaigns, and crowds screaming at one another. In other words, it is a mess" (p. 2).

Second, to the extent that these degraded forms of communication fill the space for public discourse, many citizens do not want to or cannot figure out how to participate in public discourse without simply adding to the cacophony. Third, because these degraded forms of communication do fill the space for public discourse, many citizens "learn" that this is the way to participate in democratic processes. As a result, when they do join in, they reproduce these unfortunate patterns of communication.

Moral conflicts are those in which the participants not only differ about what they want, believe, or need but also lack shared procedures for arguing their claims and standards for judging the validity of those arguments. For this reason, the conflict often escalates to a second level. Not only do disputants disagree about whatever was the originating cause of the conflict, they disagree about how the opponents argue their case, often to the point of repugnance. The discourse in moral conflicts often turns quickly from the originating issue to the inadequacies or perfidy of the other side. So, for example, we hear one side tell the other it is stupid for using the Bible as proof, and the other responds that the first side is immoral for using science!

The following hypothetical conversation is roughly based on the creationism debates that occur in school board hearings to determine the content of textbooks:

Pro: Yes, it is!

Con: No, it is not!

Pro: The best scientific evidence shows . . .

Con: There you go again! Trusting science instead of God's Word. Your Godless, heathen attitudes have caused the deterioration of society.

Pro: You narrow-minded bigots aren't going to restrict what my child studies!

Con: You arrogant fool!

Pro: You benighted throwback!

At this point, we leave the conversation as it turns into a form of a reciprocated diatribe in which each side vilifies the other and the originating cause of the dispute gets momentarily forgotten.

How did public discourse get so bad? There are probably many explanations. Here is one way of telling the story of how moral conflict has become one of the most serious challenges to public discourse.

At the time of the American Revolution, the primary challenge to a public discourse was seen as the long arm of King George III in the form of censorship. The colonies were, by current standards, media deprived. The only means of mass communication were oral speech and print, the supply of orators and books was relatively small, and most people were illiterate. News was difficult to obtain and, when available, was often received long after the events in question had occurred. In this context, the democratic impulse took the form of freeing speech, press, religion, and assembly from the shackles of government or religious restraint. The architects of the new nation envisioned a vigorous public discourse emerging.

The founders' sanguine faith in the "free marketplace of ideas" as the context for a public discourse, however, depended on three characteristics of their society that they took for granted. First, the public was relatively small. Second, the public was culturally and ethnically homogeneous. They were all male, Protestant Christians (of varying degrees of devotion perhaps), had read all the same books, referenced the same symbols for their public experiences, and located themselves within the same set of stories as ways of identifying their personalities and political commitments. Third, they shared a particular notion of eloquence. Rhetoric was an important part of their curriculum, and this gave them a common sense of what constitutes a good argument or good reason for belief and action.

These unacknowledged assumptions were accurate enough for the founders to act as if there were a public sphere in which unrestrained communication could lead to public judgment. Those not part of this public sphere were expected to be led by their more educated and articulate betters. In other words, whatever moral differences existed— and we have reason to believe there were important ones—were suppressed or hidden by the normal discourse of the day.

Skipping ahead a century, the United States was much less media deprived at the end of the 19th century than it had been at the end of the 18th. Bennis (1989) claims that the contemporary United States has been shaped more by the industrial revolution in the 19th century than by the political revolution in the 18th (see also Boorstin, 1978; Cronon, 1991).

Although it spanned a much larger space, the country was now linked by telegraph, trains, and newspapers. The new technologies of mass transportation and telegraph gave rise to the centralization of ownership and the bureaucratization of the mass communication system.

After the industrial revolution, the freedom of the press became the freedom of the owners, not necessarily the freedom of journalists, to publish what they chose. At the end of the 19th and beginning of the 20th centuries, newspapers had become big businesses that bore the clear imprint of their owners' political commitments. A recurring irony is experienced by working journalists who champion unrestricted freedom of the press when talking to the public and then submit their stories to an editor or producer, who decides whether, in what form, when, and where their stories will be published.

Culture and communication technology combined to create a new sense that the nation was one place; the 1890s saw the formation of a sense of "a national economy, a national polity and a national culture" (Carey, 1993, p. 180). Not only were the borders connected to the center, but the spaces in between were, whether they wanted it or not, integrated into the common public. Carey's analysis is worth quoting at some length here:

> In 1892 it was announced that the frontier had closed, that the society had been fully enclosed in space. The expansion of the railroad and telegraph had, first of all connected the major cities into a national system of transportation and communication. Then, in the later years of the nineteenth century, the vacant spaces were "backed and filled," hooking "island communities" into a national society. This process everywhere met local resistance, but the "system was the solution" and communities everywhere were either integrated into it or circumvented by it and left to die.
>
> The closing of the frontier represented larger closings and transformations. Space was enclosed in two senses: first the nation was enclosed, reaching its manifest destiny as a prelude to a leap beyond its own borders in imperial expansion. Second, space was enclosed institutionally as national networks of communication invaded the space of local institutions. That is, local institutions of politics, commerce and culture were reconfigured as end points or nodes in national structures. Local political organizations became outposts of national parties; local business became elements in chains; local newspapers, lectures, performances, concerts and educational institutions became, in a manner of speaking, stops on a national circuit. They lost their autonomy increasingly, their local identity.
>
> Time was also transformed and opened as a new frontier. Time was, first of all, standardized into a national grid so that everyone was on the same clock of awareness. The telegraph organized and controlled

time zones so that organization and activity could be coordinated
nationally. . . . Eventually, nationally produced communications would
occupy every space and every time: every office, home, street, city and
institution; every time, sacred and secular, seasonal and annual, day-
time and nighttime; we would never be out of earshot or eyeshot of
national media. (p. 177)

Several subsequent events made the moral assumptions of the
country's founders even more difficult to apply to communication in
an early capitalist economy. For example, the influence of the Hearst
newspapers in the Spanish-American War set a disturbing precedent
for the role that owners of the media might play in making national
policy, and 60 years later, the myth of objectivity permitted journalists
to be manipulated by Senator Joseph McCarthy with his unsubstanti-
ated charges of communist infiltration and influence.

These two examples bracket a period in U.S. history that raised
troubling thoughts about whether the forms of communication practiced in the media were serving the purposes required for democratic
processes. The Hearst case indicated that the media might have too
much power; the McCarthy case that it might have too little.

The 20th century has seen a communication revolution in the
United States and throughout the Western world. During the first two
thirds of the 20th century, the United States became a media-saturated
society, using as primary media film, radio, and television as well as
print. The structure of the media during this first phase of the communication revolution impelled it toward a centrist position. The production and distribution of a book, newspaper, or television show was a
capital-intensive effort made profitable only by hitting a relatively large
market segment including those with considerable disposable income.
With this market segment in view, those who participated in public
discourse tended to think of their society as culturally homogeneous
(even though it was not), sharing a common rationality (even though it
did not), and composed of stable rhetorical situations (even though new
situations were being developed and the legitimacy of old ones was
being undermined).

By the 1960s or so, however, a series of developments had begun to
undermine the plausibility of the myth that politics occurred in a public
sphere in which there was a common rationality. For example, reliance
on "expert judgment" in all areas of life increased, so that Katz and
Lazarsfeld's (1955) model of the two-step flow of information fit neatly
into conventional wisdom.

The national traumas of the 1960s brought with them clear recognition of the different cultures within the state, as well as a deep suspicion about the adequacy of information given by the government or provided by the media. Daily government briefings in Vietnam were commonly referred to "the Five O'Clock Follies," and a sustained credibility gap made President Johnson's reelection and ability to govern so difficult that he withdrew his candidacy.

Although the media were (largely) free from government influence, they were proudly and openly subject to the forces of the marketplace. Information and other cultural symbols were made into commodities, valued by their going price in the marketplace. Inevitably, the mercantile values of the owners shaped the practices of the communication industry. Consequently, the alchemy of the marketplace transformed audiences from consumers of the content of the media to the consumers of the product generated by the media and sold to sponsors. Ratings and distribution statistics became the criteria of success because these were markers that fit into the price schedule offered to sponsors.

The last third of the 20th century has witnessed a yet unfinished newer phase of the communication revolution. Like the first wave, this one is technologically driven; unlike the first wave, this one democratizes the communication media rather than centralizes them. Inexpensive computers, video and audio recorders, and other media make it possible for more people to produce and distribute messages; the Internet, specialty publications, and user-controlled media have increased the discretion of the public in what they watch or read. Several consequences of this phase of the communication revolution are apparent.

For one, competition within the communication industries has increased. In journalism, professional standards are fighting a losing battle against the demands of the marketplace. The traditional distinction between news and entertainment has been eroded by the practice of assigning nonjournalists as the corporate heads of the news departments and by the explicit slide into sensationalism as a means of capturing a larger share of the reading/viewing public.

The audience has been fragmented. As the objects of intense competition for their attention, members of the public can choose to read, watch, and listen to programming tailored for their specific interests. For example, a recent mailing from American Family Publishers listed 131 magazines that might occupy our attention, including *Alaska, Game Players: Nintendo Sega, Bowhunter, Field and Stream, Wildlife Conservation, Decorative Crochet, Woodworker, Word Wize,* and *Yachting.* Local cable companies are moving in the direction of providing 500 channels on a 24-hour-per-day basis. Already (in Chicago) there are two national and international news channels and one 24-hour local news channel, a court channel, an all-sports channel, a weather channel, and a shopping channel. There is talk of a 24-hour golf channel! Direct and electronic mail technology has created the opportunity for entrepreneurial development of private means of communicating within a group of like-minded people. We seem to be moving from the domination of mass communication to a new microcommunication in which public information needs are met in specialized, rather than generalized, ways.

Cultural diversity has changed from the awareness of discrete groups separated in space to the experience of "otherness" as a regular aspect of life. It is not that differences are being eliminated so much as the alien "other" is no longer "over there" but "here." Carey (1993) comments,

> The age of large undifferentiated total societies facing off against one another is, relatively speaking, gone. The old comparisons of East versus West, primitive versus modern, developed versus underdeveloped, anthropologist versus native do not work anymore. . . . The natives, if you will forgive me, are everywhere and so are we. If someone is predicting the weather from the entrails of a chicken, chances are he is living next door. If there is widow-burning going on, it is likely to occur outside of town rather than halfway around the world. The most recent cases of cannibalism I have encountered have not been in darkest Africa but in relatively enlightened Milwaukee. (p. 181)

Communication media have become a new "place" in society comparable with "church," "school," and "courts." We regularly talk of something getting "into the media." As a place, the media have a strange geometry: Distance is eliminated, funny things happen to time, and the usual distinctions among contexts such as private and public are drastically reduced.

This structure of the media focuses attention on definable groups and stresses the differences among those groups, both as potential audiences for specialized programming and as the content for programming itself. There is a legal and popular recognition that our society is a motley in which the practices and institutions of many cultures have not "melted." The differences in rationalities among various parts of our culturally diverse society are recognized, although various people disagree about how to think about these differences.

Some would institutionalize a common culture, generally that associated with "dead white males" (Bloom, 1987), others would celebrate diversity and accept the moral and political relativism that comes with it (Simonson & Walker, 1988), and yet others believe that we must develop and institutionalize new ways of dealing with cultural diversity and the moral conflict that it spawns (Kegan, 1994). The rhetorical situations in which public discourse occurs are recognized as shifting and fluid. For example, in the 1960 election, presidential candidates debated; in the 1992 campaign, they appeared on a talk show format; today, President Clinton is available on the Internet. What's next?

⬙ What Can Be Done to Improve the Quality of Public Discourse?

At the time of the American Revolution, it seemed that all that was needed to improve public discourse was to eliminate restrictions. At the end of the 20th century, however, the solution to the problem created by King George III is not likely to suffice for us. Today, an open discursive arena is necessary, but far from sufficient, to improve public discourse.

Contemporary culture confronts us with forms of diversity with which historical democratic institutions were never designed to cope. Carey (1993) elaborates,

> The very technology that is bringing us together physically and imaginatively is just as assuredly driving us apart. . . . To believe that we have a purchase on a new world of diversity is a delusion of those who visit difference armed only with spiritual traveler's checks. We are as confused, though often as arrogant, as the first anthropologists encountering the first natives. And we have a critical problem. Because in the midst of these unsettling changes we stubbornly cling to the hope of forming a democratic world, we wish to retain amidst globalized diversity a public space for citizenship. But what can public space or citizenship mean when Time Warner proclaims that "the world is our audience"? Having failed to create a national public space, we now are charged with the problem of creating an international one. And, closer to home, our received notions of democracy are tested by forms of public diversity they were never created to contain. (p. 183)

The freedom of speech is far from absolute, and so it should be. We rightfully prohibit marketing poisons without clear warnings and require accurate product identifications; we make slander and libel crimes and prohibit lying under oath. These restrictions are best understood as ways of regulating the discursive arena, making it possible for good public discourse to occur. But what else is possible? What else is necessary?

The very fluidity of rhetorical situations provides us the opportunity we need to create spaces in which new forms of communication can emerge. There are "fragile, fugitive moment[s]" when social worlds collide in which, "with a lot of luck," if we "describe difference in an intelligible and mutually acceptable way . . . [and] humanely articulate difference to difference," we can "produce a public space of citizenly discourse" (Carey, 1993, p. 183). The common ground in such a space is not based on agreements about issues or the worldviews that contextualize them. Rather, it is built on "an agreement about how we should contend over our moral and political differences—a public agreement over how to disagree publically" (Hunter, 1994, p. 35).

The creation of such spaces requires at least some of us, at least some of the time, to be more concerned with the process than the outcomes of political activity. This is not a matter of being uninterested in issues; it is a matter of being sufficiently invested in the quality of public discourse that we work to create the conditions for that type of "abnormal discourse" in which we acknowledge that the participants do not have "an agreed-upon set of conventions about what counts as a relevant contribution, what counts as answering a question, what counts as having a good argument for that answer or a good criticism of it" and in which we "attempt to make some sense of what is going on at a stage where we are still too unsure about it to describe it" (Rorty, 1979, pp. 320-321).

▧ A Position

As authors, we are taking a particular position in this book, a role that might be termed "neutral." This term is in quotation marks because it is used in a narrow sense. To be a partisan means to side with one of the conflicting parties against the other. Authors frequently do this, and appropriately so. Given the problem we address in this book, however, ours is a different role, one that comes with an obligation for fairness, open-mindedness, and catholicity in our accounts of moral conflicts. We accept this obligation, and others will judge how effectively we carry it out.

As citizens, we have our commitments. We sometimes take sides, debate, and fight for what we believe is right. When we take an activist role, we try to achieve change of a certain type that might be labeled *first-order change,* to legalize abortion, establish gay rights, and resist creation science. Activism, important as it often is, has its limits. Such work, as we explained in the previous chapter, is encapsulating because the relationships among the conflicting parties are reinforced.

Another type of change might be termed *second-order change.* Here the social arrangements in which conflict is played out are themselves modified. The history of most organizations and societies is that of perpetual first-order change and infrequent second-order change. So although we say we are neutral in this book toward the first order of change, we are definitely not neutral toward second-order change.

In our analysis of ways of managing moral conflicts, we attempt to look beyond the justifications and emotional engagements of particular partisan positions to see the structure of the conflicts themselves. We believe that most participants in moral conflict act in ways that, to the extent that they are successful, bring about only a first-order change. The problem with perpetual conflict focusing on the first order is that these means of managing conflict have extensive collateral damage. For example, gang wars about who can use certain street corners to sell drugs have wrecked whole sections of cities as residential areas for law-abiding people; international wars about who will have access to a seaport or oil field have killed millions of people and caused extensive damage to the environment; political wars between developers and environmentalists, pro-life and pro-choice advocates, and the proponents of individual rights and family values have impoverished, rather than enhanced, the quality of public discourse necessary for democratic government.

In this analysis, we strive to adopt a specific form of neutrality in which we are less concerned about the outcome of any specific conflict than we are in the means by which it is conducted. One useful analogy for what we mean by neutrality is that of a referee in an athletic event. The referee should be passionately, professionally committed to having a good game, played according to the rules, and—at least during the game—uninterested in which team wins. These neutral activities of the referee allow professional football to be played without devolving into team mud wrestling; they allow basketball players to jump and run without fear of being tripped or clotheslined. Just as the elegance of these games depends on the safety provided by a set of rules and a referee, so the elegance with which participants in conflict perform depends on the social situation in which they find themselves.

The analogy of the referee breaks down, of course, because moral conflicts are not played within the context of agreed-on rules and with explicit agreements to submit to the judgment of an impartial interpreter of those rules. Moral conflict usually develops in something like a free-market economy in which participants do everything they know to do that is not counterproductive. No wonder so many moral conflicts resemble mud wrestling!

Our perspective is simple: Moral conflicts are too important and the prospects of collateral damage too great to ignore the potential for second-order change. We are not proposing the model of a commissioner of a sport to establish a set of rules that conflicted parties must obey. To the contrary, we are describing, commending, and inviting others to join the activities of others who have become involved in specific moral conflicts not as partisans but as participants who help shape the way the conflicts are managed. By taking a referee-like perspective, we can develop a sense of how moral conflicts usually work out and develop the ability to intervene (at least sometimes) to restructure the way they are managed. If done well, the restructured way of dealing with moral conflict will produce a better public discourse.

In the following chapters of this book, we explore the type of communication necessary to establish change of the second order—to improve the quality of discourse, public and private, in moral disputes.

5

Patterns of
Expressing Difference

In 1991, the former Yugoslavia came apart. After Croatia seceded from
Yugoslavia in 1991, Serbian rebels in that region waged a bloody six-
month war for territory and drove hundreds of thousands of Croats
from their homes. In the ensuing years, and up to the time of this
writing, the various ethnic groups of the region have been battling to
draw lines between and, some believe, even eliminate one another.

As part of the regional struggle, Serbian forces in the newly formed
Bosnia-Herzegovina began what some observers called an ethnic cleansing
campaign against the Muslims there. The horror of the Bosnian civil war
has been made increasingly real by news of atrocities such as the
discovery of a mass grave containing the bodies of thousands of Muslims near the town of Srebrenica in 1995 and reports of "rape camps."

In August 1995, purportedly in an attempt to stop Serbian aggression in Bosnia, Croatia moved militarily against Serbian forces in the
occupied territories of Croatia and Bosnia. More than 200,000 Serbian
refugees streamed out of Croatia. As they fled, Croat people lined the

roads in anger to bid them a violent farewell. The Croats created a veritable gauntlet of flying bricks, manure, and ethnic hatred through which the desperate Serbs had to traverse. The Serb refugees who made it out of the country were determined to return in revenge.

The ethnic struggles in this region reproduce a pattern of interaction that has been going on there for centuries and a pattern of intergroup violence occurring throughout world history. We do not know how the Yugoslavian conflict will play itself out in the end, and we certainly do not presume to understand all the factors contributing to it. But one lesson is clear: We human beings do not always deal well with our differences.

▧ Orienting to the Other in a Postmodern World

In their treatise *The Homeless Mind*, sociologists Peter Berger, Brigitte Berger, and Hansfried Kellner (1973) explain that in most of human history, people lived in small, cohesive societies in which differences could be managed by an integrating framework, usually religious. But "the typical situation of individuals in a modern society is very different. Different sectors of their everyday life relate them to vastly different and often severely discrepant worlds of meaning and experience" (p. 64). Berger and his colleagues show how this tendency is exacerbated by urbanization, or close contact among different peoples, and mass communication, or dissemination of confusingly diffuse realities. It is also exacerbated by political and territorial interests.

We human beings find meaning in associations with others within a community. But we cannot have a community without a boundary to separate us from "outsiders." Often, as in Yugoslavia, the line between the community and the outsiders is political and ethnic. Sometimes it is territorial or regional. Sometimes the boundary is religious, sometimes it is racial, and sometimes it is ideological. Sometimes it is economic, gender based, or generational. And much of the time, it is a combination of these. Boundaries can be formed from anything that makes "us" different from "them."

All human beings use language to establish a sense of self and other, to define the boundary, and to create some sort of orientation toward others. This process is inherently social. It is accomplished through communication, as stories of "us" and "them" are told and retold. It is precisely through such stories that we create a sense of coherence about who we are. Such stories determine the way we live and the way we orient to others.

> Because they are ensconced in stories, births are political events as well as biological facts. They determine the succession of dynasties and provide the means by which mortal individuals attempt to achieve some manner of immortality. Bawling infants are central characters in stories they did not choose—stories that will shape their experience with the physical and social world. Deaths do not merely mark the termination of a particular life, but are invested with religious and legal significance. Sexuality has been endowed with so much significance that it complicates and enriches human life in everything from fashion to philosophy. The ingestion and elimination of food are surrounded by taboos and rules of etiquette in every culture, and those who do not follow these rules offend those who do. National or religious symbols become more precious than life itself, and our heroes would rather face death than dishonor. The quality of the stories we tell determines whether we confront the facts of life with equanimity, ecstasy, or dread. If we tell confused stories, we will be confused, and if we pursue confused stories too literally, they can drive us mad. If our stories are too far out of touch with the facts of life, we will experience recurrent problems; if our stories provide sufficient affordances, they facilitate coordination. (Pearce, 1989, pp. 68-69)

So facts do not by themselves drive human action, because any set of facts can be understood from the perspective of a nearly infinite number of stories. Stories become the driving force of human understanding and action. A story liberates us from mere facticity, but it also ensnares us in the world that it creates. In our stories, the lines between "us" and "them" are drawn, and in our stories we learn how to orient to "The Other."

Our ways of orienting to one another constitute forms of communication that shape the ways we treat the people around us and how we act on our stories. Sometimes, we treat other people as part of "us" and are not cognizant of differences. In this state, we assume that other people are part of our community and share our stories. Except for the most remote tribal peoples (are there any left?), this is a temporary state, at church, in the family, at work, or in any of the other transient settings in which we live.

Other times, we are aware of differences. We do not assume that other persons are like us or will understand or share our stories, as life in any city makes clear. When meeting a stranger, we ordinarily assume a boundary of some type. Sometimes, we find that the boundary is not there and fall comfortably back into whatever stories we share. Other times, we cope with the expected differences without difficulty. Other times, such differences strain our relationships and cause unpleasant conflict.

Our orientation to other people is also affected by whether we are willing to put our stories at risk. Sometimes, we hold on to our stories and protect them against risk and change. Other times, we willingly allow our stories to be challenged. When that happens, our stories may change, and we may change. When stories are challenged, boundaries change, and old enemies become new allies. "They" become "we."

Patterns of communication, then, are determined by how we treat others and whether we are willing to put our stories at risk. We have come to talk about the expression of difference as five patterns, outlined in Table 5.1.

▧ When Difference Is Not a Problem

Human differences are not always problematic, of course. Our discussion would be incomplete without recognizing such moments. The first two patterns are of this sort.

Pattern 1: Celebrating Similarity

The first pattern of communication occurs when groups work to recognize, enjoy, and bolster their similarities. At such moments, difference is either out of awareness or downplayed in a state termed *monocultural* (Pearce, 1989). It involves living with others in a shared and unchallenged social reality. In the monocultural mode, one's way of being is not challenged, nor does one expect it to be. Children are often in this state, and adults seek and find it in enclaves of many types.

Because monocultural communication is such a natural way of being human, we join groups and clubs of like-minded people to have a place to practice it, a place in which stories are shared and not questioned. This state is inviting, too, because it does not normally

TABLE 5.1 Patterns of Expressing Conflict

Pattern	Orientation to Difference	Orientation to Communication	Orientation to Change
Pattern 1	Absent or inconsequential	Celebration of similarity	Change resisted
Pattern 2	Acknowledged and sought	Celebration of difference	First-order change desired
Pattern 3	Acknowledged and problematic	Persuasion	Attempt to change the Other
Pattern 4	Major obstacle and essence of relationship	Frustration Diatribe Force and violence	Attempt to suppress or eliminate the Other
Pattern 5	Difference and similarity acknowledged and valued	Dialogue	Open to second-order change

involve conflict, or if it does, shared stories provide the means by which the conflict is understood and played out.

One of the appeals of monocultural communication is that it rarely presses us beyond relaxed thinking. We do not need to take foreign categories into account when dealing with other people because those people share our stories. This pattern of communication is easy, which makes it a comfortable mode in which to live. Within a monocultural enclave, differences are neither expected nor encountered. The monoculture is governed by a coherent moral order, and its stories do not permit difference. But every now and then, we have to look out the window, and when we do, we will see a different world there.

Of course, this pattern is not always as pure as it might seem. Sometimes, it is more like a pseudo-environment or fiction that maintains a pretense of similarity. Organizations are often like this. They appear on the surface to be monocultural, and powerful forces operate to keep moral differences under the surface (Fine, 1995; Littlejohn, 1995b).

The problem of this first pattern is that if we stay in it long, we will not change, grow, encounter new things, or expand our awareness. Important moral differences will be ignored and suppressed.

Education, at least in liberally minded democratic societies, is supposed to counteract monocultural forces by exposing students to new ideas and stories. Such expansion is believed necessary for the improvement of society, but we don't need to go to school to get exposure to

"The Other." It is virtually impossible in the world today to remain in a monocultural state for long.

Pattern 2: Celebrating Difference

Sometimes, we are willing, even eager, to put our stories at risk by interacting with individuals who are different from us. The diversity movement in schools is predicated on the healthiness of this mode of communication. It says in essence, "People are culturally different, and that is good. We need to learn from and respect one another." In Pattern 2, we deliberately seek out difference and change in a type of exploratory form of communication. Although one could spend a year traveling around the world without seeking difference, most sojourners enjoy travel precisely because it is an opportunity to explore other ways of being human, to learn new stories.

Being exploratory requires seeing connections among stories, relating one system of thought to another, and importing ideas from one community into those of another. This pattern leads one to strive for improvement, to search for the ultimate good by seeing the various ways in which peoples at different times and in different places have come to understand their experience.

Pattern 2 involves an exploratory communication and a relativistic temperament, but it also embodies an intercultural modernism. Personal improvement and the increasing approximation of truth are pursuits of modernity, and some people do this by exploring foreign ideas. Politically, those who identify with this mode of communication call themselves *progressives* because they are striving to progress toward betterment rather than conserve the outdated values and practices of the past.

In this mode of communication, conflict and change are prospects, not problems. The exploratory communicator is open to change by learning new information, adopting alternative perspectives, and changing attitudes and opinions. Such communicators recognize that conflict is a way in which such change can be achieved, and that is why they put their stories at risk. Exploratory communicators expect to be jarred, but only temporarily, while they adjust to the opposing reality.

In this form of communication, then, we search out differences, put our stories at risk, and hope for change. This can be exciting for a while, but people who stay in this mode too long begin to lose touch with who they are. They get caught in a cycle of change that sometimes feels like a runaway train. Rather than moving closer to perfection and truth, the modernistic traveler sometimes gets lost in a postmodern world of great uncertainty and loss of identity: Celebrate the new until it is no longer new, then change it; celebrate the new until it is no longer new, then change it; celebrate the new, and so on. The inveterate exploratory communicator ends up with a pastiche personality that is everything and nothing (Gergen, 1991).

Some people prefer the exploratory mode and make it a life's journey. Others try it for a while and then abandon it, and others fear it, staying as far away from it as they can. At its best, this pattern is a happy state, but when it gets old, it becomes a disillusioned one, as neotraditionalism itself stands to prove.

▧ When Difference Is an Obstacle

We all have stories we are not willing to put at risk, and some people are willing to endanger none of them. When we recognize difference but move to protect our own stories, difference becomes problematic. Actually, viewing difference as problematic is normal and good. It is a way of finding solace in a storm of difference. It is a place in which we can find truth in a field of varying versions of truth. It is a way to establish identity and community. In its soft form, resisting difference involves a healthy reliance on certain stories to inform our experience and thereby to establish a point of view from which to experience the world, but at the same time, it makes others look outdated, quaint, undeveloped, subordinate, and even outlandish.

In its hard form, resisting difference is ethnocentric, and this can lead to the worst of human abuses. Racism, sexism, hatred, and fear are the children of this mode of communication. When we take our own stories too seriously, oppression, violence, and genocide can result.

In the face of difference, we can become acutely aware of outsiders and act to shield ourselves from the damage they may do to our way of life. Categories can get hardened, and protective measures can become extreme. We do not need to look far to find examples of ethnocentric communication in its worst forms and have presented several in this book already. It is sometimes difficult to see the problem when we look at our own ethnocentric communication, but when we look elsewhere, the limits of this mode come right into focus.

How do we handle problematic differences? Here we discuss two ways, identified as Patterns 3 and 4.

Pattern 3: Using Persuasion

People express their differences in a variety of ways. At least initially, most parties rely on their own rhetorical sensibilities to make a case for their point of view. Assuming the superiority of their own story and methods of argument, they communicate with "rhetorical eloquence." In our society, initial persuasion is usually civil. Advocates assume that their visions and rhetorical standards are compatible. They believe, often correctly, that both sides will appeal to the same values and standards of judgment. In this situation, persuasion is normal discourse. Appeals are made, and decisions are rendered by whatever criteria are in force.

When we assume that our own frame of reference is superior and our own forms of argument compelling, the appropriate form of communication for resolving conflicts among compatible views seems to be rigorous demonstrations that our position properly meets the standards of good knowledge and appropriate action. As we discussed in the previous chapter, different worldviews have different forms of rhetorical eloquence. In some cultures, it consists of nonverbal demonstrations of prowess; in others, skillful wordplay; in others, excellent storytelling skills; and in yet others, the ability to adhere to rules of logic, evidence, and scientific proof. As long as disputing parties share a frame of proof, persuasion is possible.

Each form of rhetoric is like a game, governed by rules. When the rules are followed, the rhetoric is judged eloquent and effective, and when they are not, it is deemed substandard. Wittgenstein (1953) called these forms of rhetoric *language games;* Toulmin (1958) called them *fields of argument.*

Aristotelian rhetoric is in our society a paradigm case of rhetorical eloquence. Aristotle recognized that life, by its very nature, is contingent rather than certain, and thus it often is impossible to get clear rulings about the true, the good, and the beautiful in politics, economics, and the other fields. Aristotle believed that conflicting claims could be resolved by reference to logic and evidence, artfully represented in rhetoric. Used effectively and ethically, rhetoric would lead to an ability to make good judgments.

Because good judgment inevitably falls short of certainty, intelligent people of good motives may still disagree about matters of policy. According to Aristotle, the primary reasons why conflicts are handled poorly is the inability or unwillingness of rhetors to reason sharply enough or to consider the available evidence. Thus, Aristotelian rhetoric leads to an emphasis on increasing the sophistication of speakers and audiences so that they may exploit the potential of language, draw from a rich array of argumentative forms, impose rigorous critical standards on would-be persuaders, and make steady progress in becoming more competent advocates for their points of view. This has been the goal of modern courses in speech and rhetoric for years, and a whole tradition of rhetorical theory has developed through the centuries to address this concern (Harper, 1979).

Several traditional methods of conflict intervention are commonly employed as part of this pattern. Democratic processes, involving debate and election, are one way of trying to settle conflicts in democracies. But campaigns and elections are not always possible or appropriate. Adjudication through litigation or arbitration allows parties to the dispute to make their cases before a decision-making authority. Negotiation and bargaining are also common methods for achieving settlement, and mediation is increasingly popular for settling disputes.

All these forms of argument and intervention are what we call *normal discourse*. They are normal within a shared story of how to argue and settle disputes. And often normal discourse is precisely what is needed to express and settle our differences. But as we have repeatedly seen in this book, it will be effective only when the parties to a dispute share a common discourse. As long as all sides buy into the forms of argument and intervention employed, as long as these work for the parties, they create a common frame within which to discuss and settle disagreement.

But not all disputes are like this. Moral conflicts by definition involve differences in which normal discourse does not work. Simply put, the normal discourse of one group does not match that of the other. Debate, no matter how eloquent or civil, does not work because the standards of argument of the two sides do not match. Adjudication does not work because it is a form that is not permitted within the worldview of one side. (Or it works because the system forces it on the parties, but the conflict keeps coming back.) The parties do not easily engage in bargaining with one another because bargaining means different things to them.

The pluralistic state of modernity prevents any set of rhetorical standards from prevailing at all times. Rhetoric scholar Thomas Frentz (1985) writes, "Where once agents could be presumed to share a common social knowledge from which moral action might emanate, that presumption has become all but untenable in an age of increased specialization and the concomitant proliferation of technical knowledge" (p. 4). The frustration of not having such a common morality is exactly what motivates conservative education writers such as E. D. Hirsch (1987), Allan Bloom (1987), and Dinesh D'Souza (1991) to struggle to reestablish such a common frame.

Several areas in which rhetorical standards may vary from group to group have been suggested (Toulmin, 1958). In some cases, for example, the ideographs, or value terms, will be incompatible (McGee, 1980). Such terms serve as argumentative warrants, and when they are incompatible, the arguments on one side will not meet the rhetorical standards of the other. In some situations, the grammar of one side becomes abhorrent to the other, as, for example, when pro-life advocates use terms such as *murder* for abortion and *unborn child* for fetus and pro-choice advocates refer to *back-alley abortions, terminating pregnancy,* and *reproductive rights.*

Persuasive efforts may be incompatible because the stories behind them are incompatible. Narratives elicit shared experiences with particular audiences, and some narratives strike an unexpected chord in audiences holding incompatible stories. In an analysis of two antiabortion films, *Eclipse of Reason* (1984) and *The Silent Scream* (1987), Branham (1991) found heavy use of the conversion story. Both films are narrated by Bernard Nathanson, who is a physician and former abortionist, a convert to the pro-life position. The films feature medical personnel who began to oppose abortion because of their experiences. In contrast, narratives on the pro-choice side tend to center on the horrors of illegal abortion: "Here's what happened to me, and I don't want it to happen to anybody again." These incompatible stories reveal incommensurate moral structures in the discourse on abortion (Littlejohn, 1993).

The metaphors of competing discourses may also be incompatible, as *silent screams* and *coat hangers* certainly are. What happens when the elements of persuasion are indeed incompatible? Sometimes disputing parties agree to live with the incompatibility and create a contract of civility (Branham & Pearce, 1987). In a civil arrangement, the pattern of rhetorical eloquence remains the same, but within an atmosphere of toleration. Each side insists on expressing its ideas while allowing the other the right to do the same. Kennedy's Lynchberg address, "Tolerance and Truth in America," came after a vicious period of attack and counterattack between spokespersons from Religious Right organizations and opposing groups. Among its many functions, this speech extended a contract of civility to Falwell and his supporters, as Kennedy managed to invite Falwell into a continuing relationship in which the two could talk civilly with one another (Branham & Pearce, 1987). A year and a half later, the two met again and spoke at the National Religious Broadcasters convention in Washington.

Although this event was not a reunion of allies, a definite atmosphere of toleration was apparent. Civility makes it possible to live with the difference for a time, and it can even provide respite from the stress of battle. But civility seems to have a short life span. As we noted elsewhere, "Despite the surface civility of the [Kennedy-Falwell] debate, it is interesting to speculate . . . on how each side of this debate would interpret the other. . . . The debate provides no foundation for resolution of the conflict. The worldviews remain incommensurate" (Pearce et al., 1987, p. 190).

Civility requires worldviews in which tolerance is possible, but as is often the case in moral conflict, one or both of the parties cannot sustain it. In the case of the Religious Right, for example, the traditionalists often reject tolerance out of hand. Although the liberal critics espouse tolerance, they are often incapable of dealing with the paradox involved in "tolerating" an "intolerant" group because in so doing they would have to accept that which they reject.

For these reasons, civility is frequently illusive. After a particularly rancorous period at the University of Massachusetts in the early 1980s, a civility commission was formed to suggest ways for the university community to patch its differences and work together without bigotry. The commission consisted of faculty, staff, and students committed to the goal of peacemaking. On the surface, they seemed to have consensus on what this goal meant. However, Freeman (1985) found that the members held vastly different ideas about civility and the ways of achieving it. The commission's own "civility" covered up deep differences that were either unexpressed or unperceived.

Traditional rhetorical methods are indeed effective in many disputes, but because of their restrictive character, such methods do not work in cases of moral conflict. Indeed, they often serve only to harden the division and create frustration. Rhetorical strategies may themselves become important moral issues within the traditions of the advocates. As often happens, then, civility can lead to frustration, transforming rhetorical eloquence into diatribe, even violence. When the best persuasive efforts of the parties fail, they enter the frustration phase, and uglier forms of expression result.

Pattern 4: Moving to Repress

At some point, the parties and public become aware that conflicting moral orders in some cases are incompatible. For activists, this often happens when their best arguments are turned against them. The frustration that results from failed rhetorical eloquence and played-out civility often leads to *reciprocated diatribe*, in which participants protect their most precious beliefs by expressing their perceptions of the faults of the other. We expect others to follow the moral rules we believe govern society, and we invoke harsh sanctions for not following such rules, including ostracism and damnation (Freeman et al., 1992).

Diatribe is *vilification*, "a rhetorical strategy that discredits adversaries by characterizing them as ungenuine and malevolent advocates" (Vanderford, 1989, p. 166). Diatribe involves ad hominem arguments that are simplistic, undeveloped, and inflammatory. As we saw in the previous chapter, otherwise intelligent speakers for the New Christian Right and its critics made inane comments that questioned opponents' morality or intelligence. One observer wrote that it is

> not surprising that the Moral Majority's actions tend to provoke intense reactions. However, while the more vitriolic of these responses may express adequately the moral indignation of their authors, they do little to illuminate either the Moral Majority or its rhetoric. (Conrad, 1983, p. 159)

In its extreme forms, this type of communication is confrontational, agonistic, and redressive, a "moral dramaturgy intended to assault sensibilities, to turn thought upside-down, to turn social mores inside-out, to commit in language the very same barbarisms one condemns in society" (Windt, 1972, pp. 7-8). Although many moral conflicts do not contain this degree of offensiveness, some level of intemperate moral indignation is often encountered.

Diatribe seems to be a natural result of frustration in having one's best arguments ignored or rejected by opponents. In the pro-life/pro-choice debate, for example, diatribe serves to clarify the enemy as target, to characterize the conflict as a fight against evil, to mobilize the movement against a threatening outside group, and to magnify the opponent's power (Vanderford, 1989).

Diatribe is essentially nonphysical, but we all know that the old adage about "words will never hurt me" is wrong, and hurtful words can and do sometimes lead to physical violence. As any police officer can testify, there is often a fine line between verbal and physical assault. Diatribe is a type of dehumanization of the opposition, which can make violence seem like a natural and appropriate response. Domination, subversion, repression, and violence too often occur in this pattern of communication. When rational discourse appears to be impossible, forceful tactics designed to secure compliance become more attractive.

The question of when frustration spills over from diatribe to violence is complicated, and we do not presume to be able to predict when violence will result. Many people attribute intergroup violence to psychological factors such as uncontrolled emotion or pathological tendencies. Within the frame of moral conflict, however, the problem of violence is surely more complicated than this.

Ascher (1986) makes a compelling case for the role of moral positioning in intergroup violence. Ascher found various positions on violence within two activist groups in the United States supporting violent organizations abroad. In general, the belief structure of those who defended violence in these two groups had three characteristics. First, they had a strong identity with the in-group, even though they were not personally present with the group. Second, there was a strong sense of moral indignation. And third, these individuals believed that the enemy had disdain for their group as evidenced by a history of perceived persecution. But even for those who support violence, this option is not taken as gratuitous vengeance but as an instrumental means of accomplishing well-defined goals. It is a case of ends justifying the means. Ascher concludes that "emotions and principles are generally mutually reinforcing. The presumption that support for intergroup violence serves psychological needs *rather* than expressing moral positions is, at least for long-standing confrontations, misguided" (p. 421).

Repression and violence signify the ultimate failure of traditional administrative, judicial, and democratic forms of decision making. They reflect society's inability to work through differences. In his well-known book, *The Uses of Disorder,* Sennett (1970) points out the irony of violent confrontation. We Americans have come to believe that although there are differences, our society is basically coherent, and we expect traditional methods of conflict resolution to keep the peace in a unified world. Our desire for community solidarity leads us to reject ways of thinking that threaten that sense of unity:

The myth of community solidarity disposes men, I believe, to escalate
discord with other communities or with outsiders too powerful to be
excluded to the level of violent confrontation. Essentially, communities whose people feel related to each other by virtue of their sameness
are polarized. When issues within or without the community arise that
cannot be settled by routine processes of bureaucratic administration,
it seems that the whole fabric of the myth is in jeopardy because of an
intractable issue or event that cannot be assimilated. . . . In situations
like these, everyone's dignity is threatened, and people can't ignore it.
They feel that the very survival of the community is at stake, and in a
sense they are right. (p. 44)

To illustrate the moral basis of violence, we quote at length from a
fascinating and startling short story written by one of our students, Rob
Hampson, in 1986:

Warrior of God or Terrorist?

Kavosh Dehpanah was born on a small family farm on the plains to
the south of the small city of Semnan. Semnan is no more than an
oversized walled watering hole 150 miles along the old highway east
from Tehran. The city is nestled against the Elburz Mountains, whose
runoff provides the city's water. From Semnan, the barren plateau of
Iran stretches for many hundreds of miles over the horizon to the
south and east. This is the Dasht-i-kavir Desert, much of which is
composed of salt rather than sand. In the spring, the mountain steams
flow into the Dasht-i-kavir and form small salt deposits; when the
lakes and swamps evaporate in the long, hot, dry season, a layer of
salt is left to blow across the plains. The salt blasts the gray walls of
the Dehpanah farm for most of the year, wearing away the clay stone.
Kavosh's family is fortunate because they have a well that provides
their water for most of the year. In the driest part of the season, they
must pay for their water from the local *kanat* system, an ancient
network of deep mountain wells and long tunnels that carry this water
to the farms.
   Kavosh's family has grown wheat as its main crop for genera-
tions. They have also maintained a crop of poppies for opium and an
orchard of a few dozen small lime trees. They also maintain a meager
flock of sheep and goats. In prosperous years, they may have a donkey,
cow, or camel to raise for food or extra income.
   On the farm, Kavosh's family consists of his parents, his two
brothers and two sisters, his grandfather, both of his grandmothers,
an aunt and uncle, and two cousins. Kavosh's family, like almost
everyone around Semnan, are Shiite Muslims, as is 95% of the Iranian
population. They follow the Shari'ah (Divine Law) as their guidelines

in which to live by; they pray to Allah five times a day, pay alms, and fast; everyone has paid at least one pilgrimage to Mecca, the Holy City of Islam. Their politics define God as the only Legislator and believe that their leaders only carry out the laws but do not create them. Shiites put their complete faith in the Imam as the sole executor of God's law. The Imam is the ruler of the community and the inheritor of the prophet's teachings. The Imam is the enlightened one. His position has three duties: to rule the Muslim community as the representative of Muhammad, the prophet; to interpret religion, science, politics, and the law to the masses; and to guide men in the spiritual life. Because of the light within him, the Imam's authority goes unquestioned, and his decisions are infallible on spiritual and religious matters.

The Dehpanah family, like most Iranians, characterize themselves as a people in an environment of constant fluid change. They have survived outside invaders from the early Greek and Romans and the Persians, through the Crusades, English and Russian colonization, and finally, Western civilization's insatiable quest for oil. They have also survived the unpredictable farming and irrigation conditions inherent in their country, as well as a myriad of inept governments. To them, the only stability in their ever changing lives is their historical pride, their religious dedication, and an ancient sense of social hierarchy.

With these inner resources of stability, Iranian people, like the Dehpanah family, stubbornly hold tight to their cultural heritage and have resisted foreign influences for decades. They have become stationary farmers with their agriculture assuming top priority in their lives. The foreign invaders and the governments have come and gone, but to these people, the law of the land and of Allah reign as supreme.

What the Imam says is the will of Allah. He speaks for Allah to the Muslim people; so when he called for the overthrow of the Shah, it was the will of God. He called upon "all Islamic nations [to] join us in the fight which is between ourselves and America, between Islam and blasphemy."

This is a powerful statement, alone, to a people who equate the Shah's downfall and the subsequent decline of their state to the American influence in their country, but the Shiite perspective is a dichotomous one that sees only black and white, good and bad, and no in-betweens. Combined with this philosophy, there is no room for compromise. The Imam represents the ultimate good of Allah; and the enemy, which he points to as the United States, is the opposition to Allah, the devil.

In order to save their country, the Middle East, and Allah's land, they must eradicate the devil from the world. Therefore, with Kavosh's unquestioning devotion to Allah, and especially to the Imam as the sole interpreter, when he is sent to a training camp by the ILF, he goes for Allah. He learns to smuggle and detonate explosives and to handle small arms. He becomes a warrior of Allah. His ultimate contribution would be to die for Allah in the struggle to destroy the devil.

His first mission for Allah was to drive a van that assisted in the escape of some more seasoned brothers from western devils after an attack on an Israeli shopping center. Then the ILF allowed him to participate directly in a coordinated attack on two airports in Greece and Italy. Several of his comrades died for Allah, but he escaped. Next came his ultimate mission; the ILF sent him and three other brothers to southern Europe in order to hijack a jet full of devils. Their plan was discovered before they were ready to take over the plane and they had to act prematurely. The jet was still on the ground and they had to take 53 hostages and issue demands. The jet was quickly surrounded by an assault team of commandos. They were in a stalemate.

With Kavosh and his comrades finding it an honor to sacrifice themselves as martyrs to Allah, and along with a strong Iranian value of *aberu* (saving face), there was no backing down, no compromise. Again, there was the dichotomous view of black and white, win or lose, and no in-betweens. They were trapped with no way out. The opposition was not giving in and they could not. Therefore, they set explosives on the jet and pulled the pins on incendiary grenades.

▧ Transcending Moral Conflict

So far in this chapter, we have described four patterns of communication commonly associated with difference. Transcendent discourse, the fifth pattern of interaction in our model, is important enough to develop in some depth, so we address it more completely in the following two chapters. As a preview, let's take a brief look at this pattern now.

Each of the precursors to Pattern 5 is predicated on the creation, conservation, and change of stories. The fifth pattern, in contrast, aims to acknowledge and work within and between multiple stories. Its goal is not to preserve or change stories but to coordinate them.

In short, transcendent communication aims to express moral difference eloquently in ways that build understanding and respect. Can we work with people different from us? Those who use the fifth pattern believe that we can.

This mode of communication recognizes both difference and no difference. It acknowledges that human beings are richly different and are defined in large measure by their differences. We all share a common life as social beings, unfinished at birth, who achieve full realization only by learning the stories of our communities and cultures. We all base our realities on stories, and we all seek coherence in those stories. Transcendent communication, then, brings a metastory to light, an overarching notion of human beings as social, linguistic, story-defined agents.

Transcendent communicators are not willing to put this metastory at risk because it is the very thing that makes peacemaking possible. In this regard, transcendent communicators may or may not be willing to alter their position on the presenting issue, or undergo first-order change, but they are willing to accept the metastory, to change their approach to the conflict, or undergo second-order change. This sort of change is a movement of primary commitment from the community's story to a new story that will make communication with the other side possible.

This type of communication admits the possibility of creating new categories by which one side can compare itself with the other. It admits to the possibility of developing a creole language in which one side can communicate with the other. Unlike the rhetorical eloquence embedded in the normal discourse of Pattern 3, which relies on one's own established vocabulary to help outsiders "see the light," it creates a new language in which each side can understand the moral order of the other. Unlike the reciprocated diatribe resulting from the frustration of Pattern 4, it creates conditions in which a new form of *transcendent eloquence* might prevail. As such, it is very much a form of *abnormal discourse* (Rorty, 1979).

⋈ Moments in the Development of Moral Conflict

Moral conflicts develop like a tree. Growth and movement occur along several branches at the same time. At a given moment, several things may be going on within the various branches. In the case of moral conflicts, the three major branches are persuasion (Pattern 3), schism (Pattern 4), and transcendence (Pattern 5). *Persuasion* involves attempts to influence. Rhetorical eloquence is precisely this type of activity: Give them your best shot, and your superior logic will win them over. *Schism* is the breach. Following the realization that persuasion has failed, advocates now communicate in ways that distance themselves from the "enemy" and attempt to win by isolating, outnumbering, overpowering, or eliminating the opposition. Diatribe, repression, and violence are examples. Finally, *transcendence* is the attempt to create new ways of thinking about the conflict, forms of communication explored in some detail in the next two chapters.

It is tempting to think about the development of a moral conflict as a linear passage from one of these to the next: First, persons try to persuade; failing that, they behave in ways that create a schism; then, in the end, they are able to transcend their differences. But obviously, moral conflicts are not this simple.

We hypothesize that all three of these processes are going on simultaneously, albeit in different places and by different people. The development of a conflict is probably a complicated affair, and depending on recent perceptions, actions of the other side, outside influences, and personal psychological factors, people will try different things at different times. Sometimes, they will attempt to convince; sometimes, in exasperation, they will drive wedges; sometimes, they will attempt to bridge differences.

Like the growth of a tree, then, we should think of the development of a moral conflict as a multitrack process. Through time, changes occur in these three tracks at different rates and in different directions.

It may happen in certain conflict situations that different people specialize in different development tracks. Some people are inveterate persuaders. They live by the code of civic virtue. They see it as their duty to speak out clearly, forcefully, and eloquently on the causes in which they believe. The persuaders are not discouraged by the lack of success, and even temporary gains fuel their fire.

Other activists may see themselves as angry dissenters. They feel righteously indignant, and their goal is to distance themselves and their movements as much as possible from those who oppose it. They seek not to persuade but to divide. They are interested not in winning converts but in standing up for what they believe. These individuals see respect of one's enemy as a weakness and co-optation. They will not respect, they will not transcend, and they will not compromise. They see schism as an important instrument in the ultimate goal of social change and progress.

Finally, there are the peacemakers, those who fear war and violence. They are diplomats, mediators, arbitrators, and social scientists. They are the ones who keep the transcendence track moving.

On the other hand, it may also happen that certain people involved in a conflict are not specialized, not tied to one of these roles. They find themselves changing from time to time. They may be compelled to attempt to influence the other side at times and to strike out in indignation on other occasions. Sometimes, such individuals may try new forms of eloquent communication designed to transcend. Some may accuse such individuals of being confused; others may praise them for being adaptive and flexible.

As authors, we are most interested in peacemaking, which can happen in the context of transcendent eloquence. The activities and development of the interaction along the transcendence track is therefore of utmost importance to us in this book. We do not mean to suggest that the other tracks are unimportant or morally reprehensible. Our goal instead is merely to make sure that along with persuasion and schism, transcendence remains viable and healthy as a development track. In practical terms, this means that someone is always making an attempt to see the conflict in a new way, to make new connections and comparisons, to create dialogue and rapprochement, to remain constructively critical, and to reconstruct the context of the conflict.

Postmodern times often present complex situations, and as Kegan (1994) expresses the problem, we are frequently "in over our heads." Kegan shows that the loss of foundational truth and the conflict among incommensurate moral orders require a level of thinking not taught well by the "curriculum" of society. This higher level of consciousness involves an awareness of the socially constructed nature of reality, the recognition that moral conflict is inevitable and that it can be constructive, the willingness to live with unfinished conversation, the creativity to construct places in which that conversation can occur, and the inventiveness of new transcendent categories for comparing and critiquing otherwise incommensurate moral orders. This is a tall bill of goods, but it sets a standard for all of us who would make peace in a postmodern world. We turn now to a closer look at transcendence as a form of peacemaking.

6

Fighting and Making Peace

On January 16, 1991, the United States attacked Iraq. While most Americans that evening sat immobile in front of their television sets eagerly awaiting any news from the Persian Gulf, the city council of Arcata, a small northern California town, held its regularly scheduled meeting. Before the meeting was closed, the council unanimously passed a resolution that declared the city a sanctuary for anyone refusing to participate in the war for moral, ethical, or religious reasons.

The council's decision came as a surprise to the residents of the quiet coastal college town. Some were euphoric when they heard the news, feeling that they had been properly represented by elected officials. Others were irate, calling the council's action irresponsible, unconstitutional, and unpatriotic. Within 48 hours, everyone in the town had heard of the council's action, and the battle lines were drawn. The

AUTHORS' NOTE: Material in this chapter quoted from Kegan (1994) is from *In Over Our Heads: The Mental Demands of Modern Life*, by Robert Kegan (Cambridge, MA: Harvard University Press). Copyright © 1994 by the President and Fellows of Harvard College. All rights reserved. Reprinted by permission.

town was divided in their support over the council's action, and there was virtually no middle ground. Arcata made national news.

The conservative faction of the town, the residents who viewed the council members as knee-jerk liberals, wasted no time in organizing a coalition to ensure that the town not be taken over by the liberals. The "Concerned Citizens" collected 6,000 signatures on a petition, bought radio spots, took out newspaper ads to express their embarrassment over the sanctuary decision, urged citizens to pressure the council to rescind the measure, and petitioned for a recall election.

While the Concerned Citizens were busy circulating petitions and gathering a flock of supporters, local peace activists continued to hold vigils in the town square. They realized the emotionality of the issue and understood that it could erupt into something that could bring physical harm to the people living within the once harmonious city. Although the conflict never came to blows, there were some ugly scenes and shouting matches, as various threats of violence were heard.

The city council members were certainly not sleeping easy after their decision. The most disturbing issue facing them was the schism their decree had created within the community. They hated to see the town torn apart. People who used to do business together were not talking, neighbors were turning an icy shoulder, and a boycott was threatened. Council members did not want this atmosphere in their city, and they realized that they had acted too hastily and without sufficient input from the community.

Four days after the council's decision to become a sanctuary, three of the five council members publicly apologized on the steps of the town hall for their "hasty reaction." This action did not mollify either side. The pro-sanctuary group was hurt by what it perceived to be an accommodation to the pro-war group and a betrayal of their cause. The anti-sanctuary element did not think the apology addressed the real issue—the continued liberal stands of the council on a variety of issues the conservatives considered inappropriate.

Because of the frustration and the tension brewing between the two sides, the council decided to hold a town meeting so the residents could voice their opinions publicly on the matter. Approximately 3,500 people attended the town meeting. Because of the size of the hall, the large majority were forced to wait outside the building during the nine-hour hearings. As a first item of business, before the hearings began, the council formally rescinded the sanctuary resolution, bringing cheers from some and jeers from others. The recision order did not defuse the crowd, and about 170 persons addressed the council before the meeting ended at 4:00 a.m. the next day.

The hearings and recision of the resolution did not reduce the tension that had built up. The war stirred up too many emotions kept dormant for at least 20 years. Concealed anger had been brewing over growth initiatives, nuclear-free zone propositions, a Nicaraguan sister city action, and, most recently, the conflict over logging the redwoods. The war issue was the catalyst that released capped hostility.

After the town meeting, the conservative group wanted to continue the move toward more changes. The Concerned Citizens elected officers and began to hold regularly scheduled meetings. They seriously considered a recall election and established a watchdog committee to attend council meetings. At a gathering attended by hundreds, they installed a huge three-story-long American flag as a war memorial.

During all this activity, some members of the community banded together to undertake peacemaking activities. A quilt project received about 30 squares. A blood drive was started but never made it off the ground. A peacemaking dinner was held, but the Concerned Citizens did not attend.

The conservative group had no confusion about their goals; they were out to silence those who opposed U.S. policy in the Gulf. The liberals, in contrast, were less confident about what voice to use in the conflict. On the one hand, they were angry at the conservatives for being so belligerent, and they were committed to opposing the Gulf War. On the other hand, they wanted to model a peacemaking style that would open an exchange of views and establish mutual respect.

To no one's surprise, it was the liberal faction that proposed various peacemaking events, designed to establish dialogue between the two city factions. The liberals seemed confused about whether to fight against the conservatives in open clash, a move that would contradict their peace-seeking goals, or to be more open toward their opponents, a move that would contradict their commitment to fighting those who favored the Gulf War.

℞ The Dilemma

In the first four chapters of this book, we characterized moral conflict by its harmful consequences. We have been advocating the need to develop ways of transforming such conflicts. But there is something troubling about this position. Anybody who has been actively involved in a movement knows that the compulsion to fight for what he or she believes is right is sometimes overwhelming, and history is replete with examples of oppression and repression that at some point had to be resisted violently. History also teaches that well-meant attempts to transform conflicts, listen differently to the other side, and make peace can be co-opted and turned into appeasement. That is precisely what happened in 1938 when Prime Minister Chamberlain conferred with Hitler and Mussolini, declaring on his return to England that he had achieved "peace for our time."

Moral differences sometimes lie under the surface and smolder and other times ignite into open clash. In this chapter, we use the term *suppression* to designate those conditions in which difference is left unexpressed, silent, hidden, glossed, smoothed over, or quashed and the term *expression* to designate engagement, confrontation, debate, and other forms in which the moral difference is uncovered and made explicit. Because they are disturbing and polarizing, moral splits tend to be fought out hostilely or suppressed altogether, and neither eventuality is desirable.

Faced with an apparent dilemma, many people perceive that they must make a choice between "being silenced" and "going to battle" on issues that matter to them. Peacemaking is too frequently viewed as another form of surrender.

In this book, we take the contradiction between expression and suppression seriously as a dialectic that must be managed in every case of moral difference. Moral difference, then, is a problem in dialectical management, a challenge of living with the contradiction between expression and suppression of moral difference.

❧ The Consequences of Moral Difference

The social reality of a group or culture is based on certain moral assumptions, and in the ordinary course of events, people expect these to go unchallenged. A reality is reproduced through some version of a normal discourse, a set of rhetorical practices and claims that are taken as normal and true by a culture or group. Given the power of normal discourse in the formation and reproduction of a culture's beliefs, such discourse legitimizes the group's forms of life (Wittgenstein, 1953).

Normal discourse can suppress moral difference in a number of ways and create structural constraints to its expression. Organizations, for example, often establish policies and practices that make the expression of moral difference difficult, if not impossible (Littlejohn, 1995b). Fine (1995) shows that until recently, diversity went essentially unrecognized in most organizations. The result of normalization is the promotion of the interests of dominant groups over those of marginalized ones, resulting in a type of oppression of thought and interest (e.g., Deetz, 1992).

Hiding important differences brings about a *secrecy relationship*, according to Roth (1993). Here, some members of the group believe that their differences are important, but they are unable or unwilling to make this feeling known to the group as a whole because others in the group do not take those differences as seriously. People think, "We are troubled by our difference from you, but we will keep this concern a secret rather than being open about it."

Because moral challenges shake at the foundation of established truth, they are often suppressed. The oppression of homosexuals is a clear example. Because the discourse of heterosexism dominated our society until recently, the interests and ideas of homosexuals were hidden, marginalized, and suppressed. Only after gays and lesbians began to come out and speak out did they have a chance of changing this state of affairs. The gay rights movement, like so many others, provided a forum in which to express moral difference and counteract the suppressive tendencies of dominant discourse.

The solution to the problem of suppression seems to be to allow conflicts to be heard fully, to expose hegemony by engaging in something like a completely free "ideal speech situation" (Habermas, 1970). Indeed, history is full of examples of the rise of certain radically new ideas through public moral clash, and society does provide "spaces" in which such clash can occur (Evans & Boyte, 1992). Some argue that without open clash, social change would be impossible.

Although moral conflict can be suppressed by the mechanisms of domination, the history of movements shows that moral disharmony is often quite open and can result in havoc. The hate speech, assault, repression, deprivation, and war that can result from moral clash become forms of domination in their own right as they turn quiet oppression into direct repression and overt aggression (e.g., Pearce, Cobb, Cano, & Freeman, 1991).

The contradiction between suppression and expression plays out somewhat differently for activists than for peacemakers. In general, once an activist has made the decision to "go fight," the contradiction becomes momentarily resolved. If genuine change results, it may seem worth the battle, but when the clash is prolonged and seemingly interminable, the activist may return again to the quandary.

For those who take a peacemaking role, the contradiction between expression and suppression remains acute. Peacemakers face a paradox; a better society requires that opposing moral positions be expressed, but the clash resulting from this expression can damage society. To avoid the harms of open moral clash, peacemakers must calm, override, or eliminate the conflict, but by doing this, they may end up suppressing moral differences and unwittingly perpetuating unhealthy power arrangements.

For example, mediators believe they are providing a valuable service by helping people solve their disagreements, but some observers worry that mediators sometimes perpetuate power imbalance and that the adversarial system is the only way to provide justice in these situations (Abel, 1982). In attempting to overcome one set of harms, then, another set can be created inadvertently.

To avoid taking sides, the peacemaker cannot resolve the issue, must leave it an open question, and must admit the potential legitimacy of both sides. For individuals who do not have much of a stake in the issue, this type of intervention seems an eminently wise course of action, but for those who have strong interests in the issue at hand, peacemaking stifles expression of their points of view and prevents the achievement of valued goals. As Barber (1984) puts the matter, "Tolerance is a beneficent and admirable posture, but in itself it can stop nothing. It refrains from doing harm but may permit harm to be done" (p. 105).

Take the peacemaking efforts of Jimmy Carter as a current example. An associate describes Carter's style as one in which he suspends judgment about the parties and their ideologies (Kelly, 1994). Carter's approach is viewed by many critics as problematic because it legitimizes U.S. enemies and cripples the administration's ability to meet important commitments and policies. Carter's supporters, however, contend that he may have prevented unwanted war on at least two occasions in 1994 (Kelly, 1994). On an international scale, then, Carter's diplomacy illustrates the contradiction between the need to promote what are believed to be important interests and the need to avoid the damaging outcomes of doing so. The same contradiction exists on every level, from the personal to the international. The management of this dialectic sometimes requires sophisticated types of thinking not readily available to participants in these conflicts.

▧ Levels of Consciousness in the Management of Dialectic

Once moral difference becomes prominent, those who care must make some fundamental decisions, and their choices become moves in the management of the contradiction of suppression and expression. Any strategy—withdrawal, clash, compromise, negotiation, or transcendence—is but a momentary move in a stream of events that enables one to cope with the tension through time.

How we cope with the tension, the choices we make, depends on how we think about human differences. In his book *In Over Our Heads: The Mental Demands of Modern Life*, Kegan (1994) addresses this problem and outlines five levels of consciousness that can be developed in human beings for dealing with difference.

Kegan takes a developmental perspective, viewing consciousness as increasing with cognitive maturity and education (Tables 6.1 and 6.2). He uses the metaphor of the school curriculum and questions how particular forms of consciousness can be taught not only in real schools but in the metaphorical curriculum of society and life. How well does society prepare its citizens to cope with and understand the increasingly complex experiences with which they are faced?

Kegan's first level of thought is infantile, impulsive perception, in which children see objects as independent entities without connection. As children undergo more socialization and maturation, they enter the second level, which involves relating objects to one another in "durable categories." Here concepts are formed and connections made. The categories of children of, say, 10 years of age, are durable in that they are assumed immutable and universal. A tree is a tree.

Distinguishing most adult thinking from childish thinking is consciousness of a higher order of things. In the third level of consciousness, people become aware of different ways of understanding and conceptualizing experience, and categories lose their durable character. Realizing that different people have different points of view, self is distinguished from other. Here one learns to express a point of view and adapt to audiences that may hold different views. The third level of consciousness is required to live in traditional society, in which social roles are crucial.

In contrast to traditionalism, modernism requires yet another, higher order of consciousness. At the fourth level, we come to realize that our categories are not merely personal, but social. We see that realities are

TABLE 6.1 Kegan's Levels of Consciousness 1 and 2

LEVEL	SUBJECT	OBJECT	STRUCTURE
Level 1			
Cognitive Dimensions	Perception/fantasy	Movement	Single point/Immediate/Atomistic
Interpersonal Dimensions	Social Perceptions		
Intrapersonal Dimensions	Impulses	Sensation	
Level 2			
Cognitive Dimensions	Concrete—actuality, data, cause-and-effect	Perceptions	Durable Category
Interpersonal Dimensions	Point of View—role-concept, simple reciprocity	Social Perceptions	
Intrapersonal Dimensions	During Dispositions—needs, preferences, self concept	Impulses	

SOURCE: Adapted from *In Over Our Heads: The Mental Demands of Modern Life*, pp. 314-315, by Robert Kegan (Cambridge, MA: Harvard University Press). Copyright © 1994 by the President and Fellows of Harvard College. All rights reserved.

TABLE 6.2 Kegan's Levels of Consciousness 3, 4, and 5

LEVEL	SUBJECT	OBJECT	STRUCTURE
Level 3: Traditionalist			
Cognitive Dimensions	Abstractions—ideality, inference, generalization, hypothesis, proposition, ideals, values	Concrete	Cross-categorical Trans-categorical
Interpersonal Dimensions	Mutuality/Interpersonalism—role consciousness, mutual reciprocity	Point of view	
Intrapersonal Dimensions	Inner States—subjectivity, self-consciousness	Enduring dispositions, needs, preferences	
Level 4: Modernist			
Cognitive	Abstract Systems—ideology, formulation, authorization, relations between abstractions	Abstractions	System/Complex
Interpersonal Dimensions	Institution—relationship-regulating forms, multiple-role consciousness	Mutuality Interpersonalism	
Intrapersonal Dimensions	Self authorship—self-regulation, self-formation, identity, autonomy, individualism	Inner states Subjectivity Self-consciousness	

Level 5: Postmodernist

Cognitive	Dialectical—Trans-ideological/post-ideological, testing formulation, paradox, contradiction, oppositeness	Abstract System Ideology	Trans-System Trans-Complex
Interpersonal Dimensions	Inter-institutional—Relationship between forms, interpenetration of self and other	Institution Relationship-regulating forms	
Intrapersonal Dimensions	Self-transformation—Interpenetration of selves, inter-individuation	Self-authorship Self-regulation Self-formation	

SOURCE: Adapted from *In Over Our Heads: The Mental Demands of Modern Life*, pp. 314-315, by Robert Kegan (Cambridge, MA: Harvard University Press). Copyright © 1994 by the President and Fellows of Harvard College. All rights reserved.

given meaning from within the confines of a system, and we move from seeing the world from concrete categories to abstract ones, or what Kegan calls *relations of relations*. Roles give way to institutions, and individuals are understood no longer as merely having categories but as living within the constraints of a larger set of institutions.

Kegan makes clear that most of what we must do in society today can be handled easily within the fourth level of consciousness, but he shows that not everybody is able to think in this way. Those who are limited to the third level may face obstacles and challenges easily overcome by those who have achieved a higher, systems level of thinking. Still, the contemporary world is exceedingly complex, and the fourth level of consciousness itself is limited, making yet another level necessary.

At the fifth level, our consciousness moves from an awareness of institutions and groups to a trans-system cognizance. Reality not merely is constructed within a tradition, institution, or system but is a complex product of a transaction among traditions, institutions, and systems. At the fifth level, we no longer confine our analysis to the differences between groups and perspectives but begin to question the ways in which systems affect one another, creating contradictions, conflicts, and paradoxes. Our lives are influenced never by only a single system but by multiple and contradictory ones.

Difference, even cultural diversity, is easily recognized at the fourth level of consciousness, but this level does not allow us to step out of a system of thought to take a metalevel view. When we can do so, we find ourselves unable to privilege one system of thought over another, and truth evaporates.

If the fourth level of consciousness characterizes modernity, the fifth level characterizes postmodernity. In a time of uncertainty and loss of truth, citizens can function more effectively if they can learn to hold multiple and contradictory truths simultaneously.

To complicate matters even more, postmodernism has two versions. Relying largely on the work of Burbules and Rice (1991), Kegan distinguishes between *deconstructive* and *reconstructive* variants. Deconstructive postmodernism is essentially nihilistic, leaving no foundation on which to stand. In reconstructive postmodernism, differentiation and ambiguity lead to reintegration, or the *making of* places to stand.

The purpose of reconstruction and integration is not to achieve a super theory or Truth-for-all-time, which would be nothing more than a return to the fourth level. Rather, such work leads to a temporary resolution of contradiction, diversity, and ambiguity, a resolution that may be useful but never ultimate. This work, in Kegan's view, is necessary to sustain life in postmodern times, in which certainty cannot exist. If we cannot use talk to find truth, we can at least keep the conversation going (Rorty, 1979).

Kegan makes clear that how we handle conflicts is a result of the level of thinking at which we are operating. His analysis of consciousness is therefore useful in understanding the dialectic of expression and suppression.

▧ Manifestations of Expression and Suppression

The dialectic of expression and suppression can be experienced on three tiers, which we label *silence and engagement, clash and peacemaking,* and *encapsulation and transformation*. These are depicted in Figure 6.1.

Silence and Engagement: Level 3 Consciousness

The most fundamental issue for parties interested in a moral dispute is whether to remain silent or to confront others publicly. Although the advantages of each option may be weighed, for passionate activists, the question is when, not whether, to engage in public dissent. Not all interested individuals actually participate personally, but their sympathies may lie with those who do. And as moral disputes heat up, more and more people take to the streets, carry signs, attend rallies, or view such events sympathetically on television.

The first tier of the dialectic, then, will almost certainly be managed by making a clear choice. Either we speak up or shut up. The perception of moral difference and the classification of positions into two opposing groups—pro-life and pro-choice, gay rights and homophobia, evolution and creation science, environmentalist and industrialist, Christian and humanist—are products of Kegan's Level 3 thinking.

At this level, we become conscious of the difference between self and other. We assume ownership of our own point of view, and we attempt to sell it to others. Indeed, the third level of consciousness requires us to take others into account and to adapt our messages to the perspective of the other. In moral conflicts, however, we will probably

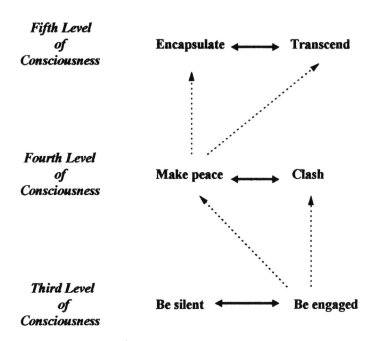

Figure 6.1. The Dialectic of Expression and Suppression

find this difficult and end up valorizing our own position and demonizing that of the opposition.

In this dialectic, we will predictably engage in debate when we perceive that the difference between self and other is significant and important to us as individuals or as a group. To remain silent is to fail to recognize the difference, fail to recognize its significance, or fear the consequences of engagement with the other side, all negative consequences of the suppression of moral difference.

Once the torch is taken up, however, a fairly predictable negative pattern results (Freeman et al., 1992). Each side makes use of its most eloquent forms of rhetoric in a type of civil discourse. Discovering that this is neither impressive nor persuasive to the other side, the rhetoric of moral clash begins to degrade into frustrated and mutual diatribe. The verbal and sometimes physical violence that results is eloquent in no way, a consequence discussed at some length in the following chapter.

The abortion conflict is an excellent example of what happens when moral difference gets expressed in this manner (Tribe, 1990). Each side has its own good reasons and rhetoric, eloquent in its own way, but each also completely bypasses the rhetorical standards of the other side. The frustration of having one's best arguments ignored, or worse, turned against one, lead to the extreme forms of verbal and physical violence so common in this dispute.

Concerned about abusive events such as these, some participants and other observers may hope for and even become involved in peace-making interventions, as if to say, "Come, now, settle down and be nice." At this point, we see the second contradiction—between open clash and peacemaking.

Clash and Peacemaking:
Level 4 Consciousness

Peacemaking is problematic for many people. If peacemaking means talking in kinder, less aggressive ways, then it appears attractive, but it can also give credence and some legitimacy to the other side. Those who hold authoritarian views do not accept outsiders on any level, and within such sealed-off moral systems, peacemaking is tantamount to defeat. Silence or clash is the only option, and peacemaking is wholly unacceptable.

In contrast, those who describe their moral orders as "progressive," such as the liberals in the town of Arcata discussed above, find the question of peacemaking paradoxical because they want to promote their cause but do so in a way that is open to other views. How can we both respect and attempt to overcome those who would oppress us? How can we be open to views that are not themselves open? How can we tolerate intolerance?

Thus the choice between clash and peacemaking is frequently prob-lematic. It is often confusing, especially for those who want their own interests heard but are discouraged by the perceived silencing moves of the other side. For instance, gay rights activists are moved to go to battle for legitimacy, while delegitimizing their opponents as hatemongers. They want dialogue but find it difficult to assume a position toward the opponent necessary for such dialogue to occur. They struggle with ways to have their moral position expressed without the negative conse-quences of all-out battle (Littlejohn, 1994a).

In their video *The Great Divide*, Fort and Skinner-Jones (1993)[1] document the clash over gay rights in Oregon and Colorado in 1992. Both states put measures on the ballot that would have excluded gay and lesbian persons from antidiscrimination laws. This was an extremely dynamic issue because both sides took it up in a cause célèbre. The battles in Oregon and Colorado were strident as gay activists fought for what they perceived to be their basic human rights and anti-gay activists fought for what they perceived to be basic moral values.

As the campaigns of both sides became increasingly hostile, dialogue movements emerged to attempt a more respectful and probing exploration of the issue. This peacemaking movement was led by "progressives" who sought to find a way in which differences could be expressed respectfully, to increase understanding and find common ground. In the video, Theresa Jensen of Community Conversations explains the goal in these terms:

> We did stress that we were asking people to try having a real dialogue, a conversation, with each other in a real way. If you can create a safe atmosphere where they can really be honest and talk about how an issue affects them, how an issue impacts them, their lives, then those two people, I think, can start seeing each other in a new way and some individual empathy can start to happen.

Indeed, this attempt was somewhat successful. A minister whose sympathies lay with the anti-gay side said, "I know that the community as a whole was invited to participate in this kind of reconciliation model. All I can say, my hat's off to the people who put this together." At the same time, notable failures also occurred. Lesbian Marcy Westerling describes her attempt to get together with members of pro-initiative representatives in Colorado, only to find them unwilling to talk. Yvonne Benitex of Community Conversations in Oregon relates a similar incident, quoting a member of the opposition: "In all moral conscience, I cannot agree to come and talk about this with someone who may think differently than I do. I just can't do that."

This objection brings us right back to the contradiction between the expression and suppression of moral difference. Many activists are afraid that by having a conversation with someone who holds different moral views, their own commitments will be compromised, and they will lose the benefits of expressing difference in open clash and lose ground in the advancement of their interests. It seems that this fear is based in the lack of understanding of transcendent discourse, a confusion of transformation with suppression.

The choice between clashing and making peace is not unlike that of silence versus engagement, but peacemaking is more active. Level 4 thinking invites us to see options other than polarizing clash. Because different groups have different needs and values, a single solution may not be possible, which means that new forms of interaction between groups may be necessary. Peacemaking attempts to create an overarching frame within which the disputants can discuss their differences, a frame consisting of values, assumptions, interests, goals, or procedures.

A case of Level 4 thinking in moral conflict is the gay rights movement within the church (Littlejohn, Higgins, & Williams, 1987; Littlejohn & Wright, 1987). Virtually every mainstream Christian denomination and Reformed Judaism includes such a movement. Religious gay men and lesbians who have not left their church are seeking the acceptance of homosexuality within the structure of their own churches, which takes an entirely different form from public political gay rights campaigns.

Both sides in these conflicts are acutely aware of their differences, which are debated in church forums, newsletters, and councils. The gay rights activists seek to change church teachings, and the traditionalists resist doing so. Striking about this issue is that it is almost always argued in the common frame of scripture, because scripture is the basis of the institution. The gay rights activists use scripture as a justification for acceptance, and their opponents use it as a rationale for rejecting homosexual behavior. The debates are usually quite civil and respectful because of the common heritage of believers, but nothing gets settled. Each side, however, is still seeking to promote its view of truth, and there has been little movement or change in gay rights within the church.

Encapsulating and Transforming:
Level 5 Consciousness

Encapsulating strategies—such as selecting one side of a contradiction over another, switching between sides, wavering, or compromising—work by separating the contradictory elements (Baxter, 1988; Rawlins, 1989). When people choose to remain silent, to clash, or to make peace, they are adopting encapsulating strategies.

In contrast, transformative strategies attempt to transcend the contradiction in some way (Rawlins, 1989). This type of move reframes the contradiction to eliminate, at least temporarily, the tension between the sides, to incorporate both simultaneously. Sometimes this means putting the two opposing forces together in opposition to something else. *Fast* and *slow* are no longer opposites when both are put into a new category called *movement* (in contrast to *stillness*). *Happy* and *sad* are no longer contradictory when combined into the category of *feeling* (as opposed to, say, *apathy*).

Such transformative moves can be made in the management of moral difference as well. One of the things we can do to promote such common ground is to transform the context for understanding the issue. For example, people often approach an issue from the standpoint of winning. "If we organize skillfully, do enough research, plan well, argue hard, and stick to it, we will prevail." That is fine if we define winning as prevailing. What would happen if we redefined winning as avoiding violence? What if winning came to mean achieving peace? The entire context for the dispute would be transformed. Instead of asking, "How can the pro-life side win?" we could ask, "How can better choices be made available to women so that fewer abortions are performed?"

In his book *The Soul of Politics*, Wallis (1994) makes a transformative move in the clash between conservatives and liberals throughout our society:

> The "liberal structuralists" and "conservative behaviorists" are both right and both wrong. To speak only of moral behavior, apart from oppressive social realities, just blames the victim; and to talk only about social conditions, apart from moral choices, is to keep treating people only as victims. . . . The culture war that is raging between the advocates of social justice and the preachers of moral rejuvenation must come to an end, not simply to make a truce between embattled intellectuals but also for the sake of our endangered children, who have become the chief pawns and victims of our absurd bifurcations.
>
> Why must we constantly choose whether to stress responsibility or oppression? Must it be either/or? . . . It's time to start talking to one another instead of just at one another; or, more accurately, it's time to stop our ideological battles in political process, which are often motivated by the competition for power and scarce resources. What is called for now is that particular combination of which the prophets most often spoke—justice and righteousness. (pp. 20-21)

Wallis wants to transcend old economic, political, and social categories by fusing their best parts into new categories. He wants a new set of values, including conversion, compassion, community, reverence, diversity, equality, peacemaking, justice, contemplation, courage, responsibility, integrity, imagination, reconstruction, joy, and hope.

In a classic social psychology experiment, Sherif, Harvey, White, Hood, and Sherif (1961) worked on eliminating intergroup prejudice at a boys' summer camp. After building thorough hatred between the groups and finding all the customary methods for resolving conflict inadequate, the researchers posed a problem to the two groups that they could not overcome without cooperating. In the summer camp situation, the supraordinate goal involved restoring the water supply from a broken reservoir. In the world of moral conflict, it consists of establishing new ways of thinking that make old hostilities obsolete. That's what the transformative peacemaker tries to do.

Therapist Sallyann Roth (1993) was once asked to conduct a consultation with a gay and lesbian counseling service that employed both gay and heterosexual staff members. Some tension had been experienced in the organization because of a statement made two years earlier by two heterosexual staff members that homosexuality was wrong. Although hurtful to the gay and lesbian staff at the time, the issue was quickly submerged and not openly discussed, except "secretly" in small groups. Those who wanted the consultation felt that the issue needed to be opened up, but some members of the staff feared that such a discussion would create conflict and make the situation worse.

Certainly, an encapsulating debate on the morality of homosexuality would not have accomplished any salutary effect, but Roth did not make this the focus of her intervention. Instead, she took the issue of difference itself as a theme and developed a climate that would make it possible for the staff members to discuss their differences safely and productively. In this transformative move, group members were encouraged to come together on the side of exploring their differences in opposition to hiding them. Roth made use of dialogue around an extended role reversal, in which both understanding and alienation could be experienced and discussed.

Laudable as they are, transformative strategies are not always possible. The first tier of the dialectical model presented here, that between silence and engagement, is necessarily handled in an encapsulating way. On that level, if people decide to stay here, they must decide to remain silent or speak out. The thing is, they don't have to stay here. They can set themselves to rise to a higher level of consciousness.

Several transformative methods are available and have been used in the face of moral difference (Kriesberg, Northrup, & Thorson, 1989).

These methods share the attempt to establish new forms of discourse in which moral difference can be expressed in integrative ways. Barber (1984) defines this type of discourse as

> a public language that will help reformulate private interests in terms susceptible to public accommodation; and it aims at understanding individuals not as abstract persons but as citizens, so that commonality and equality rather than separateness are the defining traits of human society. (p. 119)

When one realizes that truth is complex and sometimes contradictory and that new possibilities for truth can be created, the contradiction between expression and suppression softens.

The aim of transcendence is to express difference in ways that neither promote diatribe nor smooth over important differences. Transformative methods attempt to build an understanding of the clashing moral orders and the type of life experiences that may lead activists to adopt one or the other. This type of peacemaking aims to show how a moral order is socially constructed within the life space of a group, to uncover both the powers and limits of each constructed order, and to develop a critical attitude toward one's own and other worldviews.

When these methods work, participants have a deeper understanding of the conflict and a more respectful understanding of their opponents. They can discuss their differences on a level that reveals the underlying moral assumptions of each. They can share their misgivings about their own positions as well as the good reasons held by their opponents. They will see their own views as incomplete and open to change. The outcome can be one in which a new form of civility and a new vocabulary for expressing difference without rancor, disgust, hatred, and verbal and physical violence are possible. Most important, participants will come to conceptualize the difference in less polarized terms and may even find common ground.

The distinction between "game mastery" and "game playing" (Pearce, 1994) hinges on transformation. In "game playing," the player works within a system of rules and is effective in doing so. The game master, on the other hand, may choose to play the game by the rules, to change the rules, or to switch to another game entirely. Good activists, negotiators, mediators, trial attorneys, and diplomats are game players, but they are not necessarily game masters. Only Level 5 consciousness reveals the limits of one's own games and opens the field for the possible creation of new ones.

Level 5 involves the suspension of belief and the recognition that any version of truth is a construction within a system. Level 5 consciousness realizes in the spirit of reconstructive postmodernism that new categories can be created from old ones and that these can make possible a dialogue across systems, a synthesis of expression and suppression that allows the virtues of both to be realized in a single move.

There is sometimes a fine line between encapsulating and transcendent forms of peacemaking. As long as the peacemaker treats the two sides in a conflict as single, separate, and coherently different positions, the conflict is kept in an encapsulating frame. Even mediation, in which win-win solutions are sought, is still encapsulating if it fails to take a trans-system view. Mediation still treats each side as separate, with individual interests and goals. Barber (1984) helps us understand the difference between encapsulating and transcendent forms by discussing them in political terms:

> The basic difference between the politics of bargaining and exchange and the politics of transformation is that in the former, choice is a matter of selecting among options and giving the winner the legitimacy of consent, whereas in the latter, choice is superseded by judgment and leads men and women to modify and enlarge options as a consequence of seeing them in new, public ways. For this reason, decision without common talk always falls short of judgment and cannot be the basis of strong democratic politics. The test of legitimacy is whether an individual value has been changed in some significant way to accommodate larger—that is, more common or public—concerns. (p. 136)

Transcendent discourse requires that we deconstruct not only the opponent's moral order but also our own. From a Level 5 perspective, those engaged in a struggle reason like this:

> The protracted nature of our conflict suggests not just that the other side will not go away, but that it probably should not. The conflict is a likely consequence of one or both of us making prior, true, distinct, and whole our partial position. The conflict is potentially a reminder of our tendency to pretend to completeness when we are in fact incomplete. We may have this conflict because we need it to recover our truer complexity. (Kegan, 1994, p. 319)

In sum, then, Level 5 transcendent peacemaking is a way of managing the dialectic of expression and suppression without perpetuating the contradiction. It refuses to treat these as opposites and instead creates a new position within which both can be brought to bear.

▧ The Meta-Dialectic: Ambiguity and Commitment

The three tiers of the dialectic—silence and engagement, clash and peacemaking, and encapsulation and transformation—are akin to different entry points of the same basic contradiction. Permeating the contradiction between expression and suppression is a more fundamental difference that can be viewed as a meta-dialectic, a tension between ambiguity and commitment. This dialectic is generic in the sense that it seems to underlie most contradictions.

Warren (1984) says that the tension between ambiguity (or openness) and commitment (or adherence) is fundamental to the human condition. He puts the matter this way:

> Without the act [of commitment to a point of view], our inquiry remains ghostly and impotent, but without the recognition of ambiguity, our knowledge degenerates into ideology and our acts so easily lead to systems of totalitarian oppression, irrational indifference, and human sorrow. (p. 195)

This state of tension seems to characterize the expression of moral difference. Either we fight for what we believe, or we acquiesce. Either we promote the values of our way of life, or we admit their possible flaws. This is the meta-dialectic of fighting and making peace.

But what of transformative moves? Are these merely another form of ambiguity and subjectivity? In Figure 6.1, transformation appears in the commitment column, because it is a new type of commitment, commitment to a synthetic position that enables both expression and suppression to occur side by side, promoting the salutary values of each. It is a commitment not to a position in the debate but to a certain form of peacemaking.

Traditional peacemaking methods (court, mediation, arbitration, negotiation, etc.) usually involve the selection of ambiguity over commitment. They separate the sides in a dispute in an encapsulating way and leave as an open question which side is right. This means not that the outcome of an intervention will be ambiguous but that the enterprise itself does not take sides, does not presume one to be superior to the other, and grants potential legitimacy to both sides. In the cases of negotiation and mediation, the result itself may be ambiguous in a win-win or integrative way.

Transcendent forms of peacemaking certainly appear to share this sense of ambiguity. But there is a difference because this is a commitment to a new way of looking at disputes and a new form of discourse. It is commitment not to a cause or point of view, nor to expression or suppression, but to the values of reconstructive postmodernism itself. Kegan (1994) explains this commitment as a type of leadership. Such a leader might say,

> But that's exactly why I think I *am* a leader, why I think I'm actually *being* a leader right now in refusing to treat my ideas and plans as whole and complete, however internally consistent and comprehensive they may be in their own terms. I *am* standing up for something right now, for the importance of our suffering through this inevitably frustrating and awkward process of cobbling together a collectively created plan for getting where we want to go. And once we have the plan, you know what? I'll want to lead by continuing to stand up for the likelihood of its incompleteness, and for our need to keep seeking the contradictions by which it will be nourished and grow. (p. 323)

Postmodernism requires a commitment to the rejection of absolutes and the celebration of difference, and reconstructive postmodernism adds to this a commitment to reintegration and new ways of knowing.

This ideal is never something that one person can do alone. It is something we must achieve together. In a real sense, then, transcendent responses to moral difference are social constructions of the greatest import. In the final section of the book, we explore the characteristics of transcendent discourse.

ℵ Note

1. Quotes from the video *The Great Divide* by Deborah Fort and Ann Skinner-Jones used with permission of DNA Productions, Santa Fe, NM. Copyright © 1993.

PART III

Toward a
Transcendent Discourse

7

New Forms of Eloquence

Sally Miller Gearhart (1995), by her own description, is a retired activist. As she describes herself, "I've marched and rallied and picketed, raged and wept and threatened, crusaded and persuaded and brigaded" (p. 8). But something has changed in Gearhart's life. She now lives by a credo that she would have scorned in previous years. Instead of confronting, she is joining. We can think of no better way to introduce the subject of transcendent discourse than with her story.

> Five years ago when I'd see a logging truck loaded with redwoods or old oak, I'd shoot the driver a finger. He'd (could it ever be a she?) shoot one right back at me and then go home and put a bumper sticker on his truck that would read, "Hey, Environmentalist, try wiping your ass with a spotted owl!" Three years ago, I was a shade more gentle. I would stop dead in my tracks, glare at the driver of a logging truck and make sure he read my lips: "Fuck you, mister." Then he'd go home and add another bumper sticker to his truck: "Earth First! We'll log the other planets later."
> These days . . . I'm practicing acknowledging loggers as "fellow travellers on Planet Earth," as Trudy the bag lady would say, doing what they do just as I do what I do; I'm laying off any attempt to change

or even judge them, and I'm trusting that acknowledgment of our kinship can make a positive difference in the texture of all our lives.

When I meet an erstwhile "enemy," instead of moving immediately into horse posture or splitting the scene entirely (fight or flight), . . . I look for the joining point, the place where we are the same, where we can meet each other as beings who share the experience of living together on this planet. I introduce that into the conversation, and we talk about the thing that belongs to both of us. . . . When I can't find any common ground upon which to stand with some "enemy," like a logger, then I ask him to take me into his world for a day or two so I can hear him and his buddies talk about what it means to be out of work in a poor country with a family to feed.

When all's said and done, I measure these encounters by my feelings, I like "joining" better than fighting or running away, better even than marching for or rallying to a cause. . . . I've learned a lot. I've learned that it is never individual men/people who are my "enemy" but complex systems of exploitation that have emerged from centuries of alienation and perpetuation of violence; it is these systems and that consciousness—not the people—that I can, with integrity, hope to change. I've learned that my pain, anger, and/or hatred accomplish nothing except to render me ineffectual and to increase the problem by adding to the pain, anger, and hatred that already burden the world. I've learned that whole parts of my identified "enemy" are really my own self, walking around in different costume. And in the moments where we've found some joining space, I've learned that, though I still may not choose to spend time with him, I do feel kinship or love for that killer, that exploiter.

To tell the truth, I don't regret a single day of my past as an activist. I figure that the desire to stop injustices and heal the earth is an honest and an honorable one. It's a big part of who I have been as a being incarnated on this planet. That's why I've been here: to speak out and confront, to crusade and fight, to be involved in those struggles up to my eyeballs. I wouldn't know what I know, and probably wouldn't be making the changes I'm making, without those experiences of activism. But right now, I'm getting clear and unmistakable signals that it's time for another approach. If I can still hold strong to my standard of what is just and decent and appropriate behavior for human beings and yet to go about my life with a new awareness, with joy in the process instead of my former debilitating pain, and if I can do all this without creating and maintaining "enemies," then I have to try it. (pp. 8-11)[1]

◙ Beyond Normal Discourse

Normal discourse consists of attempts to persuade, frustrated diatribe, threats, and sometimes even violence. Is it possible to transcend these customary responses, to break the pattern, to engage those with whom we disagree on a new level, and to avoid the seemingly unavoidable spiral toward schism, degradation, and violence? We believe that these achievements may be possible if certain forms of transcendent discourse are employed.

Transcendent discourse goes beyond the normal communication of moral conflict. It can lead to the possibility of constructive dialogue, new contexts in which to understand differences, and new ways to compare and weigh alternative choices. Where normal discourse in moral conflict is condemnatory, transcendent discourse suspends execration. Where normal discourse tries to persuade, transcendent discourse aims to probe. Where normal discourse is designed to prevail, transcendent discourse seeks to compare and critique. Transcendent discourse can be employed by a mediator as a means of intervention, by a judge as a means of comparison, by a critic as a means of commentary, by an audience as a means of analysis, or by the disputants themselves as a means of transforming the conflict.

Intractable moral conflicts are not easily resolved and, in many cases, may not be resolvable. Indeed, many such conflicts should not be resolved, but they can be argued in more humane, enlightening, and respectful ways, at least "continuing the conversation" (Rorty, 1979, p. 394). Needed is a format or setting in which trust can be built between conflicting parties, a forum in which issues and options can be explored without attempts by one party to influence the other, and an atmosphere in which beliefs are put at risk of change, not by influence from the other party but by self-reflection.

Psychologist Herbert Kelman (1972) isolates three aspects of communication in conflict-transcending events that may change the dynamic of interaction:

> The participants can learn new information about how the other side thinks; new ways of thinking about the issues and the conflict itself can be introduced; and participants can come to see their own communication patterns up close and to understand some of its problems. (pp. 192-194)

International relations scholar Terrell Northrup's (1989) analysis of intractable conflicts suggests that frozen conflicts can begin to thaw when two types of change come about. The first of these is a change in the dynamics of the relationship between the parties; the second, and most profound, is a change in the sense of identity by one or both sides in the conflict. Transcendent discourse is a form of communication that has the potential to accomplish either or both of these. In recent times, several attempts to achieve this level of communication have been made.

The Burton Experiment

As part of a program of studies on innovations in conflict resolution, Burton (1969) and his colleagues at the Centre for the Analysis of Conflict at University College, London, conducted a workshop in 1966 on the Greek-Turkish conflict in Cyprus. The weeklong session brought together two representatives from the Greek community, two from the Turkish community, and six social scientists.

The sessions were informal and relatively unstructured. The participants first presented their own views of the conflict, and the social scientists asked questions designed to clarify these positions. Next, the social scientists presented a number of models of conflict and asked the participants to discuss these and to apply them to their own dispute. Finally, toward the end of the week, the participants discussed possible ways to overcome the conflict. The social scientists provided insights into why a solution favored by one side was objectionable to the other. Throughout the workshop, the facilitator attempted to move the discussion away from accusation and blame toward analysis, self-reflection, and mutual understanding.

The session itself was at least partially successful in that the participants were able to talk to one another respectfully, make use of newly shared frames of reference, and gain information about one another's perspectives. At the least, certain citizens representing groups that had not been able to communicate with one another spent a week together exploring mutual concerns.

The Fermeda Workshop

The Fermeda Workshop was the brainchild of psychologist Leonard Doob (1970) and his colleagues at Yale University. It dealt with an intractable border dispute between Somalia, Ethiopia, and Kenya. After much difficulty securing government approval, Doob and his associates organized a workshop at the Hotel Fermeda in Switzerland. Participants included six Somalis, six Ethiopians, and six Kenyans, along with a small group of social scientists.

The workshop was two weeks in length and included sessions in which various theories of leadership and conflict were presented by the leaders. Unlike the Burton experiment, the Doob workshop did not begin with a discussion of the dispute itself. During the first few days, every attempt was made to avoid the topic. Instead, the leaders worked on creating an atmosphere in which the participants could get to know one another as individuals and to talk freely among themselves.

Then, in a second stage, the topic turned to the dispute. During this period, a role reversal exercise was used to help each participant develop empathy for the others. Finally, attention was directed at creating specific proposals for resolution of the conflict itself.

The workshop was successful in helping the participants to see the humanity of each of the parties in the dispute. Especially in the first phase, the participants did communicate freely. The experiment was less successful, however, in dealing with the conflict itself. Several of the participants refused to participate in the role reversal exercise, and, in the end, no consensus was reached on solutions.

The Doob experiment illustrates how difficult intractable conflict can be. Dealing on a higher level with the real issues that divide us and that involve us emotionally is hard to do, and many people simply refuse to cooperate in this type of exercise.

National Coal Policy Project

The National Coal Policy Project was an ambitious attempt at environmental conciliation, negotiation, and policy making in 1977 (Alexander, 1978). It followed a model known as policy dialogue, in which interested and conflicting parties attempt to resolve their differences on matters of general policy (Amy, 1987). The idea is that if a group can discuss ideas in the abstract out of the heat of a particular dispute, group members may be able to gain insights and generate acceptable ideas not possible in more immediately threatening circumstances.

The coal project was the brainchild of Gerald Decker, an industry executive with considerable credibility among both environmentalist and industrialist camps. He was interested in experimenting with policy dialogue and making use of a number of conflict resolution techniques. Decker met with leading environmentalists early in 1976 and, after considerable difficulty, persuaded most of them to participate in the talks. A number of industrial representatives were also induced to participate.

The talks were sponsored by Georgetown University's Center for Strategic and International Studies, which raised more than half a million dollars to support the project (Alexander, 1978). The participants were divided into five task groups. They went on a number of field trips to see the potential sites and impacts firsthand and respond to these as a group. In their talks, they were required to use "the rule of reason," which consists primarily of avoiding the deceptive tricks so commonly found in litigation: "Opponents should not . . . withhold data from each other or employ misleading tricks. They should not impugn motives or characters. They should avoid dogmatism, acknowledge uncertainties, and disclose personal interests and biases" (p. 101).

Although the bargaining was hard and the project certainly had its critics, the results seem to have exceeded all the participants' expectations. The two sides came to have a good deal of mutual respect, and a number of difficult issues were resolved. This project shows that deep conflicts can be transcended, at least on occasion, and such discourse can have a practical impact on the way things are done in the future.

Syracuse Area Middle East Dialogue

The Syracuse Area Middle East Dialogue (SAMED) has been a highly successful program bridging the Arab and Jewish communities in the greater Syracuse area on the Israeli-Palestinian problem (Schwartz, 1989). In fact, SAMED began something of a movement, which includes a variety of programs, including the American Coalition for Middle East Dialogue and the Seminar on Palestinian-Israel Reconciliation Efforts.

SAMED was a grassroots experiment in "Track II diplomacy," the involvement in ordinary citizens in informal and unofficial negotiations. The idea is that officials engaged in primary, or Track I, negotiations are unable to explore a full range of options because of political constraints. Citizens, who are somewhat removed from the immediate setting in which the dispute is occurring, however, do not have such constraints and may be somewhat freer to pursue a variety of alternatives (Davidson & Montville, 1982).

SAMED made use of the dialogue-group model, in which citizens sat together to discuss on a deep level the issues that separate them. The SAMED groups met regularly during an extended time, explored the issues, and attempted to reach consensus on certain ideas or courses of action.

SAMED began with only six persons in a pilot group—two Palestinians, two Jews, and two others—and they met frequently to plan the program and solicit members. An expanded dialogue group then met for more than a decade from once a month to once per quarter. The convener alternated between representatives from the two sides.

The group attempted to sort issues and tackle them systematically. Certain issues proved unmanageable at certain times, some were difficult but possible, and others fairly easy. Some issues had to be dropped and revisited later, and some remained intractable through a long period.

This project was highly successful. SAMED continued for a number of years, made contact and shared ideas with other dialogue groups, and even developed a consensus statement. Because of the duration of the project and the frequency of meetings, the members came to know one another well and appreciate the unique backgrounds and insights of each person. The members of the group did not always agree, but they continued to respect and talk to one another.

SAMED shows us that transcendent dialogue can be continual and long-term. People do not necessarily run away from it, and it can actually attract people and bring them back again and again. Once people see a new way of handling conflict, they may easily give up old patterns that seemed for so long to lead nowhere.

The projects discussed here represent ambitious and brave attempts to transcend difficult conflicts. They demonstrate that this is not an easy job but that with creativity and tenacity, it can be accomplished.

℞ A Different Form of Eloquence

As we saw in Chapter 5, *eloquence* is the exemplary use of discourse within a rhetorical tradition. To be eloquent is to represent the highest form of expression within the frame of rules adopted by a moral community. Within a moral community, eloquent speech elicits attention, respect, and compliance. Between moral communities, however, it can create frustration, hatred, anger, and even violence.

Transcendent eloquence is an answer for people who are frustrated by the interminable character of moral disputes and long for something other than more of the same. As a form of speech that bridges or encompasses various moral communities, transcendent eloquence has five general characteristics; it is (1) philosophical, (2) comparative, (3) dialogic, (4) critical, and (5) transformative.

First, *transcendent eloquence is philosophical.* By this, we mean that it attempts to uncover the assumptions about knowledge, being, and values that lie behind the positions in conflict. As a philosophical discourse, transcendent eloquence is educational, aiming to help those involved to understand the basis of the conflicting belief systems on a deep level. It has the potential to create constructive reflection because it attempts to move the discussion from intractable struggle over issues to a more fundamental level at which the parties must pause and reflect.

The philosophical nature of transcendent discourse contrasts sharply with many traditional methods of dispute management, which are oriented toward interests, issues, and power and require disputants to itemize their objectives, make arguments for their interests, and use power. These methods are appropriate and effective in cases of conflict in which the disputants agree on the standards and means by which the conflict is to be conducted and settled, but they do not work well in cases in which the disputants' realities are incommensurate.

Many common methods of dispute resolution, including direct and representative democracy, litigation, and bargaining, fail to recognize just how deep many conflicts are. These methods certainly recognize the passion and commitment in moral disputes, but they often neglect the assumptive differences that lie behind this entrenchment. Political scientist Mona Harrington (1986) states that the failure to look at deep divisions "precludes real bargaining" and produces only superficial and temporary benefits. She concludes that "in the long run, by denying the seriousness of differences in society, the myth solidifies those differences and polarizes the groups bearing them" (p. 26). Ironically, then, if we ignore our axiomatic differences, we may end up more divided in our clash than might otherwise be the case.

The second characteristic is that *transcendent eloquence is comparative.* It attempts to create categories that can be used to compare otherwise incommensurate systems. It conceives a language with which people can talk with one another about their assumptions and see the relative powers and limits of each side. Stout (1988) refers to this type of language as a *creole,* a vocabulary in which two divergent groups can communicate and reason together.

We have already noted the inherent difficulty of comparing incommensurate systems. According to philosopher Richard Bernstein (1985), incommensurate and incompatible ways of thinking are not normally comparable because *from within either system,* there is no conceptual or logical frame sufficient to account for their differences. Therefore, such frames must be *created outside the conflicting positions.* This does not mean that the disputants themselves cannot do this, only that they have to get out of their own frame of reference to do so. Transcendence, thus, is a wholly creative act. It is a movement of the mind that enables one to surpass customary limits (Zwiebach, 1988.)

Comparability is an interpretive process of coming to understand each reality separately. It is a creative process of inventing a set of dimensions along which the two systems might be compared. As Bernstein (1985) expresses the process,

> The task of understanding an alien culture may require the imagina-
> tive elaboration of new genres, or the stretching of familiar genres, in
> order to compare what may be incommensurable. The art here is one
> of knowing what are the right questions to ask in approaching the
> strange practices of an alien culture. (p. 65)

Such comparison is always local and specific to the dispute in question because there can be no single, universal scheme that compares all systems.

Stout (1988) refers to this process of creating new categories as *bricolage,* which involves putting elements of a new moral language together. Like laying brickwork, it is the building of a new structure:

> My claim is simply that how the various fragments of moral language
> are related to each other and to the whole can be every bit as important
> as which parts are selected for retention or available for use in the first
> place. (p. 75)

Stout shows us that differences are created in discourse and that new discourse based on fragments of the old can and should be created to search for common ground.

Comparative ethnography is a discipline that creates models to compare cultures (Hymes, 1974; Philipsen, 1989). In comparative eth-nography, incommensurate cultural systems are analyzed by creating a comparative model. In a sense, the parties in a moral conflict are different cultures, making the procedures of comparative ethnography apropos.

Transcendent eloquence, like comparative ethnography, aims to find or create a context within which the two sides can be compared on some dimension. Disputants themselves may then confront their differ-ences on this new level. The aim is to transform the pattern of interaction between the conflicting parties so that it becomes more productive. The process involves a reconceptualization of the nature of the conflict and makes rational discourse between the parties possible. The transformed conflict forces spokespersons to deal directly with their own assumptions, which may give pause to see the rationality of the other side and even to open disputants to change.

In essence, this type of move is a shift from experiencing the conflict from within one's own moral order to viewing it from an outside, more objective position. Cooper (1981) refers to it as taking an "antidote" to one's own morality to understand how it compares with other, diverse forms (p. 31).

Spokespersons in the abortion debate normally speak different languages. The pro-choice advocates speak a language of individual rights and social welfare, whereas the pro-life advocates speak a language of scriptural authority and sanctity of biological life. This debate could be transformed into a dialogue about ethics and moral decision making, apart from the limited issue of abortion. Here a common language of moral decision making would need to be created. In this type of discussion, the parties would have the opportunity to understand the moral assumptions on which the claims of each side are based. Such an analysis would not center on whether a woman has the right to have an abortion; instead, it would focus on the criteria one uses to make a moral decision, any moral decision.

Another transcendent category that might be employed in the abortion debate is the definition of personhood apart from the specific question of whether a fetus is a person under the Constitution. As each side struggles to define personhood and to hear the definitions of the other side, both sides would be able to compare the conflicting positions on this issue (Gert, 1988; Goodman, 1988). The aim would be not to reach agreement but to understand better the basis for disagreement.

In sum, then, productive comparisons cannot be made in intractable conflicts until higher-level categories are created for this purpose, and when that is done, true dialogue on radical issues may occur. This experience can provide concepts that the participants never considered before, ideas that might be used as a common reference point in analyzing the statements and actions of each side.

The third characteristic is that *transcendent eloquence is dialogic.* It attempts to move the debate from statements designed to convince to statements designed to explore. It transforms a debate in which attributions are hurled back and forth into an interaction in which the relationship itself can be discussed. This approach changes from accusing and belittling and an attitude of exclusiveness to realizing that both sides are limited by the axioms of their respective realities and an attitude of inclusiveness.

The distinctive features of dialogue have been summarized by comparing it with monologue:

> In monologue, questions are asked to gain a speaking turn or to make a point; in dialogue, questions are asked to invite an answer. In monologue, one speaks in order to impress or impact on others; in dialogue, one speaks in order to take a turn to an interpersonal process that affects all participants. (Pearce, 1993, p. 61)

Thus, when we enter dialogue, we risk being changed.

Bernstein (1992) says this type of discourse "presupposes moral virtues—a certain 'good will'—at least in the willingness to really listen, to seek to understand what is genuinely other, different, alien, and the courage to risk one's more cherished prejudgments" (p. 51).

Transcendent eloquence fulfills Rorty's (1979) call for an open-minded conversation between disputants to construct a truth that is acceptable to the larger community within which the conflict occurs. Hill (1991) refers to such discourse as a conversation of respect:

> Conversations of respect between diverse communities are characterized by intellectual reciprocity. They are ones in which the participants expect to learn from each other, expect to learn non-incidental things, expect to change at least intellectually as a result of the encounter. . . . In such conversations, one participant does not treat the other as an illustration of, or variation of, or a dollop upon a truth or insight already fully possessed. There is no will to incorporate the other in any sense into one's belief system. In such conversations, one participant does not presume that the relationship is one of teacher to student . . . , of parent to child, of developed to underdeveloped. The participants are co-learners. (p. 43)

Frentz (1985) refers to this type of dialogue as *rhetorical conversation:*

> A rhetorical conversation is a narrative episode in which a conflict over opposing moral viewpoints re-unites the agents with their own moral histories, with the moral traditions of which they are a part, and—perhaps most important—with an awareness of the [Aristotelian] virtues. As a practice, the goods internal to rhetorical conversations are an awareness of the moral unity of individual life and a sense of the quest for the ultimate good for self and humanity. (p. 4)

In its ideal state, this type of dialogue creates the understanding that although we have deep moral differences, we are intelligent, well-meaning, and moral people. Showing that other people do not meet our criteria for intelligent moral probity and trustworthiness serves no good purpose. As such, transcendent eloquence should make participants aware and respectful of the moral tradition of opponents, even though they may continue to disagree.

We do not mean to suggest naively here that all participants in conflicts are well-meaning and moral people. Some are out to subvert others deliberately for personal gain, and such people can probably be found on both sides of most issues. If we start with the assumption that the other is mad, bad, or sick, however, we block ourselves from transcendent ways of dealing with the conflict and risk initiating a self-fulfilling prophecy in which the other becomes as despicable as we treat them. Starting assumptions are always risky; sometimes it is worth taking different risks for peace, as the Arab-Jewish dialogue well illustrates.

The dialogue-group model can be a practical means of transcending moral conflict. Legal scholar Richard Schwartz (1989) suggests that in dialogue groups, people with diametrically opposed views really can learn from one another, that such dialogue and intergroup learning can be expanded by creating a network of groups, and that official policy can even be affected by communicating ideas generated in such groups to policy makers.

The effect that dialogue can have on conflict is illustrated by this anecdote from the National Coal Policy Project (Alexander, 1978) described earlier:

> At first, the industrial members of the mining task force were horrified when they heard that one of the members picked for the environmental side was Robert Curry, professor of geology at the University of Montana. In the past, Curry's biting testimony before courts and hearings had often lacerated the technical competence and the motives of his industrial opponents. But by the time the mining task force had completed its first field trip through the lignite fields in the Gulf states, Curry's expertise and evenhanded attitude had earned the industry men's profound respect. "If I wanted to open a mine in the West," says lawyer John Corcoran, co-chairman of the mining task force and a former board chairman of Consolidation Coal, "Bob Curry is the first man I would go to about the environmental problems." (pp. 101-102)

The fourth characteristic is that *transcendent eloquence is critical*. It exposes the powers and limits of each side in a controversy, and, more important, it exposes them to the advocates on both sides. It enables participants and viewers to weigh alternatives on the basis of these strengths and weaknesses. It deconstructs the assumed truth value of conflicting claims so that choices must be made, not on the basis of which side is correct according to some set of criteria or whose interests will be promoted or how decision makers happen to "feel" about the issue but on the basis of the powers and limits of the various positions when they are held up side by side. Transcendent eloquence, then, does not seek adjudication based on any foundational truth, nor does it employ the emotive method of choice deplored by MacIntyre (1981), in which one simply does what feels right.

Transcendent eloquence is critical, then, in a way that most traditional forms of discourse are not. Customary methods of managing disputes in our society are designed to clarify goals, articulate reasons, make choices, and compromise. They rarely compare the powers and limits of conflicting views directly, and they almost never allay assumed truths.

The National Coal Policy talks illustrate the critical nature of transcendent eloquence. To talk on the level of policy rather than specific disputes enables the participants to weigh the strengths and weaknesses of various actions in the abstract without the threat of consequences within an actual situation. The Syracuse project is another good example because it employs a set of rules that make criticism of ideas, not persons, both acceptable and expected.

The final characteristic of transcendent eloquence is that it is *transformative.* It reconstructs the context in which the conflict is to be understood. Any action or object—a wave of the hand, a facial expression, a manuscript, a piece of graffiti, a videotape—is always understood in relation to some context. Actions and contexts are closely related to one another. What we do and how we understand what is done depend on context, but the action in turn also serves to define the context in which it occurs. Each influences the other.

Within a moral conflict, then, what spokespersons say is interpreted within some context, which is in turn affected reflexively by their talk, gestures, writings, and actions. The Religious Right, for example, understands its dispute within a context of good against evil. In turn, statements made by advocates of the Religious Right, as well as those of their opponents, further bolster the context—a struggle of morality versus immorality. The other side, however, understands the struggle differently. For the liberals, the conflict is one between freedom of speech and religion and narrow-minded forces of repression. Their statements and actions and those of their conservative opponents are understood in this light and in turn reinforce their understanding of what is going on.

Most moral conflicts are stable. The patterns of understanding and acting are repeated over and over, and the participants rarely change their understandings of what is going on. Indeed, the context constitutes the accepted social worlds of each side. It is the moral imperative that galvanizes their actions. It is what they are. They become what they do. Their identities as warriors are determined by how they respond to the struggle. If people act toward others in hateful ways, they become filled with hate. Hate becomes the context.

It sometimes happens that people will speak and act in ways that transform the context so that their acts can be understood differently. To change the context means to change the identity of the community in which one acts.

For example, mediators can create new contexts within which the disputants can understand what is going on in new and more productive ways. In child custody disputes, for example, the mother and father may have different ways of understanding the situation, each in its own context. The wife may suggest that she should receive custody because of the sanctity of the mother-child relationship. The husband, on the other hand, may suggest that his wife has shown herself to be unfit and that he must therefore take custody. In this type of conflict, a mediator may attempt to create a new context that will change the issues, such as "the best interests of the child." This context does not focus exclusively on the mother-child relationship or the fitness of this particular mother but does focus on what is best for the child in these particular circumstances, which may be a more complex issue than the earlier framings would admit (Wynn, 1989). The notion of joint custody, now the option of choice in most states, grew from this type of contextual reconstruction.

The Burton and Doob experiments described earlier in the chapter attempted to reconstruct the context of the conflict from certain intractable issues to the personal relationship between conflicting parties. The National Coal Policy Project is another example of a different type. Here the context is changed from a specific dispute to general policy. As this case shows, when issues are raised to a higher level than those of a specific disagreement, words and acts are interpreted differently, and disruptive patterns of conflict interaction can be broken.

Transcendent discourse reconstructs contexts in large measure by changing the meaning of winning. In contemporary American life, winning as a cultural prescription has become a central virtue in the national culture. The self-help section of any bookstore contains shelf after shelf of books offering advice on how to win. We are deeply troubled if we do not have the most powerful military, the highest standard of living, the largest market share in computers and automobiles, and the most gold medals at the Olympic Games.

Many areas of life are expressed in the metaphor of winning. We do not simply want to reduce the use of drugs; we have a war on drugs. Political campaigns are not straightforward ways of presenting alternative candidates and platforms; they are contests in which the participants have game plans and that result in the declaration of a winner. The infatuation with winning causes us to focus on the "thrill of victory" and the "agony of defeat." In other words, winning is a pervasive context that defines our identities and drives our actions.

There are at least three positions we can take on winning. The first is to win at any price, the second is to count the costs and win if we can afford it, and the third is to rethink what winning means. The third option is contextual reconstruction.

The moral algebra of winning changes when we shift from being a partisan to looking at the conflict from outside. Whether Bill has more marbles than Betty does not really matter if the competition to take marbles is either irrelevant or itself the problem to be examined. In a transcendent mode, winning in the sense of prevailing over those who do not share our moral position may really equate to losing because in the process, we lose something more important. Winning in such situations can come to mean refusing to play the game of fight to the death.

Transcendent eloquence holds out the hope of transforming the context so that parties to the dispute can understand themselves, the opponent, the issues, and the relational patterns in different terms. This is what we mean by contextual reconstruction (Branham & Pearce, 1985).

We have seen that transcendent eloquence is philosophical, comparative, dialogic, critical, and transformative. Although a full-blown transcendent discourse possesses all these features, many forms of discourse display only some of them. In the *Roe v. Wade* (1973) decision, for example, the Court received amicus curiae briefs and arguments addressing some higher-level moral and theological differences between the two sides. To some extent, then, certain participants in the litigation did raise the argument to a philosophical level. The parties did not, however, have a dialogue about their differences, nor did the

Court make any concerted effort to compare the positions on this level or to outline the powers and limits of the two sides. The decision in *Roe v. Wade* explicitly refused to consider theological arguments about personhood and relied strictly on Constitutional precedent and interpretation to make its judgment as to the personhood of a fetus (Faux, 1988).

℞ Values and Limits
of Transcendent Discourse

Another way to understand the nature of transcendent eloquence is to consider what it is not. First, transcendent eloquence is not a method for resolving moral disputes, although, as the cases presented earlier in this chapter show, a number of resolution techniques may employ it in an attempt to deal more humanely, respectfully, and intelligently with moral conflict than is often the case. Transcendent discourse extends the hope of managing and coordinating moral conflicts without degradation, repression, or violence. When choices must be made between two morally incompatible positions—a frequent occurrence in contemporary society—transcendent discourse can provide a more rational basis for such decisions. Transcendent eloquence is also a way to promote constructive dialogue. It is a way to reduce harmful or destructive patterns of interaction. It can sometimes even lead to local, temporary solutions, where none have been found before.

Second, transcendent eloquence is not a neutral ground without values and commitments. It can create a new ground so that conflicts can be viewed in fresh ways, but that ground is never value-free. Transcendent eloquence is committed to reflection, to tempered judgment, and to humane talk.

Third, transcendent eloquence is not blindly relativistic. It lies somewhere between MacIntyre's (1981) *wistful alienation* and *utopian criticism* and Rorty's (1979) *smug approval* and *liberal apologetics*. It attempts to understand each position on an assumptive level before evaluating the powers and limits of the position. It makes judgments about positions by appropriateness in historical situations, and it promotes deep reflection by all participants so that they can make their own judgments.

Fourth, transcendent eloquence is not a panacea. It is a form that is appropriate in some situations and not in others. We are not suggesting that transcendent eloquence is the only appropriate response to moral conflict. Sometimes civility, tolerance, and rhetorical eloquence are appropriate. In the face of extreme oppression or violation of human rights, resistance and revolution will sometimes be judged the only alternative. Moral conflicts do not usually necessitate such an extreme form, however, and transcendent eloquence becomes an appropriate and fruitful option on these many occasions.

We believe that when the salutary powers of transcendent eloquence are known and when it is made an option, this avenue often will be taken. We also suspect that those whose commitments lie with conflict management—people such as mediators, judges, counselors, and managers—will find this type of response inviting. It is especially appealing in situations in which the disputants are stuck in a rigid and harmful pattern of interaction or a pattern that prevents decisions from being made.

We believe transcendent eloquence is the best option in situations in which both conflicting parties subscribe to the Kantian ideal that human welfare must be an end in itself and never merely a means toward some other end. Most of the well-known moral conflicts in our own society fit these criteria.

Transcendent eloquence, then, is worthy of our consideration as a response to moral conflict. It can transform contempt into respect. It can minimize unreflective condemnation, and it can reduce violence. If we can see the rationality behind our opponent's position, we will no longer be able to characterize the opponent as insane, stupid, or misguided. When we realize the limits of our own philosophical assumptions, we will have more respect for the powers of our opponents' views. And, in the end, we will find the ability to disagree without silencing the other side through repression, injury and pain, or death.

This type of discourse is uncommon in our society. It is what Rorty (1979) calls "abnormal." But it does have value and needs to be nourished. It is, as Bernstein (1992) asserts, "the basis—perhaps the only honest basis—for hope" (p. 53).

◈ Note

1. First printed in *Sojourner: The Women's Forum*, Vol. 21, No. 1 (September 1995).

8

Model Projects in
Transcendent Discourse

Birmingham, Alabama, has come a long way since Dr. Martin Luther
King Jr. wrote his famous letter from the jail there. One of the most
notable achievements has been the development of an enthusiastic
network of citizens deliberating across racial and class lines about the
issues affecting their daily lives.

This type of interaction has not always been possible in Birmingham. Even 15 years ago, the city was divided, with little communication
between the groups affected by national and city issues. Wanda Minor
wanted to change this state of affairs and, at the suggestion of David
Mathews of the Kettering Foundation, instituted a series of public
forums and study circles in which citizens could talk among themselves
and across group lines.

Since the early meetings sponsored by Ms. Minor in Birmingham,
more than 40,000 citizens have participated in broad-based community
forums sponsored by a coalition of nearly a hundred neighborhood
associations that cut across the entire fabric of Birmingham society. Each

year, the coalition sponsors about 20 forums involving 200 people each. At tables for 10, each group and a facilitator discuss a significant public issue.

As these groups talk, they consider a number of viable options, or choices. They question the trade-offs and costs of each option. They explore their respective positions on these choices and, in the process, uncover the basic values underlying each. They share stories from their own lives as they reveal to one another the experiences that have led them to favor one choice over another.

Sometimes minds are changed in these Birmingham groups, but often they are not. What does happen is that the participants leave the forums stewing and mulling over the options.

This activity is the heart of true citizen democracy, and it is one way in which people and groups with deeply held opposing moral convictions can express and explore their differences constructively and humanely. Through these forums, people can construct a frame within which to compare their incommensurate positions and even find common ground.

This chapter showcases three projects that deal with moral conflict in new and productive ways. The story of Birmingham comes from one of these, the National Issues Forums (NIF). We have chosen to include the NIF because of its established history of work in the improvement of public discourse and citizen democracy. Like the other projects featured in this chapter, it provides an alternative to contentious debate, solidified polarization, reciprocated diatribe, and violent clash.

The National Issues Forums

A Collaboration

Charles F. Kettering is famous for getting people out of the mud by inventing a car starter that could be operated from the comfort of the driver's seat, but he accomplished something else of great import. In 1927, Kettering established a foundation to promote research and practice in politics. Throughout its history, the Kettering Foundation has been interested in addressing persistent problems in politics. Endowed with $130 million, the foundation seeks joint ventures with other organizations to find productive ways for democracy to work.

In addition to its active publication program, Kettering promotes unofficial citizen dialogues between countries; studies the manner in which citizens, the press, and government officials address major issues; and investigates the way in which policies on technically complex issues get worked out.

One of Kettering's most ambitious and important collaborations is with the National Issues Forums. The NIF and its 3,000 local partner organizations annually sponsor thousands of public forums and study circles such as those in Birmingham, in which citizens deliberate about significant national issues. These groups are not unlike old-fashioned town meetings, in which citizens weighed their choices and expressed opinions on important public policy decisions.

> **Information about the National Issues Forums is available through the NIF at 100 Commons Rd., Dayton, OH 45459-2777.**

The NIF model assumes that there is something not quite right about American politics. Politics, of course, involves activities necessary for the management of community problems and issues, including deliberation as well as voting and influence. "Politics as usual," which seems preoccupied with special interest appeals and vote winning, seems to leave out the citizen as the ultimate source of direction for public policy and the legitimate authority in society. In democracy at its best, citizens are more than individuals with separate needs and wants, vote casters. Citizens should speak as an interdependent "public" with many common concerns. The problem is to find those common concerns.

The public, of course, does not speak as a unitary voice but as a series of communities with some shared and some differing values. The issues dividing the country are really defined by those differing values, and politicians do not always understand this basic fact of democracy. Too often, the public is considered a thing to win over to get elected so that the "real business" of the country can get done.

That real business involves defining problems, seeking expert advice, learning the "facts," and choosing the best "solution." Missing from this formula are public knowledge and judgment. The public knows what is important to individuals and communities, and when citizens have an opportunity to deliberate, an informed public judgment can develop.

Public judgment is not the same thing as the public opinion discovered in quickie opinion polls. Opinion polls may tell a politician what to say to win votes, but policy making requires an understanding of public judgment.

The NIF believes that ordinary citizens have a wisdom that experts often do not have. They may not understand the technical aspects of building a bridge, but they know that the increased traffic a bridge would bring into their neighborhood would be unpleasant and unhealthy. Citizens may not have training in professional education, but they know when their children are learning and when they are not. Citizens may not understand nuclear physics, but they do understand the health consequences of a nuclear accident.

Such basic citizen understandings have always been the heart of democracy, making citizen input vital in policy making. But informed public judgment cannot develop without deliberation, and NIF forums and study circles are a means for moving deliberation, most often associated with the lofty halls of Congress and the Supreme Court, down to the grassroots level.

To provide a setting in which deliberation can take place, the NIF annually identifies a few significant issues that seem to be emerging on the national scene, such as poverty, the family, or affirmative action. Table 8.1 lists many of the NIF issues covered through the years.

For each issue, three or four choices are identified, and videos and issue booklets are written to provide information about the issue and the choices it entails. Then, special events ranging from forums and study circles to regional and national conferences are planned to explore the issues. Some of the partners for these events are the National Archives, presidential libraries, The Learning Channel, National Federation of State Humanities Councils, National Council for the Social Studies, and numerous local colleges and universities, schools, libraries, churches and synagogues, senior centers, and community groups.

Whether in a study group, forum, or televised event, citizen deliberation involves "choice work." Viable choices must be weighed against one another for an informed judgment to be reached, and this cannot be done superficially. Participants in deliberation learn that there are good reasons for each choice, that people have lived experiences that lead them to favor one choice over another, and that positions on important issues involve core values, some of which are shared and some of which are not.

TABLE 8.1 NIF Issues

1995-1996

Mission Uncertain: Reassessing America's Global Role
Pocketbook Pressures: Who Benefits From Economic Growth?
The Troubled American Family
How Can We Be Fair: The Future of Affirmative Action

1994-1995

Kids Who Commit Crimes: What Should Be Done About Juvenile Violence?
Admission Decisions: Should Immigration Be Restricted?
Values in the Schools: The Collapse of the Commons

1993-1994

The Poverty Puzzle: What Should Be Done to Help the Poor?
The $4 Trillion Debt: Tough Choices About Soaring Federal Deficits
Health Care Costs: Why Costs Have Exploded, What Can Be Done?

Earlier years

Education: How Do We Get the Results We Want?
People and Politics: Who Should Govern?
The Health Care Crisis: Containing Costs, Expanding Coverage
Criminal Violence: What Direction Now for the War on Crime?
Prescription for Prosperity: Four Paths to Economic Renewal
Energy Options: Finding a Solution to the Power Predicament
The Boundaries of Free Speech: How Free Is Too Free?
America's Role in the World: New Risks, New Realities
The Battle Over Abortion: Seeking Common Ground in a Divided Nation
Regaining the Competitive Edge: Are We Up to the Job?
Remedies for Racial Inequality: Why Progress Has Stalled, What Should Be Done?
Growing Up at Risk
The Day Care Dilemma: Who Should Be Responsible for the Children?
The Drug Crisis: Public Strategies for Breaking the Habit
The Environment at Risk: Responding to Growing Dangers
Health Care for the Elderly: Moral Dilemmas, Mortal Choices
Coping With AIDS: The Public Response to the Epidemic

SOURCE: National Issues Forums. Used by permission.

By carefully listening to the perspectives of others and sharing their own, NIF participants work through the issue to come not to agreement but to an informed judgment. In the process, they find out that people who disagree with them are not mad, bad, or stupid; that they may share some common concerns and values with people who favor a different option; and that every option has its costs. The question in looking at any choice is what must be given up to get what is wanted.

The result of citizen deliberation is not consensus on specific choices but a clearer understanding and consideration of the values involved. From deliberation comes a type of complementary action in which even opposing choices are viewed as moving in a common direction.

For example, if townspeople were debating whether to build a bridge over their river at point A, point B, or not at all, they probably would not reach consensus on the answer, but in talking about it, they might discover some common set of concerns that the city should take into account in deciding whether and where to build the bridge. If, for example, economic well-being, safety, and neighborhood quality emerged as important values, then the decision makers would be seeking that solution that would best accomplish these three things in concert. The decision would not be easy, but it would be informed by a public wisdom.

In short, deliberative democracy involves a logic with seven elements: *Actors* make *choices* by *deliberative dialogue* to come to *public judgment* and thereby establish a *public voice* through *common ground* and *complementary action*. This ideal is explained in more detail in Table 8.2.

Normally, when we encounter differences on important public issues, we have a tendency to take sides and argue to win. The objective in such situations is to make arguments and persuade those in power to support our position. This is a frame within which one view is pitted against another.

The NIF creates a different frame, one in which the discussion itself is central. Deliberation is the means by which public judgment emerges. And public judgment is not predicated on one side persuading the other. It is an outcome in which people continue to hold different views but with a fuller, more complete understanding of the powers and limits of each view. In the NIF, democratic process is more important than winning. Uncovering common ground and understanding real value differences are more important than showing how one view is superior to all others. Consequently, in NIF sessions, listening is just as important as speaking.

The goals of NIF sessions and the types of questions that moderators ask can create a set of synthetic categories in which people with otherwise incommensurate moral orders might communicate. Opposing views no longer constitute a contradiction because their expression and exploration, not the difference itself, are important. People with opposing views end up on the same side, that of promoting deliberative democracy and the improvement of public life for us all.

TABLE 8.2 The Logic of Deliberative Democracy

1. For "politics" to work as it should—to have the qualities we want it to have—citizens have to be ACTORS. The political system won't change by itself. People have to claim their responsibilities and act on those responsibilities, both by setting directions for government and by joining together in public action.

2. People can't act together, either to set directions or to join together as citizens, without making CHOICES, or decisions, which are always difficult because choices about what kind of community or country we want to have force us to deal with the pulls and tugs of all that is deeply valuable to us.

3. This "choice work" requires a DELIBERATIVE DIALOGUE. Deliberation is that particular form of reasoning and talking together in which we weigh carefully the costs and consequences of our options for action—as well as the views of others. Forums have to be deliberative if they are to lead to sound decisions.

4. Deliberation changes first opinions into more shared and reflective PUBLIC JUDGMENT about how we should act. Deliberative forums create public knowledge (new information about the public) and a PUBLIC VOICE.

5. The information or public voice that comes from a forum about how citizens see issues and what they are or aren't willing to do to address them is essential information for officeholders. When governments act in accord with public judgment, they acquire public legitimacy.

6. Deliberation also helps people find connections among varied purposes and a shared sense of direction. Though not complete agreement or consensus, this COMMON GROUND FOR ACTION that deliberative forums create is the basis for public action, which is a rich array of citizen-to-citizen actions that are mutually reinforcing or COMPLEMENTARY because they serve compatible purposes. Public action makes governmental action effective.

SOURCE: National Issues Forum. Used by permission.

Through the years, several NIF projects have emerged as particularly noteworthy. The Birmingham project is certainly one of these, as are those mentioned below.

Various Catholic groups have been involved in the NIF almost from its inception, but in 1989, the church expanded its involvement with the establishment of the National Issues Forums in the Catholic Community (NIFCC). This project is distinctive because of its size and because it employs materials of special relevance to the church, including scriptural concerns, church history, and church social documents.

One of the largest NIF programs is in El Paso, in which English and Spanish forums are regularly held. Among its most interesting projects were the international forums involving Mexicans and Americans divided by the Rio Grande, which flows between El Paso and Juárez. The issue was the environment, a significant point of contention between the two cities.

TABLE 8.3 Goals of Issues Forums

1. Identify the range of realistic alternatives and move toward a choice.
2. Make a good case for those positions one dislikes as well as the position one likes, and consider choices one has not considered before.
3. Understand others have reasons for their choices and that their reasons are very interesting—not dumb, unreasonable, or immoral.
4. Realize one's own knowledge is not complete until one understands why others feel the way they do about the choices.
5. Consider the underlying values of each choice.
6. Leave the forum/study circle "stewing" over the choices. (Sometimes this is called "thinking.")

SOURCE: National Issues Forums. Used by permission.

NIF has become quite popular at community colleges around the country. Various programs are offered, including cross-generational miniforums, televised forums, student-club sponsored forums, multi-day conferences, study circles for senior citizens, forums for high school and junior high school students, a Spanish language forum for Hispanic farmworkers, and credit courses on NIF issues.

The Process

The centerpieces of the NIF model are community forums and study circles. Forums are public events lasting about two hours, in which members of the community gather to talk about an issue. Study circles do essentially the same thing but are limited to a smaller group of people and meet several times to go into the choices in greater depth than is permitted in a forum. In both settings, participants attempt to achieve six goals, as outlined in Table 8.3.

NIF sessions are most fruitful if participants have read the issue booklets in advance. (This level of preparation is not always practical in forums, but use of the booklets is standard practice in most study circles.) These booklets, written by the Public Policy Institute, are really quite good. They are written in an accessible style at about the 12th-grade level, cover all the basics of the issue, and are available for less than $5. (Simplified books at the 5th- to 7th-grade level are also available.) The booklets address each choice in some detail, including the evidence and reasons used by proponents and the chief objections of those who oppose the option. Often, the various positions on an issue are incommensurate, and the booklets do a good job of relating the moral orders from which the positions stem.

At the beginning of the forum, participants are asked to complete a pre-forum ballot as a way to get everyone focused on the issue. Comparing the data from the pre-forum ballot with a similar form completed at the end can provide useful information about how the group may have changed as a result of the deliberation.

After participants have reviewed the goals and philosophy of NIF (which are called the ABCs of NIF) and sometimes viewed a video or participated in an icebreaker, the moderator asks participants to share stories and perspectives as part of a brief exploration of the issue before moving to the choices. The heart of deliberation is consideration of the actual choices. Each choice is put on the board and discussed one by one and at some length. (In study circles, a separate meeting may be devoted to each choice.) Participants are always given a chance to add options in addition to the standard ones. They are also encouraged to look at ways in which choices might be combined.

Participants are encouraged to probe the arguments in favor of and against each alternative, and those in favor are asked to consider what they would be willing to trade off for their favored choice. In a good forum or study circle, participants are pushed to contribute more than standard arguments, to share their own experiences that led them to favor one position over another, and to identify the values underlying the choices.

After the group explores the choices, it engages in a process of "harvesting," in which deep value differences and common ground are identified and discussed. The most important question at this point is whether any shared values can be communicated to policymakers as a direction for decision making on the issue.

The moderator obviously plays a crucial role in a forum or study circle. The "Do's and Don'ts" for moderators are listed in Table 8.4. Table 8.5 lists sample questions for deliberation, and questions for harvesting are included in Table 8.6.

Selecting and Developing the Issues

The issue year corresponds to the academic year (e.g., 1995-1996), and new-issue forums begin in the fall and run through the spring. Issue selection at the NIF begins late in the summer before the year in which the issues are used, so that, for example, the process for establishing the

TABLE 8.4 Do's and Don'ts for Moderators

DO'S:

DO create opportunities for all Forum participants to discuss issues on an equitable basis. Create a climate for nonevaluative and noncritical audience participation and encourage active audience listening skills.

DO stay personally neutral. Resist "straw votes" and other moves to "resolve" the issue.

DO clarify your role with the group in advance.

DO make sure the group understands the Forum guidelines.

DO play the role of timekeeper by moving the group when a point has been fully discussed.

DO summarize the group's discussions from time to time—or call on the recorder to do so.

DO be prepared to intervene to interpret questions and points of discussion and to handle controversies.

DO help the group explore deeper dimensions of a topic. Each person arrives at his or her own judgment after extensive discussion of the choices and trade-offs involved.

DO return a question to the person who asked it or to another person so that the moderator does not take responsibility for the question.

DON'TS:

DON'T let any one resource person or Forum participant dominate the discussion.

DON'T take sides.

DON'T insert your personal feelings.

DON'T allow the group to make you an "expert" or "answer person."

DON'T drive the group too rigidly.

DON'T allow the group to drift without guidance.

DON'T resort to such formal processes as *Robert's Rules of Order*—you are not seeking a majority opinion.

DON'T talk too much.

DON'T moralize about what individuals have to say or about the group process.

SOURCE: National Issues Forums. Used by permission.

1995-1996 issues began in the summer of 1994. At this time, the various community organizations affiliated with the NIF are sent a list of about six possible issues for the following year. These organizations discuss the list and add other possible issues. The expanded list is returned to the NIF with an indication of the group's top three. The NIF then uses these local preferences to establish the following year's issues.

After the issues are chosen in the early fall, the NIF gets busy with the Public Agenda Foundation to outline the chief options for addressing the issue and researching material for the issue booklets. By summer,

TABLE 8.5 Sample Deliberation Questions

You indicated you wanted to take all these actions, but if push came to shove, what would you do?

What would be your priorities?

Could you tell me a story to illustrate that?

What might that mean in your life?

What are your criteria for judging?

What are the consequences of that choice on all the citizens?

How would someone make a case against what you just said?

I understand you do not like that position, but for the persons who hold it, what do you think they deeply care about?

What is there about this choice that you just cannot live with?

How do you separate what is a private matter and a public matter on this issue?

What values might people hold who support that position?

Would someone identify the values that seem to be clashing? What is really happening here?

SOURCE: National Issues Forums. Used by permission.

the new fall issues and choices are ready to announce, and booklets are completed and available for distribution.

Issue definition and choice generation are complex and thought-provoking processes in their own right. From a fuzzy problem statement, a more precise wording of an issue in the form of a question must be developed. The issue must be worded in such a way that its answers are the chief choices facing the nation. For example, one of the issues in 1995-1996 was affirmative action. The question turned out to be, "How Can We Be Fair?" Three choices were generated as answers to this question:

1. *Eliminate affirmative action—People, not government, can ensure fairness.* Society is ready to judge all people on their individual merits. We must abandon government controls that force us to treat people as members of competing groups.

2. *Provide support so that people can compete equally, but do not discriminate in favor of any group—Level the playing field, but don't fix the game.* The best way to promote fairness is to give all people the nurturing, education, and training they need to compete fairly for jobs and advancement.

3. *Continue affirmative action—We need to finish the job we started.* We've made progress in bringing about fair treatment for minorities and

TABLE 8.6 Sample Harvesting Questions

Now that we have considered this issue, how do we see the problem?

Given that each of us has a somewhat different personal perspective on the problem, can we restate it in a way that takes account of each of our perspectives?

What are the understandable concerns we have about the consequences of resolving this issue one way rather than another? What are the downsides to each of the choices open to us?

Given that each of us is motivated by things we attach great importance to, can we redescribe the issue in a way that highlights what each of us values? What are the things we care about deeply that pull us in different directions, that make this such a hard choice?

What are the values we believe a widely accepted public policy ought to respect as far as possible?

What consequences do we consider unacceptable? Are there ways of resolving the issue that we can reject because the consequences are unacceptable?

Is there any general way of proceeding that would address everyone's most serious concerns and protect the things we care about most deeply?

Is there a range of actions we all might be able to live with, even if they are not ideal from our personal point of view? Could we all go along with some actions and rule out others?

SOURCE: National Issues Forums. Used by permission.

women, but discrimination is still pervasive. We can't stop the progress now. (National Issues Forums Institute, 1995, p. 1)

Although the NIF is most known for developing its annual public issues, non-national issues are also possible, and the NIF encourages local groups to use its methods to define and deliberate on state, regional, and local issues. (Theoretically, there is no reason why the method would not work for international issues as well.) The NIF process is especially appealing for local issues, and the issue definition process itself is educational for the participation of local citizens. Kettering helps to make this possible by offering issue-framing workshops to teach the skills necessary to define and develop issues and to write issue booklets.

Special Programs

In addition to regular forums and study circles, the NIF and Kettering have other noteworthy projects. We summarize several of these here.

Literacy Program. In the 1980s, literacy programs began moving in the direction of greater emphasis on critical thinking skills. At the same time, the NIF was becoming well established but mostly among middle-class and upper-middle-class citizens. Certain literacy project directors became aware of the NIF and began to consider using the concept in their work. Unfortunately, at that time, the NIF materials were too difficult to be used for literacy training. To solve this problem, some literacy programs "translated" the booklets to a lower grade level, and subsequently the NIF itself began to develop the abridged, lower-level booklets.

Once appropriate materials had begun to be produced, the NIF recruited six literacy programs to begin a pilot program. In 1986, the regular literacy program was launched, and by the 1990s, bolstered by growing enthusiasm and significant grant money, it had become established.

Public Voice. Every spring, the NIF, in conjunction with PBS, sponsors "Public Voice," a television program designed to communicate insights gained from the year's forums to journalists, politicians, and the general public. The program features a panel of high-level political leaders and reporters. In 1994, for example, Senator William Cohen of Maine appeared with E. J. Dionne of the *Washington Post*, Barbara Cochran of CBS News, and Michel McQueen of ABC News. The panelists view clips from various forums and discuss the implications of what citizens express there. The event takes place at the National Press Club.

National Issues Convention. Early in 1996, a National Issues Convention was held in Austin, Texas. Although it was not actually organized by the NIF, the annual NIF issues were discussed on a major scale. A randomly selected sample of the American public framed questions on these issues for Republican and Democratic candidates for national offices during a five-hour public television program. This was followed a week later by a 90-minute broadcast in which the deliberation itself was reviewed and discussed.

The national convention is just one sign of the recognition the NIF has deservedly received. The NIF is an inspiration for everyone interested in establishing new forms of discourse in our society.

❦ Public Conversations Project[1]

In December 1989, Laura Chasin was watching a television debate on abortion. As the exchange degraded into slander, the moderator noted, "There's nothing going on here but a lot of noise." Chasin, a family therapist, realized that this program was like some of the heated exchanges she had witnessed in family therapy. Indeed, the similarity seemed striking to her.

When families get stuck in unproductive conflict, their conversations become predictable. Negative patterns of interaction repeat themselves when family members become uncreative and limited in how they communicate with one another. Chasin also knew that therapists have skills for helping such family members engage one another in new, constructive ways. She wondered if methods adapted from family therapy could be applied to the improvement of public discourse on divisive issues, so she got together a group of therapists, a writer, and a television producer to brainstorm ideas for interventions in these political debates. With this, the Public Conversations Project (PCP) was born.

Information about the Public Conversations Project is available through the PCP at 46 Kondazian St., Watertown, MA 02172.

The PCP group members met for several months and identified abortion as their first topic. In 1990, they began organizing a series of actual dialogue groups. After working with 18 small groups of pro-life and pro-choice participants, they felt reasonably confident that they had a somewhat repeatable, field-tested model for opening dialogue on abortion in small groups. They were unsure how much the model would need to be adapted for use in more "natural communities" of activists or for groups in conflict over other issues, but they felt that the general approaches they took in their initial work held promise for other topics and other contexts. The PCP now employs a variety of methods in groups that vary in size and duration.

The PCP transcends predictable oppositions in a variety of ways. The conveners resist the idea that there are two simple sides to conflictual issues. Instead, they acknowledge that individuals who normally oppose one another may have important shared concerns and that those who normally side with one another may have significant differences. They focus not on the sides of a debate but on the personal experiences of participants in relation to the conflict. Most important, they create a "stage" on which people who care passionately about an issue can talk about it in a new way. In sum, the PCP team members accomplish four things:

First, they prepare people for a journey into the new. In all their pre-session contacts, they clarify what is new about the event and present it as a true alternative. Participants are told that like any adventure, the experience may feel odd but that a shared sense of strangeness is exactly what makes the foray an adventure.

Second, team members create a safe context. The agreements and ground rules, as well as the thorough preparation that individuals are provided, make an otherwise risky proposition safe enough to try. There will be no surprises in the *process*, although, like any adventure, there will probably be some surprises in *content*. The conveners and facilitators avoid contributing content and make a commitment to facilitate in an evenhanded manner. At the same time, the facilitators are not neutral on processs because they aim to create a new, constructive conversation.

Third, PCP events discourage old patterns of interaction. The physical space, discussion format, questions, and facilitator's role preempt debate and confrontation. Participants speak only for themselves and without making attributions to other persons. This makes old patterns easier to avoid. The group has learned the importance of providing structure that promotes new forms of discourse and preempts old, dysfunctional patterns of interaction. To do this, facilitators must know something about the old patterns and become educated on the subject and conflict being dealt with.

Finally, the PCP team aims to foster the co-creation of a new conversation. The discussion proceeds at a slow pace, and the tone is personal and heartfelt. Questions are framed from a position of curiosity and respect. Answers are often complex and unpredictable.

The members of the PCP have produced a series of creative and powerful techniques for transforming moral conflicts. In their several projects, they have developed a set of guidelines and principles that can serve any group desiring to become engaged in this field.

In summarizing their work, Chasin and Herzig (1993) have written,

For the dream of democracy to be realized, we need more than voting booths and a free press. We also need a revitalized process of public discussion. We need to hear not only from experts and leaders, who are given equal time to present polarized speeches, but from the ordinary people in the next house, the next town, and the next continent. We need to hear not only about pointed arguments, but also stories about complex human experiences. We need not only constraint from impinging on the rights of others, but also the compassion to understand threats to their dignity. We need not only the freedom to speak, but also the curiosity to listen. The personal is political and the political is personal. As politics embraces the personal—as authentic dialogue finds a place in public exchange—democracy becomes a living and breathing organism, not a machine or a formula. Family therapists can make a major contribution to enriching democracy through dialogue. (p. 190)

The Dialogue Group

All the meetings designed by the PCP share one thing in common. They are *dialogues.* Dialogue differs from debate in a number of ways (Table 8.7). Debate features the persuasive presentation of a case; dialogue features sharing personal experiences and listening to the experiences of others. Debate emphasizes predetermined arguments; dialogue relies on spontaneous sharing of personal perspective. Debate is designed to present a solid case; dialogue admits doubts and gray areas. Debate is presentational and monologic; dialogue is interactive. Debaters ask questions designed to reveal the flaws in the opponent's case; participants in dialogue ask questions from genuine curiosity and the desire to know more. Debate assumes a united front; dialogue uncovers important differences among those who share a point of view. Debate aims to persuade; dialogue aims to understand.

An important characteristic of dialogue is the search to discover deep differences and shared concerns. Debate will tell what the different positions are, but it will not reveal the personal experiences that have led to different values and social realities. Dialogue, in contrast, can. Participants in dialogue can also learn that people who share a public position may have different experiences and may not necessarily share the same assumptions and values.

At the same time, dialogue can also expose shared hopes and concerns among people who would otherwise come to blows in public settings. The PCP avoids the term *common ground* because it is often understood to denote a static middle, a new position, or even a traitorous

TABLE 8.7 Debate and Dialogue

Polarized Debate	Dialogue
Pre-meeting communication between sponsors and participants is minimal and largely irrelevant to what follows.	Pre-meeting contacts and preparation of participants are essential elements of the full process.
Participants tend to be leaders known for propounding a carefully crafted position. The personas displayed in the debate are usually already familiar to the public. The behavior of the participants tends to conform to stereotypes.	Those chosen to participate are not necessarily outspoken "leaders." Whoever they are, they speak as individuals whose own unique experiences differ in some respect from others on their "side." Their behavior is likely to vary in some degree and along some dimensions from stereotypic images others may hold of them.
The atmosphere is threatening; attacks and interruptions are expected by participants and are usually permitted by moderators.	The atmosphere is one of safety; facilitators propose, get agreement on, and enforce clear ground rules to enhance safety and promote respectful exchange.
Participants speak as representatives of groups.	Participants speak as individuals, from their own unique experience.
Participants speak to their own constituents and, perhaps, to the undecided middle.	Participants speak to each other.
Differences within "sides" are denied or minimized.	Differences among participants on the same "side" are revealed, as individual and personal foundations of beliefs and values are explored.
Participants express unswerving commitment to a point of view, approach, or idea.	Participants express uncertainties, as well as deeply held beliefs.
Participants listen in order to refute the other side's data and to expose faulty logic in their arguments. Questions are asked from a position of certainty. These questions are often rhetorical challenges or disguised statements.	Participants listen to understand and gain insight into the beliefs and concerns of the others. Questions are asked from a position of curiosity.
Statements are predictable and offer little new information.	New information surfaces.
Success requires simple impassioned statements.	Success requires exploration of the complexities of the issue being discussed.

TABLE 8.7 Debate and Dialogue

Polarized Debate	*Dialogue*
Debates operate within the constraints of the dominant public discourse. (The discourse defines the problem and the options for resolution. It assumes that fundamental needs and values are already clearly understood.)	Participants are encouraged to question the dominant public discourse, that is, to express fundamental needs that may or may not be reflected in the discourse and to explore various options for problem definition and resolution. Participants may discover inadequacies in the usual language and concepts used in the public debate.

SOURCE: Public Conversations Project of the Family Institute of Cambridge. Reprinted by permission of the Public Conversations Project.
NOTE: This table contrasts debate as commonly seen on television with the kind of dialogue we aim to promote in dialogue sessions conducted by the Public Conversations Project.

compromise. "Enemies" often fear that agreeing on anything is tantamount to submission. In contrast, people who can discover shared concerns and hopes are unlikely to feel threatened by this discovery and may derive a sense of hopefulness about relationships previously frozen in conflict. People do not have be in agreement to have a shared concern, and dialogue has the advantage of keeping the focus on the process rather than the position.

In its experiments in dialogue, the PCP has employed three sets of processes—preventive, facilitative, and collaborative.

Preventive Processes. Preventive processes are actions that minimize the possibility of debate. Such processes begin with the initial contact and include the type of agreements into which participants are asked to enter.

Fully informed and voluntary participation in a dialogue process is essential. In the original dialogue-group model, potential participants were contacted well in advance and provided a complete orientation to the dialogue process. A carefully drafted letter was mailed to potential participants, followed by a phone call. The letter and phone call emphasized the nature of the event and how it would be different from traditional debate. Those contacted were asked to consider participating in an unusual and alternative conversation on the issue. They were told of the importance of personal sharing and listening. The phone call

TABLE 8.8 A Sample of Orienting Guidelines Mailed to Participants and Discussed on the Telephone Before the Dialogue

---

The spirit of dialogue is likely to exist in a group to the degree that those involved in a conversation do the following:

- Agree to abide by a set of communication ground rules
- Speak personally—as individuals, rather than as representatives of groups or organizations, and from their own experiences and views rather than about the experiences and views of those not present
- Have as their goal the exploration and building of relationships rather than persuasion or confirmation of their own views
- Speak to communicate their own reality fully rather than to attack the reality of others or to persuade them to change that reality
- Listen to understand accurately rather than to rehearse a response or prepare a rebuttal
- Take responsibility for making themselves understood
  - Choosing words that do not raise their listener's defenses
  - Expressing their feelings so they become sources of contact and learning rather than alienation and antagonism
- Listen with respect to each speaker—regardless of how different that speaker's views are from those of the listener
- Are genuinely interested in discovering what they share as well as understanding more accurately how they differ
- Are willing to be surprised

SOURCE: Public Conversations Project. Reprinted by permission of the Public Conversations Project.

was never rushed, and participants were given as much time as they needed to ask questions and have their concerns addressed.

In different situations, the specific methods involved in PCP's preparatory work with participants differ. For example, with large groups, extended telephone conversation may take place only with a small planning group, but all who receive a letter of invitation are encouraged to call if they have any questions or concerns or if they have anything to share with the facilitating team that may help the facilitators design and guide the meeting more sensitively. In all cases, agreement to participate is based on an understanding of the nature of the event and the type of ground rules that will be proposed and a willingness to participate. (See Tables 8.8 and 8.9.) They also understand the event to be a collaboration between the facilitators and participants. They know that the conversation will be *their* conversation and that the facilitators will participate only on the level of process.

Preventive approaches are used during, as well as before, dialogue sessions. For example, in the abortion dialogues, the groups are ar-

TABLE 8.9 Suggested Ground Rules

The spirit of dialogue is fostered by the observance of a set of ground rules which foster a culture of respect and reciprocal interest. We recommend that each of you agree to abide by a set of communication ground rules that you collectively decide on and to authorize the facilitators and each other to see that what is agreed on is adhered to.

Ground rules which have often proved helpful include the following:

1. Keep the contents of these meetings completely confidential, that is, agree that outside this room you will speak only about your own experience, not about anyone else's even in a disguised fashion, unless you have explicit permission to do so.

2. Use considerate language. For example, refer to others in terms they prefer to have used to describe themselves (e.g., pro-choice and pro-life, rather than anti-life and anti-choice).

3. Refrain from attempts to persuade or convert.

4. Avoid interrupting. Allow others to complete their thoughts before responding.

5. Speak for yourself, from an "I" position that minimizes talking about what "we" and "they" think and feel.

6. Talk *to* rather than *at* one another.

7. Check the accuracy of your assumptions about what others' words mean. Avoid attributing thoughts or feelings to people that they have not previously stated they have.

8. Pass if you are not ready or willing to speak and respect the exercise of this right by others. (That is, a participant may decide not to respond to any question he or she is not ready or willing to answer. No explanation will be expected or need be given. No negative connotation will be attached to such decisions.)

9. Avoid side conversations.

10. Avoid rhetorical questions.

11. Work together to see that "airtime" is shared equitably.

SOURCE: Public Conversations Project. Reprinted by permission of the Public Conversations Project. NOTE: This is one sample. Proposed ground rules are always tailored to the needs of the group as understood by those who design the meeting, and they are presented to the participant group as proposals, open to revision.

ranged in a circle or semicircle if possible, and confrontational arrangements are avoided. The facilitator puts name cards on the seats to ensure that participants will sit next to individuals who take different positions than they do on the issue. The chairs are never divided into two sides with opposing members across from one another.

Facilitative Processes. Once the discussion is under way, several facilitative processes help to promote dialogue. Facilitators help the group design and guide its own process. They enforce the ground rules to maintain a safe, respectful environment. They intervene as necessary to make sure that everyone has a chance to say what he or she wants to say, to keep the group on track, and to sort out possible misunderstandings. They ask questions that create openings for new types of interaction. The facilitators also gather feedback at the end of and between meetings.

The dialogue sessions on abortion began with dinner. The participants and the facilitator shared a light meal before the hard work of dialogue began. At the dinner, participants were encouraged not to disclose their position on the issue but to get to know one another as persons first. Participants reported that when they realized they could not figure out which side of an issue someone was on, their stereotypes began to fade away.

Whether or not a dialogue session is preceded by a meal, an informal and welcoming atmosphere is created. Once participants are seated in the dialogue room, the ground rules and guidelines are proposed, discussed, and modified as desired. In addition to preempting debate, the ground rules also promote dialogue. They encourage personal sharing, establish a safe and confidential environment, and highlight respectful communication.

In the dialogues on abortion, the next step involves three opening questions. Although these questions are not always used in other contexts, they are suggestive of the general approach taken by PCP. In particular, they illustrate the power of carefully worded and sequenced questions.

The first of these questions encourages the participants to think about and share their personal experience: "We'd like to begin by asking you what personal life experiences have shaped your current views and feelings about abortion? Could you tell us something about one or two of these events or experiences?" In the customary pattern, the facilitator goes around the circle and invites each person in turn to address this question. The pass rule allows a member to decline to answer without explanation.

After all participants have had a chance to answer this question, they are asked, "Now we'd like to hear a little more about your particular beliefs and perspectives about the issues surrounding abortion. What is at the heart of the matter for you?" Again, this question is discussed by going around the circle, and the pass rule applies. Once this has happened, a third, more complicated question can be asked:

Many people who have participated in dialogues such as this have said that within their general approach to this issue they have some dilemmas about their own beliefs—for example, some conflicts of values or ambivalent feelings, perhaps about "hard cases." It has been productive when participants have shared some of their dilemmas. So—the next question is this: Are there any mixed feelings, value conflicts, uncertainties, or other dilemmas within your overall perspective on this issue that you are willing to mention?

This question may be answered "popcorn style," in which individuals speak whenever they are ready.

Because dialogue is personal, a period of personal questions is almost always included in the process, often after the stock questions are discussed. Anyone can ask another member a question, although the pass rule still applies. The personal questions must be asked in the spirit of true curiosity and a desire to know, and rhetorical questions are not permitted.

Collaborative Processes. The PCP is best known for its single-session dialogue groups on abortion, which followed the format described above. These single-session groups normally consisted of about six participants who had not known one another before the event. In recent years, the project has worked with continuing groups, larger groups, and groups of people who interact regularly in personal, professional, and political contacts outside the dialogue.

Whatever the context, the PCP team always builds collaborative elements into the design of the process—from invitation, to meeting, to follow-up. Participants are viewed as collaborators in a joint effort to create a constructive conversation. In addition, they provide feedback that guides the PCP team in improving the methods employed in future groups. When working with groups through time, the PCP team seeks to maximize opportunities for the participants themselves to monitor and make suggestions about their own processes and to promote adherence to group agreements, with less reliance on the facilitator. As an example, Table 8.10 presents guidelines that the PCP team offered to one of its continuing groups.

In most cases, toward the end of the session, participants are asked to reflect on their process. They may be asked what they have done or refrained from doing to make the conversation go as it did. This gives them an opportunity to identify and acknowledge their specific contributions to the dialogue. A final open-ended question usually elicits allusions to aspects of the dialogue that were especially valued.

TABLE 8.10 Sharing Responsibility for Our Process
                (Self-Help Suggestions and Tools)

---

1. If you feel *cut off*, say so or override the interruption. ("I'd like to finish . . .")

2. If you feel *misunderstood*, clarify what you mean. ("Let me put this another way . . .")

3. If you feel *misheard*, ask the listener to repeat what he or she heard you say and affirm or correct the statement.

4. If you feel *hurt or disrespected*, say so. If possible, describe exactly what you heard or saw that evoked feelings of hurt or being disrespected in you. ("When you said X, I felt Y.") If other words are not available, say "OUCH" to flag your response while it is fresh.

5. If you feel *angry*, express the anger *directly*, rather than expressing it or acting it out *indirectly*. (e.g., "I felt angry when I heard you say X," rather than trashing another person's statement or asking a sarcastic rhetorical question.)

6. If you feel *confused*, frame a question that seeks clarification or more information and/or paraphrase what you have heard. ("Are you saying that . . . ?")

7. If you feel *uncomfortable* with the process, find a way to comment that will move things forward, or state your discomfort with or without a suggestion of what might work better for you. ("I think we have been talking past each other for the last five minutes. Does anyone else have a similar perception?" or, "I'm not sure what to do about it"; or, "I'm not comfortable with the intensity of this conversation, it does not feel constructive. I suggest we have a one-minute Time Out to reflect on what we are trying to do together.")

8. If you feel the conversation is *going off track*, make a process observation or refocus the conversation. ("We seem to have moved away from the topic at hand; I suggest we refocus this conversation on . . .") Another option is to call for a moment of silence in which everyone can reflect on how things are going in relationship to the goals of this section of the conversation.

SOURCE: Public Conversations Project. Reprinted by permission of the Public Conversations Project.

Private feedback is also solicited. In large groups such as a 90-person group on biodiversity, most feedback will come to the team on forms, but telephone interviews are used to the greatest extent possible. Facilitators often hear in these follow-up calls that the dialogue had a profound effect, not so much in changing minds but in building respect, understanding previously demonized opponents, and, indeed, creating a more complex understanding of the issue itself.

Related Projects

Members of the PCP have undertaken some ambitious and fascinating large-scale programs. In this section, we describe briefly three of these—stereotyping workshops, brainstorming meetings, and conferences on population and family planning. Each of these has had worldwide impact well beyond what could reasonably be expected from a single dialogue group. At the same time, however, each is predicated on the same basic principles operating in any small dialogue group.

Workshops on Stereotyping. In 1987, as a precursor to the PCP, Richard Chasin, Maggie Herzig, and Paula Gutlove began a series of remarkable international workshops on "Assumptions and Perceptions That Fuel the Arms Race." The workshops, conducted under the auspices of the Nobel Peace Prize-winning International Physicians for the Prevention of Nuclear War, examined potentially dangerous stereotypes related to the arms race.

The workshops brought together citizens from various countries to reveal and discuss their stereotypes of one another. The workshops varied in format, but they all centered on the intriguing question, "What stereotypes do you think citizens of the other country have of you?" This type of question, inspired by a form of circular questioning used in family therapy, helps participants learn about the perspectives and sensitivities of others. This question was presented in a variety of fascinating ways at the different workshops.

The first workshop was held in Moscow in the spring of 1987 for 42 participants from 15 countries. The participants were divided into five subgroups consisting of Americans, American allies, Soviets, Soviet allies, and nonaligned countries. The first four groups were asked to list six negative stereotypes they thought "the other side" had of them that might have contributed to the arms race. The nonaligned group listed six such stereotypes on both sides. Groups were asked to include stereotypes based on personal, social, and cultural characteristics as well as on national and international goals.

In a plenary session, the stereotypes from the groups were combined into an American and a Soviet list. Then the groups met again to select four from their respective lists that they wished to disavow. (Members of the nonaligned group were asked to disavow two from each list.) In addition, the groups were asked to select one stereotype that was especially offensive and to tell the entire group why. For example, one perceived stereotype was that the Soviet Union wanted to dominate the world by force. In disavowing this stereotype, one woman spoke of Soviet citizens' experience with the realities of war and the death, pain, and suffering that war had caused them to endure.

The second workshop in the series was held in Montreal in 1988. By this year, the Cold War was coming to an end, and bipolar arrangements seemed less appropriate. Consequently, the 80 participants were grouped according to their actual country, 10 in all. Each national group was asked the following questions:

1. Many people from (name of an adversary country) assume that many people from my country have the following personal or cultural characteristics or values, which, if true of us, could fuel the arms race and/or retard the progress of developing nations.
2. Many people from (name of an adversary country) assume that the leadership of my country has the following policies, goals, or intentions, which, if true, could fuel the arms race and/or retard the progress of developing nations.

The resulting lists were put up on sheets, and the groups created a visual display by putting colored stickers on those stereotypes most inaccurate or offensive.

The third workshop was held in Hiroshima in 1989 for 71 participants from 16 countries. Because the world situation had changed even more and the participant group was the most culturally diverse yet, a number of modifications in the format were made. In a warm-up exercise, the participants listed three aspects of a hoped-for global future and three of a feared future. They then explored the strengths their country possessed that could help bring about the desired future and avoid the feared one.

After these points were discussed, the stereotype task was done in a fashion similar to the other workshops, but the disavowals were more complex. Groups could classify items on the list as untrue, mostly true, or mostly untrue but understandable. In recognition of the hosting culture of Japan, these three choices were framed as gifts. Designating a stereotype as untrue was a gift of *reassurance;* saying a stereotype was mostly true was a gift of *acknowledgment;* and explaining why a stereotype was understandable was a gift of *understanding.* The third type of disavowal was an especially interesting transcendent move because it allowed for some disavowal of the stereotype but indicated that "we can see why you might think this."

The fourth workshop was held in Stockholm in 1991. Following essentially the same format as Hiroshima, this meeting involved 40 delegates from 15 countries.

Brainstorming Meetings. Like the stereotyping workshops, the brainstorming meetings were not officially part of the PCP, but they were conducted by PCP members, privately and in concert with other organizations. The brainstorming work had creative and productive results.

The idea behind these meetings was to bring together individuals with shared concerns but different professional orientations and perspectives—individuals who, for a number of reasons, would not normally engage in dialogue and collaboration. Participants were chosen to create a group of "strange bedfellows," individuals from a variety of professions, with different skills, varying perspectives, and separate fields of influence. Participants were invited as individuals, not as representatives. The purpose of the meetings was to garner the creativity of diversity to produce new strategic ideas for solving a problem.

Brainstorming is a process of creative idea production, not limited by criticism or editing. Its goal is to produce a large quantity of ideas, many of which might not be considered in the normal course of events. Brainstorming is followed by a more critical refinement period, in which the least promising ideas are eliminated and the most promising ones are identified, combined, and organized.

The brainstorming meetings usually followed a three-day format. On the first evening, the participants talked about their background and resources, and the brainstorming method was explained. Then the following morning, a common experience was provided, usually an informal presentation by a resource expert. The larger group was then divided into three to five smaller groups. Each group brainstormed with the help of a facilitator and recorder.

Returning to a plenary session, each group offered a brief report. The next step often involved participants writing on small cards one or two topics each would like to pursue in greater detail. These cards were then clustered into a small number of subtopics. Participants chose which group to join according to subtopic, and the new groups met, brainstormed, and reported back. This process was repeated at least twice.

In this process, a few major themes typically emerged. These were often hot issues around dilemmas, conflicts, and proposed projects. When disagreement was expressed, the facilitators worked with participants toward understanding and renewed solidarity.

In the final segment, some type of resolution sometimes emerged. On occasion, concrete proposals or actual products of some sort were created.

Dialogue Retreats and the Cairo Project. In recent years, the PCP team has had many opportunities to draw on its experiences with small dialogue groups, stereotype workshops, and brainstorming sessions to design dialogue retreats in a collaborative manner with groups in search of less polarized interactions. These efforts often involve collaboration with other facilitators and with a planning group or steering committee of participants.

One example is the Northern Forest Dialogue Project. This continuing project, which PCP conducts in partnership with an organizational consultant, Grady McGonagill, involves a series of regional and site-based gatherings of stakeholders in the northern forest of New York, Vermont, New Hampshire, and Maine. Most of these meetings have been two days in duration and involved 15 to 30 people. Participants were usually involved in environmental organizations, the forest product industry, or local communities.

Another example is the Maine Forest Biodiversity Project, involving a series of retreats for approximately 90 stakeholders in the biodiversity of Maine. It has been conducted through partnership between a steering committee of eight participants and the project's two lead facilitators, Maggie Herzig from PCP and Grady McGonagill. Participants include forest product industry managers, environmental activists, managers of public land, small-woodlot owners, and scientists.

Among the most important and ambitious projects of the group is the Cairo Project, a series of four meetings with nongovernmental organization leaders who were preparing to participate in the United Nations Conference on Population and Development in Cairo in October 1994. About 25 participants with interests in family planning, population, international development, and women's health and rights attended these meetings. Holly Carter, a political scientist from Northwestern University, worked with the PCP's design and facilitation team.

Specific methods used in the meetings on family planning will be described briefly here to convey a flavor of PCP's approach to dialogue retreats, although PCP's methods vary from project to project. In 1993, it was clear that relationships among some pivotal leaders of the family planning and population networks in the United States had become too strained to allow effective planning for the Cairo event. The PCP was recruited to facilitate a one-day exploratory meeting in Washington, D.C., involving 15 leaders of these networks. The result of this meeting was consensus that environmental groups were tangential to the major obstacles in the way of improved collaboration and need not be equally included and that the next meeting should be longer.

The PCP secured funding to convene what turned out to be the first of three dialogue weekends. The invitation to the first of these weekends (Cairo One) on Martha's Vineyard in July 1993 stated the goals of the event. These were to clarify participants' shared concerns, to develop better understanding of what their differences actually were, and to explore ways in which differences might become a resource rather than a restraint.

Two other dialogue weekends were held subsequently—one in July 1994 (Cairo Two) and a post-Cairo retreat in January 1995 at the Pocantico Conference Center in Tarrytown, New York. Each conference was about three days in length. With a few exceptions, the same participants attended all three of the weekends plus a one-day reunion between sessions, in Washington, D.C., in November 1993.

At each weekend retreat, an agenda was created by the group with the help of facilitators, and PCP principles were used to guide the dialogue. Each began by exploring participants' expectations for the meeting. At Cairo One, they shared their hopes and fears for the meeting. At Cairo Two, participants created a "map of the landscape" of their own interests and hopes. At Pocantico, they created a verbal collage of images to bring back the spirit of the past meetings.

Agenda building was accomplished differently at each conference. At Cairo One, the group was divided into smaller groups that generated lists of the topics, themes, and issues that members wanted to discuss. These subjects were then compiled and discussed in a plenary session, which ended by having each participant fill out two index cards. On the first card, they indicated "the theme, title, or question for a small group that would capture the edge of my curiosity." On the second card (a different color), they completed the sentence: "I'll be really irritated if we don't find a way to talk about _____ before we leave." The facilitators clustered the cards during lunch, and three overarching themes were posted on newsprint around the room. Participants milled around and gravitated toward one of the posters to form a theme-focused group. Additional agenda items mentioned on the cards were brought up in various ways later in the conference.

Participants in Cairo Two were asked to bring agenda nominations with them. The meeting began by asking the participants to identify interests, hopes, and concrete agenda items. Overnight, the facilitators organized these suggestions into a "map," or outline of topics and concerns. Next morning began with the participants working together to organize the list and plan their agenda for the rest of the weekend.

The agenda-setting process at Pocantico was done in yet another way. The participants were asked to address three questions: (1) What has or has not happened since Cairo that is relevant to your goals for this meeting? (2) What could happen this weekend that would make you very glad that you came? (3) What questions and issues do you passionately want the agenda to include? Answers were listed on newsprint, and each participant indicated his or her priorities by marking a few items on the list with colored stickers. The facilitators studied the sticker lists overnight and created a proposed agenda. Their proposal was reworked in a plenary session the next morning.

The body of each conference was structured around a series of small-group and large-group discussions. In each case, the composition of the small groups changed, depending on the topic and interest of the moment.

At Cairo Two, a "fish bowl" structure was selected on the spot as a creative response to the group's conflict about whether to stay together so everyone could "hear everyone" or split up into more manageable groups in which everyone could have more "airtime." The fish bowl creates a group-within-a-group. Four to eight people are invited to sit in an inner circle and have a dialogue among themselves that is overheard by others who listen from a larger circle around them. Participants have turns as talking "fish" and as listeners in the "bowl." At Cairo Two, the group elected to continue this process for hours while its members rotated in and out of the two circles and explored a variety of topics.

Although the group retried this structure at Pocantico, it no longer fit the needs of the group, which had become more diverse in the aftermath of the Cairo conference. There was more pull to engage in sustained small-group discussions on quite different topics. This time, small-group topics were identified by inviting participants to stand up and announce a topic for a group they would like to be in. Other participants were invited to roam around, ask questions, and negotiate until satisfying groups were formed.

Another spontaneous variation was introduced later in the Pocantico weekend to address the flatness of the small-group reports. Each small group was asked to return with one or two questions or problems on which they would like large-group consultation. If the large group had useful inputs, these ideas could be built on when the small group reconvened. Although this innovation was only somewhat successful, it is an illustration of on-the-spot facilitator creativity focused on addressing an emerging group need.

All these meetings ended with a structured closing circle in which participants had an opportunity to reflect on the process and what they had learned. They were asked to speak for a moment about "what you will take away" from the experience or what "put a period on it for you."

The dialogues of the population and family planning group show that creative methods can help participants transcend customary divisions and talk about their differences and shared concerns in new ways. The feedback from the participants indicated that this work did make a positive difference in how they thought about their challenges and toward joint problem solving before, during, and after the Cairo Conference. The Cairo project is a model of how creativity, concern, and capability can be combined to create a forum in which differences can be explored in new and better ways.

◙ Public Dialogue Consortium

Back in the mid-1980s, the University of Massachusetts in Amherst was experiencing ugly incidents of racial and political strife. The situation got so bad that the administration set up a civility commission to work out ways for diverse opinions to be expressed in constructive, rather than destructive, ways. A subcommittee developed an innovative type of public forum in which opponents on intractable issues might talk to one another and to an audience about their perspectives. The committee came to call the forum *Kaleidoscope* (Carbaugh et al., 1986; Leppington, 1995; Littlejohn, 1986).

Campus Kaleidoscope, discussed in greater detail in Chapter 1, was created as an experiment in public discourse. Topics such as U.S. intervention in Central America, animal rights, gay rights, and the CIA were covered. The format used in Kaleidoscope encouraged spokespersons to listen to the others in a new and deeper way.

Kaleidoscope had mixed results and after a few years was "put on the shelf." Nearly a decade later, Kim Walters at De Anza College in California organized a group of interested professors, students, and practitioners to revive Kaleidoscope and use it as a starting place for developing a variety of new methods for transcendent discourse. With this effort, the Public Dialogue Consortium (PDC) was born.

For information about the Public Dialogue Consortium, contact
Stephen W. Littlejohn, Senior Consultant, Public Dialogue
Consortium, 1522 Wells Drive NE, Albuquerque, NM 87112.

In spring 1995, members of the newly formed group conducted two
Kaleidoscope sessions in the south San Francisco Bay area and then
spent a weekend critically analyzing what they had done. From this
process emerged a deep sense of the potential and importance of
facilitating better communication in moral conflict, a belief in the use
of some of the methods they had developed, and a strong critique of
the one-session model that they had used. They decided to continue
working together and to enlarge the scope of what they were doing
and engaged in an ambitious project of learning how other groups
worked. Among other things, they attended training sessions sponsored by other groups, established regular contact with similar projects, experimented, and did endless simulations in their own training
meetings.

The PDC is an informal group of communication teachers, practitioners, and students. Its purpose is to facilitate the institutionalization
of better forms of communication than generally exist in public and
about public issues. Members of the PDC work from a belief that
patterns of communication are the sites where the events and objects of
social worlds, including individual selves, are made. There are different
forms of communication, each of which provides particular constraints
and affordances for ways of being human, for personal and social
development, and for patterns of social relationships.

Despite grandiose goals, the members of the group approach their
task with a combination of seriousness and high humor, and they
understand that their goals will be achieved, if at all, locally and
temporarily. The members of the PDC have a common vision of the type
of persons required to thrive in the contemporary era, of the forms of
communication that create spaces for transformative peacemaking, and
of the type of society in which they would like to live and work.

The PDC has no official status, and the only bonds that keep it
together are the shared values of the members of the group and their
pleasure in working together. Members of the PDC live in four noncon-
tiguous states; they range in age from early 20s to mid-50s and in rank

from full professor to undergraduate student. There are no dues, no salaries, no annual performance reviews, and no hierarchy.

In one sense, the PDC is like literally hundreds of similar organizations that have been formed in recent years to increase public participation in political processes, create places for nonadversarial conflict resolution, and improve communication among citizens. Most of these organizations are not-for-profit; virtually all are nongovernmental; most are nonpartisan, although some focus on particular issues. There is no standard model for organizational structure, size, means of support, or even ways of working.

The PDC is eclectic and creative. It borrows established techniques from other programs, adapts these, and creates new synthetic forms. Greatly influenced by the work of the National Issues Forums and the Public Conversations Project, the PDC has adopted and adapted methods from these programs. The consortium has also been inspired by the work of the KCC-International (Kensington Consultation Centre) in London and has made use of techniques developed in the Milan school of family therapy.

A Systems Orientation

Despite its use of a variety of techniques, the work of the PDC does have coherence. Always, the group approaches a situation as a complex network of relationships among people and messages. All the techniques employed by the PDC are designed to bring to light the various social worlds created within a communication system, to find the positive resources within the system for making better worlds, and to elicit ideas for how the system might move forward in new and productive ways. This work is done by concentrating on several things.

First, the methods of the PDC never focus primarily on the psychic variables or individual differences. Communication is viewed as "between" people, rather than as a series of components. Important in PDC work are the connections among persons and ideas. The parties involved in a conflict communicate in multiple patterns of interaction that they themselves produce, and PDC methods are designed to bring such patterns to light.

Second, each of the multiple patterns of communication has its own grammar, expressed in a vocabulary of rights, duties, obligations, prohibitions, possibilities, and so on. This grammar guides the communicators in determining what to do and how to act. The methods of the

PDC attempt to uncover the rules by which the actors in the situation proceed and to imagine new and better ones.

Third, communication always occurs in time, space, and particular circumstances. The meaning of any act derives from a context, and the context is in turn produced by the actions of those in it. This type of circular reasoning is valued as an important part of a systems orientation. The members of the PDC attempt to help disputants understand better the contexts of their conflict and imagine future contexts in which transcendent discourse might occur.

Fourth, the PDC concentrates on what is done and what is said rather than on attitudes, beliefs, and values. Actions create social realities, and those embroiled in conflict need to become more aware of the ways in which their respective actions are tied to one another in a pattern of interaction that somehow makes the social world of which they are a part. New worlds are made possible by new actions, and PDC interventions invite participants to consider different actions that might be taken in the future.

Acting on this systems orientation, the PDC makes use of several techniques. Some of these, including dialogue groups and issue forums, have already been covered in this chapter. Other, somewhat different, techniques are discussed in more detail below.

The Methods of the PDC

Systemic Questioning. Systemic questions are designed to invite respondents to think about relationships and connections, not individual wants, needs, successes, and faults. This type of questioning can help break habitual ways of understanding a problem and can interrupt escalating cycles of reciprocal blame. Systemic questions can combine any of the following four features:

1. They can focus on differences between things. For example, one might ask, "How is Brent's reaction to this situation different from your own?"
2. They can ask for comparisons. For example, one might ask, "Who has the most to gain if Sara's position prevails?"
3. They can pose unusual and alternative ways of punctuating events. "If Brent were no longer called a racist, how might he respond differently?"
4. They can ask people to think about outcomes of particular types of interaction. "If the pattern you described continues, where do you think it will end up?"

Systemic questions are normally framed from the perspective of a hypothesis about what might be going on. These hypotheses stand not like accurate interpretations but more like wonderings. They are designed not to tell the disputants how they should think but to invite them to think differently about their own interactions. The questioner, then, will constantly shift from one hypothesis to another. Table 8.11 lists examples of systemic questions.

Three types of questions are included in Table 8.11. Some *reveal the grammar* of the participant. These questions help participants and observers come in touch with their moral orders. Some *consider the limits of the grammar* of the participants. These help participants consider more carefully the consequences of undue adherence to one point of view. Finally, some questions *imagine possible futures* and help participants think about new patterns of interaction.

Translating systemic ideas into practical ways of working is an exciting task. Those involved in the PDC have put some effort into learning to speak and act systemically in their interventions.

Appreciative Inquiry. Appreciative inquiry is an attitude or spirit with which questions are asked in a certain interview format. It involves a search for hidden virtues and positive resources within a system that might be used as seeds for growth and change. It is a way to help a group get unstuck from intractable and negative forms of discourse.

In appreciative inquiry, one asks for positive stories, examples of success, and ideas about what assets can be found in the system for moving forward in a positive direction. In sum, appreciative inquiry follows five principles:

1. *An attitude of awe and wonder:* The consultant is truly curious about how the system works and how it might work better. The consultant inquires about how things get done within the system, the conversations that produce the reality of the system, and mechanisms that might suggest movement to a new place. ("It is remarkable that you all care enough about your situation to come today. How was everybody's participation made possible today?")

2. *Avoiding "calling forth the pathology":* In appreciative inquiry, a minimum amount of time is spent on the "problem." Some time might be devoted to a description of the situation, to get a sense of where the system is now and understand the grammars of the parties, but the consultant wants them to look forward, not backward. ("You all seem to value respect a great deal. I wonder if we could go around and have each of

TABLE 8.11 Sample Systemic Questions

Questions That Reveal the Grammar

1. From your point of view, why do you think this subject was chosen for the Kaleidoscope session?
2. Why do you think you were invited to participate?
3. How has this subject been talked about in the past?
4. What has been your role in the conflict?
5. What do you most want to be heard as having said today?
6. How does Sara show that she does . . . ?
7. What does it do to you when Sara does . . . ?
8. Whose position is being heard best, do you think? What are the signs that it is being heard best?
9. What things do you think cannot be said in this dispute? What things cannot be heard?
10. What are you trying to say that Sara is having a hard time hearing?
11. What about Sara's position troubles you most?

Questions That Challenge the Grammar

1. Is there anything Sara is trying to say that you have difficulty hearing?
2. What surprised you most by what Sara said in her interview today?
3. Who would have the most to lose if you prevailed in this dispute? What would they gain?
4. Who would have the most to gain if Sara prevailed in this dispute? What would they gain?
5. What would you gain most if you gave up your position in this conflict?
6. What would Sara lose most if she gave up her position in this conflict?

Questions That Imagine Possible Futures

1. What would change if this conflict were discussed in a different way?
2. What would have to happen for the discussion on this topic to take a different form?
3. What would be different if Sara did . . . ?
4. What would change if you did . . . ?

SOURCE: Public Conversations Project. Reprinted by permission of the Public Conversations Project.

you tell us how things might be done differently if this level of respect were achieved.")

3. *Moving forward:* System interventions are appropriate when a group is stuck in repetitive and unwanted patterns of interaction. Appreciative inquiry invites the group to look forward. This is done by introducing

new grammars into the conversation, avoiding reproducing the problem, and inviting the parties to imagine various futures. If the intervention is successful, the parties will come to hold a variety of positive "ends-in-view." ("It is clear that you are all concerned about various kinds of disturbances that can occur in a neighborhood—like Jim's barking dog, Betty's daughter's band, and the bubbling of your other neighbor's hot tub in the middle of the night. I would like to know how neighborhoods come to manage and cope with the inevitable stimulation of living close to one another.")

4. *Nonexpert position:* The consultant avoids the position of an expert who can solve the problem or tell the parties what they should do. Instead, the consultant asks questions to inquire into how things work and how they might work better. The purpose of appreciative inquiry is to have the parties themselves think of new options. ("Jane, you have said that you would like to be consulted more often. Tell us how that might happen.")

5. *Enlarging the context:* One of the reasons that groups get stuck in old patterns is that they are unable to see a larger or different context of action. Like a good mediator, the systems consultant can ask questions about a larger set of values or a bigger system of which the conflict is a part. ("In listening to you all talk about your difficulties with moving the hospital to a new location, I'm struck by how important the quality of life seems to be in this city. It would help me if each of you could comment on what a high quality of life in a city entails. Judy, would you begin?")

Reflecting. Reflecting is a type of shared hypothesizing in which an interviewer reflects possible connections, contexts, and futures based on answers to systemic and appreciative questions. The purpose of reflecting is certainly not to give a definitive interpretation, analysis, diagnosis, or prescription but to suggest relationships of which the participants may not have thought. Because a system can be understood in a variety of ways, a reflection is a mere suggestion of one way in which the pattern might be viewed. Sometimes a reflection will spark recognition in the participants, and sometimes it will not.

The purpose of reflecting is to give the participants pause, to stimulate their own reflecting, and to open spaces for new action and forward movement. Consequently, interviewers must never become wedded to their reflections, they must be creative in the connections they propose, and they must shift and change reflections frequently. These goals make a reflecting team of three or four members especially desirable. The members of a reflecting team bounce ideas off one another while the participants listen in.

Like systemic questions, three types of reflections have been useful in PDC interventions. The first *joins the grammar* of the participant, suggesting new ways of understanding what the participants are saying. An example is, "I am struck by Brent's strong sense that despite his opposition to affirmative action, he is not a racist." The second *challenges the grammar*, not in a combative or critical way but in a fashion that suggests some of the possible limits of the participants' perspectives. An example is, "Even though she strongly supports affirmative action, I wonder if Sara ever finds herself in the position of being an oppressor." Third, a reflection can *imagine possible futures*, or verbalize possible avenues that the dialogue could take. For example, "I wonder how the opponents of affirmative action would respond differently if they were no longer called racists."

Reflecting is a sophisticated process that requires some skill to do well, but it can lead the participants in a conflict to think of new ways of discussing and acting with the other side. Table 8.12 provides guidelines for reflecting teams.

The PDC works in a variety of formats, including interviews, focus groups, dialogue circles, and public forums, often using the techniques of the National Issues Forums and the Public Conversations Project. Unique to the PDC, however, are Kaleidoscope sessions.

Kaleidoscope

Kaleidoscope sessions are public events combining systemic questioning, appreciative inquiry, and reflecting. The PDC sees Kaleidoscope as an experimental format in which a variety of approaches might be developed and tried. Recent Kaleidoscope sessions do not look much like the old ones at the University of Massachusetts. Indeed, Kaleidoscope is a method under development and is rarely done the same way twice these days.

A Kaleidoscope session is a public forum in which representatives from two sides of an issue present their perspectives on the conflict. The event never is a standard debate but invites representatives and audience members to think about and discuss the dispute in ways that are quite different from customary approaches. The session usually takes from 90 to 120 minutes and can be expanded to half-day and full-day formats. The session may or may not be videotaped for future viewing. A Kaleidoscope session can be done as a single event but is better if it occurs as part of a public forum series. At its best, the public session

TABLE 8.12 Reflecting Team Guidelines

---

1. Attune yourself to the grammar of the participants. This grammar may be best entered through words used, actions done, values cited, accounts given, etc. As much as possible, use elements of the grammar in your own discussion. (Since we are dealing with two "sides" of a conflict, we have the opportunity to compare and contrast these grammars; we will need to make sure that we use both grammars in our talk at the appropriate times.)

2. Take a stance of "not-knowing" or "curiosity" toward these grammars. Explore, extend, express wonder or curiosity about them; do not confront, instruct, argue, rebut, etc. Use phrases such as, "I was struck by the idea that . . ." or "I wonder how the idea that . . . might be acted upon in different ways . . ." or "I'm curious about . . ."

3. Develop "hypotheses" about the grammar and the connections among the elements in the grammar. The most useful hypotheses are those which suggest new or different patterns of connections than the disputants have made. Generally, the disputants will see themselves forced (by "causes" or "intentions") to act as they do and will see the others as choosing to act as they do; look for other connections and relations, for example, by reframing a "causal" relation to an "intentional" one, or vice versa.

4. Express these hypotheses as "ideas," not as "facts." The purpose is to offer the disputants an array of other "stories" within their own grammar; some of these will be accepted and not others for their own reasons, not ours. Phrases such as, "I'm getting the idea that . . ." or "One way of seeing this is . . ." are useful.

5. Do not fall in love with any hypothesis. We are not trying to explain anything or prove anything. No matter how clever, satisfying, elegant, etc., any hypothesis might be, it is a tool which we offer to the disputants. It is up to them to decide if it "connects" with their grammar and if they want to adopt it. The "best" hypothesis is that which the disputants find useful in creating a new story about themselves and their positions within their social worlds; often we will never know just which hypotheses "worked."

6. Connect your statements with those of the other RT members in terms of interest, not agreement/disagreement or even like/dislike. When introducing a different idea than that which was just said, make it another idea, not one in competition with others. Use phrases such as "that's interesting! It makes me think of . . ." or "Yes, and another way of thinking about that is . . ."

7. Maintain an upbeat tone, celebrating the development of a multiverse of ideas. Usually the disputants will be deeply in love with their own hypotheses, and we want to display the fun and utility of a less serious attachment to single ideas. Be flirtatious with ideas; not flippant or frivolous, but playful.

8. Address your comments to the other members of the RT. Allow the disputants to take the role of "third persons." This is a good time for them to be reflective rather than participating as a first person, giving them an opportunity to sample the ideas that you are generating and to think through the implications of them.

SOURCE: Public Dialogue Consortium.

should be preceded or followed by a facilitated dialogue in which participants can explore their shared concerns and deep differences at greater length in a private session.

There are several participants in a Kaleidoscope session. The floor manager introduces the session and coordinates the audience participation. The moderator then begins a series of interviews with the representatives, and the reflecting team shares insights and speculations about the perspectives of the parties and their relationship. The representatives from two sides of the issue respond to the moderator, audience, and reflecting team. Table 8.13 shows a typical agenda of a Kaleidoscope session.

One component of Kaleidoscope sessions is called *third-person listening*. The moderator works with one representative at a time, and the opposing representative is asked to sit in the audience. This setup is designed to encourage representatives to listen with a third-person perspective. This situation is unusual because advocates normally take a first-person perspective and rarely have the opportunity to view the interaction from a distance. In the first-person perspective, the focus is on making decisions about how to respond and act, but in the third-person perspective, the interaction is viewed from outside.

Kaleidoscope has five general goals—recognition, respect, understanding, social awareness, and forward movement. *Recognition* is the acknowledgment that individuals on both sides of significant issues have legitimate interests and commitments. *Respect* is the realization that both sides have good reasons for their beliefs on the basis of their own life experiences. *Understanding* involves making explicit the assumptions and values that each side takes as a matter of faith. *Social awareness* is the realization that the parties themselves, by the way they communicate with one another, determine the nature of the conflict. *Forward movement* means disengaging from negative repetitive patterns of interaction and finding new potentially constructive ones.

The goals can be met on three levels—for the parties, the audience, and the larger community. If a Kaleidoscope session is successful, the parties will increase their recognition of one another's perspectives, build their respect of others' legitimate concerns, and improve their understanding of the issue itself. This does not mean that they will come to agree with one another but that they will develop a clearer idea of shared concerns as well as of real differences. At the very best, the participants no longer will view opponents as crazy, ignorant, uneducated, misguided, or immoral but will see one another as concerned citizens with good reasons for believing what they do. Representatives also should develop new insights into their patterns of interaction and come to realize that damaging patterns can be changed.

TABLE 8.13 Kaleidoscope Agenda

Stage 1: Orientation

The floor manager presents an introduction to set audience expectations.

Stage 2: First Elicitation

This stage is designed to elicit and examine the position and perspective of one side in the dispute. It consists of four parts.

Interview: The moderator interviews the first representative.

Participation: The floor manager takes comments and questions from the audience.

Reflection: A reflecting team of four members shares observations and hypotheses based on the interview and audience session.

Response: The representative is given an opportunity to respond to the reflecting team.

Stage 3: Second Elicitation

This stage is designed to elicit and examine the position and perspective of the other side in the dispute. The above four steps are repeated with the second representative.

Stage 4: Interaction

The representatives are asked to think critically about their relationship, their patterns of communication with one another, and the system in which they conduct their struggle. Again, this stage consists of four parts.

Interview: The moderator interviews both representatives together and invites them to respond to one another.

Participation: The floor manager takes comments and questions from the audience.

Reflection: The reflecting team shares observations and hypotheses about the interaction between the two sides in the conflict.

Response: The representatives are given an opportunity to respond to the reflecting team.

Stage 5: Closing

The participants are given an opportunity to make a closing statement, and the moderator ends the session. In some cases a discussion may be held at this point about what might come next as a follow-up.

SOURCE: Public Dialogue Consortium.

Kaleidoscope sessions are presented in front of an audience for a reason. Because the dispute is publicly visible and has been going on for a while, there will be some general interest in the subject. The issue may have implications for public or corporate policy, and it may involve concerns on which citizens or employees must come to a judgment. For the audience, then, the event aims to provide a deeper, more respectful basis on which to understand and act on the issue. It should model for them new forms of communication and patterns of interaction.

As a public event, the Kaleidoscope session can provide a model for the types of questions that should be asked in society at large, the ways in which constructive interaction might occur, and the sorts of responses that people in conflict could make. At base, the PDC sees its work primarily as peacemaking, not to smooth over or hide differences but to express them in more humane and less violent and demeaning ways. Because they are conducting the conversation in public, then, the parties have the opportunity to participate in transforming the way in which the dispute is conducted in society at large.

Special Projects

During its brief history, the PDC has undertaken a variety of exciting projects.

Campus Kaleidoscopes. The PDC has sponsored three Kaleidoscopes on the campuses of San Jose State University, De Anza College, and the University of New Mexico. These illustrate the evolving and experimental nature of the work of the PDC. The San Jose Kaleidoscope, on the topic of intercollegiate athletics, was the first such session since the early days of Kaleidoscope at the University of Massachusetts. It was a prototype session designed primarily to try out certain innovations.

After a few adjustments, the model was transported to De Anza College to be used on the topic of campus diversity and multiculturalism. Some 40 students took an intensive two-weekend, one-unit course on moral conflict and the Kaleidoscope method and then became the audience for this session, held in the campus television studio, broadcast to an overflow audience of various other interested persons, and videotaped. This was probably the most successful Kaleidoscope of the several that have been done, including those at University of Massachusetts. It was successful primarily because of the use of new methods, such as a reflecting team and the presence of a trained audience.

Still, the De Anza session left something to be desired. Because it was a one-shot event, the participants had been left hanging, with no follow-up or continued dialogue. To test the use of Kaleidoscope in a longer, more elaborate series, a conference was planned at the University of New Mexico on the topic of affirmative action. The conference combined the dialogue-group method of the Public Conversations

Project, Kaleidoscope, and an NIF-style issues forum in a two-day, intensive format. About 30 people attended the conference and participated in the three events.

The New Mexico conference was a monumental learning experience for the PDC. It was an opportunity to look at three major methods side by side, to get a sense of their similarities and differences, and to begin discussing ways to improve the overall process in the future.

International Conference. In April 1996, the PDC sponsored an international conference titled "Improving Public Discourse: Sharing Hopes, Histories, and Ways of Working." Representatives from a variety of organizations from around the world attended the conference, held in the scenic Sequoia Seminar owned by the Foundation for Global Community near Santa Cruz, California.

About 40 individuals attended. Represented were the Public Conversations Project, the National Issues Forums, the Peninsula Conflict Resolution Center, the Kensington Consultation Centre (England), Fundación Interfas (Argentina), University of New Mexico Public Policy Institute, Stanford Center of Conflict and Negotiation, Oregon Conflict Resolution Center, the Better Government Association, the U.S.-Mexico Conflict Resolution Center, the Communication Research Institute of Australia, the Foundation for Global Community, Centro de Estudios Sobre Desarrollo Económico (Colombia), Community Conversations, Sistema Humano (Colombia), and others.

During a four-day period, the participants presented and demonstrated their methods, shared their challenges and frustrations, and explored ways to continue working together. The conference participants formed a resource network that promises to enhance the work of each program represented.

Cupertino City Project. At the time of this writing, the PDC is involved in the second of three phases of a city dialogue project titled "Cupertino Community Project: Visions and Voices." This project is designed to improve the quality of public communication in the community by involving all the conflicting voices in a climate of increased trust and respect and providing ways for citizens to hear opposing voices and explore their own doubts and commitments.

In Phase 1, 10 focus groups were interviewed to determine the issues in the minds of citizens and the various futures they imagined. Through appreciative inquiry, group members were encouraged to speak of their hopes and passions in a constructive manner. From the several themes that emerged from the focus groups, those of cultural richness and crime prevention were chosen to be explored in the second phase of the project.

In Phase 2, students are conducting appreciative conversations throughout the community with parents and other adults, and a city-wide conference and forum are being held to discuss how best to capitalize on the cultural resources of the community and to create an environment safe from crime. In addition, local media will participate in the process by publishing positive stories of cultural richness in the community. In the third phase of the project, a similar approach will be used for the other themes that emerged from the focus groups.

The Cupertino Project, like the PDC itself, is a medium in which new ideas for transcendent discourse can be tested and improved. The PDC is a neophyte group that is not afraid to play with ideas, learn from its experience, and move forward, like many similar groups, in establishing environments in which moral difference can be explored creatively and constructively.

In the following and final chapter of this book, we look again at transcendent discourse, to find in a spirit of appreciative inquiry the seeds that will enable us to move creatively into a new future.

🕸 Note

1. This section was written with the assistance of staff members of the Public Conversations Project. For additional description, see Public Conversations Project (1993, 1995).

9

Achieving Transcendence

After dinner, they began trickling into the meeting room. It was a large but inviting and comfortable space with two walls of glass overlooking the redwood forest. The sun was setting, and an orange glow filtered down through the trees. The seats were arranged in a neat circle around the perimeter of the room, just enough for the 40 people soon to arrive.

Coco and Sylvia took seats together with their interpreter, Maria del Carmen. Alejandro and Eduardo from Colombia were within earshot, just in case they needed a word or two translated. Dora, another Argentine, not needing an interpreter, sat a little distance away. Robyn, the Australian, sat grinning in the corner next to Mike from Chicago, who looked mildly skeptical. The Brits were spread out in various places. Corky and Sallyann from Massachusetts sat together opposite the windows where they could be easily seen because they would be getting first billing this evening.

After the five New Mexicans had been seated, Kevin from Texas, who had been working so hard in the kitchen, slipped into the room. People from Washington, Oregon, Ohio, and Illinois soon arrived.

Barnett and Kim, who would do a brief introduction, sat next to Corky and Sallyann, grinning and glowing in awe over the talent assembled here. They were also ecstatic that the international conference was actually under way after months of hard planning by their colleagues in the Public Dialogue Consortium.

The participants from many peacemaking programs around the world had flown in during the past few days to learn about one another's work, share ideas, and establish a supporting network. Their goals and methods varied, but they had one thing in common: All were trying to find ways to improve the quality of public discourse by creating environments in which human differences might be explored openly, constructively, and humanely.

After a brief introduction, Sallyann and Corky of the Public Conversations Project began. They wanted to do a little team building and demonstrate at the same time how the PCP works. They invited the participants to share their hopes and visions, their challenges and needs. In popcorn style, one person after another spoke, and something magical began that first hour.

In the following days at the beautiful Sequoia Seminar in the Santa Cruz Mountains, they listened and talked, demonstrated and practiced, saw a puppet show and wrote a rap, ate and ate and ate, and washed dishes and more dishes and more dishes. They practiced aikido, hiked, partied, laughed, and cried. They left after four days, filled with hope that transcendence is possible.

Transcendent conversations embody a series of turns that can allow us to discover new and positive resources for change. In Chapter 8, we looked at three models of transcendent discourse. As a group, these programs and the hundreds of others like them show us what transcendent conversations can look like.

▧ Beyond Simplicity:
Philosophical Conversation

To have a philosophical conversation is to think deeply about our respective places in the world, to consider the bases of our systems of thought, and to discover both the powers and limits of the worldviews that make us who we are. To have a philosophical conversation is to realize the rational and cultural origins of our categories and to discover the contexts from which our ideas stem. It is to understand that our actions and identities are tightly tied to our ways of thinking. To have a philosophical conversation is to look beyond surface differences to normally occult points of connection and disjunction among the peoples of the world. A philosophical conversation, then, moves us beyond old patterns to a place in which we can explore common ideas and differing assumptions.

The term *philosophical* may imply "abstract" or "theoretical," but our use of this term is not intended to be read in this way. Good philosophical conversation is grounded in the experience of the communicators.

Participants in a Public Conversations Project dialogue, for example, are encouraged to speak from their own experience and to do so in a way that shows how they came to the positions they hold. They are encouraged to probe to the heart of the matter and to identify what is most essential. That is a philosophical conversation. Moderators in a National Issues Forum ask participants to identify underlying values, to get to essential points, to identify criteria, and to express views of opponents. That is a philosophical conversation. The reflecting teams of the Public Dialogue Consortium speak in categories that reflect the grammar of the participants. That, too, is a philosophical conversation.

◪ Beyond Evaluation: Comparative Conversation

To have a comparative conversation is to create together a new language in which to see similarities and differences more clearly. To have a comparative conversation is to establish some ground on which we might weigh the powers and limits of our respective positions. To have a comparative conversation is to step outside our customary ways of talking and to cooperate in a new, more reflective way.

A comparative conversation is creative. Participants listen deeply to the social realities of others, tell their own, and together work out new ways in which their moral orders can be viewed side by side. The NIF accomplishes this by featuring choice work. The issue-framing process attempts to establish categories in the form of practical options, and the issue booklets compare various positions across these options.

All three programs discussed in the previous chapter use stories as a way of expressing the elements of a moral order. The story itself is a level on which comparison can be made. All stories have characters, settings, and narrative developments. By sharing stories, participants can see similarities and differences among these story parts. Sharing stories constitutes a new way of speaking and listening.

✒ Beyond Obstruction:
Dialogic Conversation

Dialogue is one of the central themes of this book. The idea of dialogue is particularly important because it so fully captures the notion of having a new type of conversation. To have a dialogic conversation is to value listening more than speaking, to value understanding more than explaining, and to value respect more than persuasion. The PDC first called itself the Public *Dispute* Consortium but quickly changed its name to reflect what it was trying to achieve, rather than what it was trying to get away from.

Many practitioners use group dialogue methods in their work, but we think the Public Conversations Project has turned such methods into a fine art. It has proved that dialogue can work as a new form of discourse between former opponents. The whole approach of the NIF, deliberation, is done in the spirit of dialogue—public weighing of choices, to express and hear a host of perspectives. If an NIF session is successful, the participants are supposed to leave "stewing," and that is an outcome of dialogue.

✒ Beyond Blame:
Critical Conversation

We know that the term *critical* has several meanings and that our use of the word in this book can be misread. We certainly are seeking alternatives to personal criticism of other people in moral conflicts. We are even looking for ways to avoid simplistic evaluation of ideas and actions. By now, it should be apparent that our definition of *critical* is the careful assessment of the powers and limits of a range of ideas in context.

To have a critical conversation, then, is to acknowledge that every set of ideas and actions is based ultimately on assumptions taken by faith. To have a critical conversation is to identify the basic ideas about personhood, knowledge, and value that form the basis of a moral order.

To have a critical conversation is to bring to light underlying beliefs that are not normally revealed or even clear to parties in conflict. To have a critical conversation is to look at a system of ideas and actions and recognize that every system of thought has its powers and limits, to hear the powers of one's opponent's ideas, and to express the limits of one's own. To have a critical conversation is to realize that powers and limits are constrained and contextual and to explore together the contexts in which those powers and limits apply.

The logic of deliberative democracy, used by the NIF, embodies this type of conversation. The NIF describes *deliberative democracy* as "reasoning together" and "weighing the costs and consequences" of the choices we face. The NIF says that deliberation means being able to make a good case for the choice one least prefers. In a radical way, then, NIF forums and study circles are critical conversations.

The Public Dialogue Consortium uses methods that help disputants get out of their own heads and into the larger interactional system of which they are a part. When a Kaleidoscope moderator asks, "Who would have the most to lose if your side prevails?" a critical conversation is under way. When a reflecting team "challenges the grammar" of one or both parties, a critical conversation is under way.

▧ Moving Forward: Transformative Conversation

If a conversation is transcendent, the participants must understand what they are doing in a new way. Old categories will not work for them. They will say that this conversation is somehow different from the conversations they had before. In transcendent discourse, the context of the conversation is transformed precisely because it is philosophical, comparative, dialogic, and critical.

Public debates on moral issues tend to be strategic, inflexible, and sometimes strident. But the Public Conversations Project transforms this context by changing the setting, the expectations of the participants, and the questions addressed. The NIF changes the context by a careful framing process, by providing time for citizens to speak and listen, and by establishing a different set of rules. The Public Dialogue Consortium changes the context by moving to the level of systems thinking and by refocusing from the problematic past to a positive future.

We began this chapter by revisiting a powerful experience we shared with a group of peacemakers from around the world. One of the highlights of that weekend was a presentation by Elspeth McAdam and Susan Lang from the KCC-International in London. Their work showed us the value of the positive and the need to find resources for moving forward into an uncertain future. We hope that in some small way, this book does honor the work of the KCC-International by thinking out loud about ways in which we can move forward intelligently and creatively together.

References

Abel, R. (1982). *The politics of informal justice*. New York: Academic Press.

Alexander, T. (1978, February 13). A promising try at environmental detente for coal. *Fortune, 97*, 94-102.

Alinsky, S. (1971). *Rules for radicals: A practical primer for realistic radicals*. New York: Random House.

Ames, K., Leonard, E. A., Lewis, S. D., & Annin, P. (1992, April 6). A hymn to adoption—or is it? *Newsweek, 119*, 52.

Amy, D. J. (1987). *The politics of environmental mediation*. New York: Columbia University Press.

Aristotle. (1962). *Nicomachean ethics* (M. Ostwald, Ed.). Indianapolis, IN: Bobbs-Merrill.

Ascher, W. (1986). The moralism of attitudes supporting intergroup violence. *Political Psychology, 7*, 403-425.

Averill, J. (1986). The acquisition of emotions during adulthood. In R. Harré (Ed.), *The social construction of emotions* (pp. 98-119). New York: Blackwell.

Azar, L. (1990). *Twentieth century in crisis: Foundations of totalitarianism*. Dubuque, IA: Kendall/Hunt.

Bakhtin, M. (1986). *Speech genres and other late essays* (C. Emerson & M. Holquist, Trans.). Austin: University of Texas Press.

Barber, B. (1984). *Strong democracy: Participatory politics for a new age*. Berkeley: University of California Press.

Baxter, L. A. (1988). A dialectical perspective on communication strategies in relationship development. In S. Duck (Ed.), *Handbook of personal relationships* (pp. 257-274). Chichester, UK: Wiley.

218   MORAL CONFLICT

Becker, C., Chasin, L., Chasin, R., Herzig, M., & Roth, S. (1992). *Fostering dialogue on abortion: A report from the Public Dialogue Project*. Working paper.
Bellah, R. N., Madsen, R., Sullivan, W. M., Swidler, A., & Tipton, S. M. (1985). *Habits of the heart: Individualism and commitment in American life*. Berkeley: University of California Press.
Bennett, W. J. (1992). *The de-valuing of America: The fight for our culture and our children*. New York: Summit.
Bennis, W. (1989). *Why leaders can't lead: The unconscious conspiracy continues*. San Francisco: Jossey-Bass.
Berger, P., Berger, B., & Kellner, H. (1973). *The homeless mind: Modernization and consciousness*. New York: Vintage.
Berne, E. (1964). *Games people play: The psychology of human relationships*. New York: Grove.
Bernstein, R. J. (1985). *Beyond objectivism and relativism*. Philadelphia: University of Pennsylvania Press.
Bernstein, R. J. (1992). *The new constellation: The ethical-political horizons of modernity/postmodernity*. Cambridge: MIT Press.
Bloom, A. (1987). *The closing of the American mind: How higher education has failed democracy and impoverished the souls of today's students*. New York: Simon & Schuster.
Boorstin, D. J. (1978). *The republic of technology: Reflections on our future community*. New York: Harper & Row.
Branham, R. J. (1991). The role of the convert in *Eclipse of reason* and *The silent scream*. *Quarterly Journal of Speech, 77*, 407-426.
Branham, R. J., & Pearce, W. B. (1985). Between text and context: Toward a rhetoric of contextual reconstruction. *Quarterly Journal of Speech, 71*, 19-36.
Branham, R. J., & Pearce, W. B. (1987). A contract for civility: Edward Kennedy's Lynchburg Address. *Quarterly Journal of Speech, 73*, 424-443.
Brown, M. T. (1990). *Working ethics: Strategies for decision making and organizational responsibility*. San Francisco: Jossey-Bass.
Buber, M. (1958). *I and thou*. New York: Scribner.
Burbules, N. C., & Rice, S. (1991). Dialogue across differences: Continuing the conversation. *Harvard Educational Review, 61*, 393-416.
Burgess, P. G. (1970). The rhetoric of moral conflict: Two critical dimensions. *Quarterly Journal of Speech, 56*, 120-129.
Burton, J. W. (1969). *Conflict and communication: The use of controlled communication in international relations*. London: Macmillan.
Burton, J. W. (1990). *Conflict: Practices in management, settlement, and resolution*. New York: St. Martin's.
Burton, J. W., & Dukes, F. (Eds.). (1990). *Conflict: Readings in management and resolution*. New York: St. Martin's.
Bush, R. A. B., & Folger, J. P. (1994). *The promise of mediation*. San Francisco: Jossey-Bass.
Carbaugh, D. (1985). Cultural communication and organizing. In W. B. Gudykunst, L. P. Stewart, & S. Ting-Toomey (Eds.), *Communication, culture, and organizational processes* (pp. 30-47). Beverly Hills, CA: Sage.
Carbaugh, D. (1988). *Talking American: Cultural discourses on Donahue*. Norwood, NJ: Ablex.
Carbaugh, D., Chen, V., Cobb, S., & Shailor, J. (1986). *Ceremonial discourse: From debate to dialogue* (Report to the Kaleidoscope Committee). Amherst: University of Massachusetts.
Carey, J. W. (1993). Everything that rises must diverge: Notes on communications, technology and the symbolic construction of the social. In P. Gaunt (Ed.), *Beyond agendas: New directions in communication research* (pp. 171-184). Westport, CT: Greenwood.
Chasin, R., & Herzig, M. (1993). Creating systemic interventions for the sociopolitical arena. In B. Berger-Gould & D. H. DeMuth (Eds.), *The global family therapist:*

Integrating the personal, professional, and political (pp. 141-192). Needham, MA: Allyn & Bacon.

Cobb, S. (1994). A narrative perspective on mediation: Toward the materialization of the "storytelling" metaphor. In J. P. Folger & T. S. Jones (Eds.), *New directions in mediation: Communication research and perspectives* (pp. 48-66). Thousand Oaks, CA: Sage.

Cobb, S., & Rifkin, J. (1991). Practice and paradox: Deconstructing neutrality in mediation. *Law and Social Inquiry, 16,* 35-62.

Conrad, C. (1983). The rhetoric of the moral majority: An analysis of romantic form. *Quarterly Journal of Speech, 69,* 159-170.

Cooper, N. (1981). *The diversity of moral thinking.* Oxford, UK: Clarendon.

Coser, L. A. (1964). *The functions of social conflict.* New York: Free Press.

Cronon, W. (1991). *Nature's metropolis: Chicago and the Great West.* New York: Norton.

Davidson, W. D., & Montville, J. V. (1982). Foreign policy according to Freud. *Foreign Policy, 45,* 145-157.

Deetz, S. (1992). *Democracy in an age of corporate colonization: Developments in communication and the politics of everyday life.* Albany: State University of New York Press.

Dewey, J. (1922). *Human nature and conduct: An introduction to social psychology.* New York: Henry Holt.

Dewey, J. (1929). *Experience and nature.* LaSalle, IL: Open Court Publishing.

Dispute Resolution Act of 1980, Pub. L. No. 96-190, 94 Stat. 17.

Donohue, W. A., & Bresnahan, M. I. (1994). Communication issues in mediating cultural conflict. In J. P. Folger & T. S. Jones (Eds.), *New directions in mediation research: Communication research and perspectives* (pp. 135-158). Thousand Oaks, CA: Sage.

Doob, L. W. (Ed.). (1970). *Resolving conflict in Africa: The Fermeda workshop.* New Haven, CT: Yale University Press.

D'Souza, D. (1991). *Illiberal education: The politics of race and sex on campus.* New York: Free Press.

Dunant, Jean-Henri. (1985). In *New encyclopædia Britannica: Micropædia* (Vol. 3, p. 705). Chicago: Encyclopædia Britannica.

Eclipse of reason [Film]. (1987). New York: Burnadell.

Evans, S. M., & Boyte, H. C. (1992). *Free spaces: The sources of democratic change in America.* Chicago: University of Chicago Press.

Fagre, L. P. (1995). *Cross cultural uses and means of silence in peacemaking and mediation in the Navajo peacemaker court and the Metro Court mediation program.* Unpublished master's thesis, University of New Mexico, Albuquerque.

Faux, M. (1988). *Roe v. Wade: The untold story of the landmark Supreme Court decision that made abortion legal.* New York: New American Library.

Fine, M. G. (1995). *Building successful multicultural organizations: Challenges and opportunities.* Westport, CT: Quorum.

Fisher, R., & Brown, S. (1988). *Getting together: Building a relationship that gets to yes.* Boston: Houghton Mifflin.

Fisher, R., & Ury, W. (1981). *Getting to yes: Negotiating agreement without giving in.* Boston: Houghton Mifflin.

Fort, D., & Skinner-Jones, A. (1993). *The great divide* [Video]. (Available from DNA Productions, P. O. Box 22216, Santa Fe, NM 87502-2216)

Frake, C. O. (1980). *Language and cultural description.* Stanford, CA: Stanford University Press.

Freeman, S. A. (1985). *The social construction of a moral order: A construct and discourse analysis.* Unpublished doctoral dissertation, University of Massachusetts, Amherst.

Freeman, S. A., Littlejohn, S. W., & Pearce, W. B. (1992). Communication and moral conflict. *Western Journal of Communication, 56,* 311-329.

Frentz, T. (1985). Rhetorical conversation, time, and moral action. *Quarterly Journal of Speech, 71,* 1-18.

Gearhart, S. M. (1995, September). Notes from a recovering activist. *Sojourner: The Women's Forum, 21*(1), 8-11.

Gergen, K. (1991). *The saturated self: Dilemmas of identity in contemporary life.* New York: Basic Books.

Gert, B. (1988). *Morality: A new justification of the moral rules.* New York: Oxford University Press.

Goldfarb, J. C. (1991). *The cynical society: The culture of politics and the politics of culture in American life.* Chicago: University of Chicago Press.

Goodman, M. (1988). *What is a person?* Clifton, NJ: Humana.

Gouinlock, J. (1986). *Excellence in public discourse: John Stuart Mill, John Dewey, and social intelligence.* New York: Teachers College Press.

Gunn, G. (1992). *Thinking across the American grain: Ideology, intellect and the new pragmatism.* Chicago: University of Chicago Press.

Habermas, J. (1970). Towards a theory of communicative competence. In H. P. Dreitzel (Ed.), *Recent sociology* (pp. 114-148). London: Collier-Macmillan.

Harper, N. (1979). *Human communication theory: The history of a paradigm.* Rochelle Park, NJ: Hayden.

Harré, R. (1979). *Social being: A theory for social psychology.* Cambridge, MA: Harvard University Press.

Harré, R. (1984). *Personal being: A theory for individual psychology.* Cambridge, MA: Harvard University Press.

Harrington, M. (1986). *The dream of deliverance in American politics.* New York: Knopf.

Harwood Group. (1991). *Citizens and politics: A view from Main Street America.* Dayton, OH: Kettering Foundation.

Hill, P. J. (1991, July/August). Multi-culturalism: The crucial philosophical and organizational issues. *Change,* 38-47.

Hirsch, E. D. (1987). *Cultural literacy: What every American needs to know.* Boston: Houghton Mifflin.

Hunter, J. D. (1991). *Culture wars: The struggle to define America.* New York: HarperCollins.

Hunter, J. D. (1994). *Before the shooting begins: Searching for democracy in America's culture war.* New York: Maxwell Macmillan International.

Hymes, D. (1974). *Foundations in sociolinguistics: An ethnographic approach.* Philadelphia: University of Pennsylvania Press.

Jandt, F. (1973). *Conflict resolution through communication.* New York: Harper & Row.

Johnson, D. (1990). *After certainty: A case study of moral conflict at the interface of incommensurate discourses.* Unpublished master's thesis, University of Massachusetts, Amherst.

Katz, E., & Lazarsfeld, P. (1955). *Personal influence: The part played by people in the flow of mass communications.* New York: Free Press.

Kegan, R. (1994). *In over our heads: The mental demands of modern life.* Cambridge, MA: Harvard University Press.

Kelly, M. (1994, October 3). It all codepends. *New Yorker,* 80-86.

Kelman, H. C. (1972). The problem-solving workshop in conflict resolution. In R. L. Merritt (Ed.), *Communication in international politics* (pp. 168-204). Urbana: University of Illinois Press.

Kolb, D. M. (Ed.). (1994). *When talk works: Profiles of mediators.* San Francisco: Jossey-Bass.

Kriesberg, L., Northrup, T. A., & Thorson, S. J. (Eds.). (1989). *Intractable conflicts and their transformation.* Syracuse, NY: Syracuse University Press.

Kuhn, T. S. (1970). *The structure of scientific revolutions.* Chicago: University of Chicago Press.

Kurtz, P. (Ed.). (1973). *The humanist manifestos I and II.* Buffalo, NY: Prometheus.

Leppington, R. (1987). *Radical kaleidoscopy.* Unpublished manuscript, University of Massachusetts, Department of Communication, Amherst.

Leppington, R. (1995, November). *Transforming the "undiscussable": A case study of "civil" discourse.* Paper presented at the meeting of the Speech Communication Association, San Antonio, TX.

Lev, M. A. (1994, August 28). Sports, recreation are crime-fighting attempts at body, soul. *Chicago Tribune,* Sec. 4, pp. 1, 4.

Lipset, S. M., & Raab, E. (1970). *The politics of unreason.* New York: Harper & Row.

Littlejohn, S. W. (1986). *Looking through the other end: Kaleidoscope from the inside* (Report to the Kaleidoscope Committee). Amherst: University of Massachusetts.

Littlejohn, S. W. (1993, November). *Constructing a moral order: Anti-abortion rhetoric and the "beautiful choice" campaign.* Paper presented at the convention of the Speech Communication Association, Miami, FL.

Littlejohn, S. W. (1994a, November). *The dialectic of moral difference.* Paper presented at the convention of the Speech Communication Association, New Orleans, LA.

Littlejohn, S. W. (1994b, April). *Studies in the quality of discourse: A ten-year retrospective.* Paper presented at the convention of the Central States Communication Association, Oklahoma City, OK.

Littlejohn, S. W. (1995a, February). *Ambiguity and commitment in the management of moral difference.* Paper presented at the convention of the Western States Communication Association, Portland, OR.

Littlejohn, S. W. (1995b). Moral conflict in organizations. In A. M. Nicotera (Ed.), *Conflict in organizations: Communicative processes* (pp. 101-128). Albany: State University of New York Press.

Littlejohn, S. W., Higgins, M., & Williams, M. (1987, November). *Demanding dialogue: Moral conflict in an American protestant church.* Paper presented at the meeting of the Speech Communication Association, Boston.

Littlejohn, S. W., Pearce, W. B., Hines, S., & Bean, W. (1986, February). *Coherence and coordination in mediation communication: Exploratory case studies.* Paper presented at the convention of the Western States Communication Association, Tucson, AZ.

Littlejohn, S. W., & Shailor, J. (1986, November). *The deep structure of conflict in mediation: A case study.* Paper presented at the meeting of the Speech Communication Association, Chicago.

Littlejohn, S. W., Shailor, J., & Pearce, W. B. (1994). The deep structure of reality in mediation. In J. P. Folger & T. S. Jones (Eds.), *New directions in mediation: Communication research and perspectives* (pp. 67-83). Thousand Oaks, CA: Sage.

Littlejohn, S. W., & Wright, J. (1987, February). *Forms of discourse in moral conflict: A case study.* Paper presented at the meeting of the Western States Communication Association, Salt Lake City, UT.

Lovins, A. B. (1977). *Soft energy paths: Toward a durable peace.* New York: Harper & Row.

Machiavelli, N. (1976). *The prince* (J. B. Atkinson, Trans.). Indianapolis, IN: Bobbs-Merrill. (Original work published 1513)

MacIntyre, A. (1981). *After virtue: A study in moral theory.* Notre Dame, IN: University of Notre Dame Press.

Mathews, D. (1994). *Politics for people: Finding a responsible public voice.* Urbana: University of Illinois Press.

Matson, F. W., & Montagu, A. (Eds.). (1967). *The human dialogue: Perspectives on communication.* New York: Free Press.

McGee, M. (1980). The "ideograph": A link between rhetoric and ideology. *Quarterly Journal of Speech, 66,* 1-16.

McGee, M. (1984). Secular humanism: A radical reading of "culture industry" productions. *Critical Studies in Mass Communication, 1,* 1-33.

Merry, S. E. (1989). Mediation in nonindustrial societies. In K. Kressel & D. G. Pruitt (Eds.), *Mediation research: The process and effectiveness of third-party intervention* (pp. 68-90). San Francisco: Jossey-Bass.

Mess, Z. M., & Pearce. W. B. (1986). Dakwah Islamiah: Revivalism in the politics of race and religion in Malaysia. In J. K. Hadden & A. Shupe (Eds.), *Prophetic religions and politics: Religion and the political order* (pp. 196-220). New York: Paragon.

Millen, J. H. (1992). The social construction of blame: A mediation case study. *Human Systems, 2,* 199-216.

Moyers, B. D., & Flowers, B. S. (1989). *A world of ideas: Conversations with thoughtful men and women about American life today and the ideas shaping our future.* New York: Doubleday.

National Issues Forums Institute. (1995). *How can we be fair: The future of affirmative action* [Special issues booklet] (E. J. Arnone, Ed.). Dubuque, IA: Kendall/Hunt.

Nicotera, A. M., Rodriguez, A. J., Hall, M., & Jackson, R. L. (1995). A history of the study of communication and conflict. In A. M. Nicotera (Ed.), *Conflict and organizations: Communicative processes* (pp. 17-44). Albany: State University of New York Press.

Nisbett, R. A. (1966). *The sociological tradition.* New York: Basic Books.

Northrup, T. A. (1989). The dynamic of identity in personal and social conflict. In L. Kriesberg, T. A. Northrup, & S. J. Thorson (Eds.), *Intractable conflicts and their transformation* (pp. 55-82). Syracuse, NY: Syracuse University Press.

Pearce, W. B. (1989). *Communication and the human condition.* Carbondale: University of Southern Illinois Press.

Pearce, W. B. (1993). Achieving dialogue with "the other" in the postmodern world. In P. Gaunt (Ed.), *Beyond agendas: New directions in communication research* (pp. 59-74). Westport, CT: Greenwood.

Pearce, W. B. (1994). *Interpersonal communication: Making social worlds.* New York: Harper-Collins.

Pearce, W. B., Cobb, S., Cano, C., & Freeman, S. A. (1991, November). *From terrorism to solidarity: A transformation of an oppressive discourse in rural Colombia.* Paper presented at the meeting of the Speech Communication Association, Atlanta, GA.

Pearce, W. B., & Cronen, V. E. (1980). *Communication, action, and meaning.* New York: Praeger.

Pearce, W. B., & Foss, K. A. (1990). The historical context of communication as a science. In G. L. Dahnke & G. W. Clatterbuck (Eds.), *Human communication: Theory and research* (pp. 1-20). Belmont, CA: Wadsworth.

Pearce, W. B., Johnson, D. K., & Branham, R. J. (1992). A rhetorical ambush at Reykjavik: A case study of the transformation of discourse. In M. Weiler & W. B. Pearce (Eds.), *Reagan and public discourse in America* (pp. 163-182). Tuscaloosa: University of Alabama Press.

Pearce, W. B., Littlejohn, S. W., & Alexander, A. A. (1987). The new Christian right and the humanist response: Reciprocated diatribe. *Communication Quarterly, 35,* 171-192.

Pearce, W. B., Littlejohn, S. W., & Alexander, A. A. (1989). The quixotic quest for civility: Patterns of interaction between the new Christian right and secular humanists. In J. K. Hadden & A. Shupe (Eds.), *Secularization and fundamentalism reconsidered: Religion and the political order* (Vol. 3, pp. 152-177). New York: Paragon.

Philipsen, G. (1975). Speaking "like a man" in Teamsterville: Culture patterns of role enactment in an urban neighborhood. *Quarterly Journal of Speech, 61,* 13-22.

Philipsen, G. (1989). An ethnographic approach to communication studies. In B. Dervin, L. Grossberg, B. J. O'Keefe, & E. Wartella (Eds.), *Rethinking communication: Paradigm exemplars* (pp. 258-268). Newbury Park, CA: Sage.

Public Conversations Project. (1993). *Population and family planning in context: Steps toward a shared vision* (Report on a dialogue weekend at Chappaquiddick). Watertown, MA: Author.

Public Conversations Project. (1995). *Beyond Cairo: Continuing the conversation* (Report on a dialogue retreat at the Pocantico Conference Center). Watertown, MA: Author.

Rapoport, A. (1950). *Science and the goals of man.* New York: Harper.

Rapoport, A. (1960). *Fights, games, and debates.* Ann Arbor: University of Michigan Press.

Rapoport, A. (1967). Strategy and conscience. In F. Matson & A. Montagu (Eds.), *The human dialogue: Perspectives on communication* (pp. 79-96). New York: Free Press.

Rawlins, W. K. (1989). A dialectical analysis of the tensions, functions and strategic challenges of communication in young adult friendships. In J. A. Anderson (Ed.), *Communication yearbook 12* (pp. 157-189). Newbury Park, CA: Sage.

Robbins, B. (Ed.). (1993). *The phantom public sphere.* Minneapolis: University of Minnesota Press.

Roe v. Wade, 410 U.S. 113 (1973).

Rorty, R. (1979). *Philosophy and the mirror of nature.* Princeton, NJ: Princeton University Press.

Roth, S. (1993). Speaking the unspoken: A work-group consultation to reopen dialogue. In E. Imber-Black (Ed.), *Secrets in families and family therapy* (pp. 268-291). New York: Norton.

Schwartz, R. D. (1989). Arab-Jewish dialogue in the United States. In L. Kriesberg, T. A. Northrup, & S. J. Thorson (Eds.), *Intractable conflicts and their transformation* (pp. 180-209). Syracuse, NY: Syracuse University Press.

Sennett, R. (1970). *The uses of disorder: Personal identity and city life.* New York: Knopf.

Shaeffer, F. (1982). *A time for anger: The myth of neutrality.* Westchester, IL: Crossway.

Shailor, J. G. (1988). *Conflict, communication, and culture: A review and analysis of 15 case studies.* Unpublished master's thesis, University of Massachusetts, Amherst.

Shailor, J. G. (1994). *Empowerment in dispute mediation: A critical analysis of communication.* Westport, CT: Praeger.

Sherif, M., Harvey, O. J., White, B. J., Hood, W. R., & Sherif, C. W. (1961). *Intergroup conflict and cooperation: The robbers cave experiment.* Norman: University of Oklahoma Book Exchange.

The silent scream [Film]. (1984). Anaheim, CA: American Portrait Films.

Simonson, R., & Walker, S. (1988). *Multicultural literacy.* St. Paul, MN: Graywolf.

Staub, E. (1989). *The roots of evil: The origins of genocide and other group violence.* Cambridge, UK: Cambridge University Press.

Stout, J. (1988). *Ethics after babel: The languages of morals and their discontents.* Boston: Beacon.

Thorson, S. J. (1989). Introduction: Conceptual issues. In L. Kriesberg, T. A. Northrup, & S. J. Thorson (Eds.), *Intractable conflicts and their transformation* (pp. 1-10). Syracuse, NY: Syracuse University Press.

Toulmin, S. (1958). *The uses of argument.* Cambridge, UK: Cambridge University Press.

Triandis, H. C., & Albert, R. D. (1987). Cross-cultural perspectives. In F. M. Jablin, L. L. Putnam, K. H. Roberts, & L. W. Porter (Eds.), *Handbook of organizational communication: An interdisciplinary perspective* (pp. 264-296). Newbury Park, CA: Sage.

Tribe, L. H. (1990). *Abortion: The clash of absolutes.* New York: Norton.

Vanderford, M. L. (1989). Vilification and social movements: A case study of pro-life and pro-choice rhetoric. *Quarterly Journal of Speech, 75,* 166-182.

Wallis, J. (1994). *The soul of politics: A practical and prophetic vision for change.* New York: New Press.

Warren, S. (1984). *The emergence of dialectical theory: Philosophy and political inquiry.* Chicago: University of Chicago Press.

Weiler, M., & Pearce, W. B. (Eds.). (1992). *Reagan and public discourse in America.* Tuscaloosa: University of Alabama Press.

Wentworth, W. M. (1989). A dialectical conception of religion and religious movements in modern society. In J. K. Hadden & A. Shupe (Eds.), *Secularization and fundamentalism reconsidered: Religion and the political order* (Vol. 3, pp. 45-62). New York: Paragon.

Wheelwright, P. (1954). *The burning fountain: A study in the language of symbolism.* Bloomington: Indiana University Press.

Winch, P. (1958). *The idea of a social science and its relation to philosophy.* London: Routledge & Kegan Paul.

Windt, T. O. (1972). The diatribe: Last resort for protest. *Quarterly Journal of Speech, 58,* 7-8.

Wittgenstein, L. (1953). *Philosophical investigations.* Oxford, UK: Basil Blackwell.

Wittgenstein, L. (1969). *On certainty* (G. E. M. Anscombe & G. H. von Wright, Eds.; D. Paul & G. E. M. Anscombe, Trans.). Oxford, UK: Basil Blackwell.

Wittgenstein, L. (1972). *On certainty* (D. Paul & G. E. M. Anscombe, Trans.). New York: HarperTorchbook.

Wong, D. B. (1984). *Moral relativity.* Berkeley: University of California Press.

Wynn, R. L. (1989). Custody disputes and the victims. In L. Kriesberg, T. A. Northrup, & S. J. Thorson (Eds.), *Intractable conflicts and their transformation* (pp. 83-92). Syracuse, NY: Syracuse University Press.

Yankelovich, D. (1991). *Coming to public judgment: Making democracy work in a complex world.* Syracuse, NY: Syracuse University Press.

Yoachum, S., & Tuller, D. (1993, September 13). Born-again political movement. *San Francisco Chronicle,* p. A1.

Zwiebach, B. (1988). *The common life: Ambiguity, agreement, and the structure of morals.* Philadelphia: Temple University Press.

◙ Additional Readings

Becker, C., Chasin, L., Chasin, R., Herzig, M., & Roth, S. (1995). From stuck debate to new conversation on controversial issues: A report from the Public Conversations Project. In K. Weingarten (Ed.), *Cultural resistance: Challenging beliefs about men, women, and therapy* (pp. 143-163). New York: Haworth.

Berger, P. L., & Luckmann, T. (1966). *The social construction of reality: A treatise in the sociology of knowledge.* New York: Doubleday.

Burton, J. W. (1987). *Resolving deep-rooted conflict: A handbook.* Lanham, MD: University Press of America.

Chen, V., & Pearce, W. B. (1995). Even if a thing of beauty, can a case study be a joy forever? A social constructionist approach to theory and research. In W. Leeds-Hurwitz (Ed.), *Social approaches to communication* (pp. 135-154). New York: Guilford.

Fine, M. G. (1991). New voices in the workplace: Research directions in multicultural communication. *Journal of Business Communication, 28,* 259-275.

Jones, T. S. (1994). A dialectical reframing of the mediation process. In J. P. Folger & T. S. Jones (Eds.), *New directions in mediation: Communication, research and perspectives* (pp. 26-47). Thousand Oaks, CA: Sage.

Littlejohn, S. W., & Stone, M. (1991, November). *Moral conflict in a small town.* Paper presented at the conference of the Speech Communication Association, Atlanta, GA.

MacIntyre, A. (1988). *Whose justice? Which rationality?* Notre Dame, IN: University of Notre Dame Press.

Roth, S., Chasin, L., Chasin, R., Becker, C., & Herzig, M. (1992). From debate to dialogue: A facilitating role for famiily therapists in the public forum. *Dulwich Center Newsletter, 2,* 41-47.

Author Index

225

Subject Index

About the Authors

W. Barnett Pearce is Professor in the Department of Communication, Loyola University, Chicago; Coprincipal of PearceWalters, Inc., a communication training and consulting firm; and Senior Consultant in the Public Dialogue Consortium. He received his doctorate in interpersonal communication from Ohio University. He has taught at the Universities of North Dakota, Kentucky, and Massachusetts. He served as Department Chair at Massachusetts and Loyola. He is the author of seven books, including *Interpersonal Communication: Making Social Worlds; Reagan and Public Discourse in America; Cultures, Politics, and Research Programs: An International Assessment of Practical Problems in Field Research;* and *Communication and the Human Condition.* He has written more than 100 articles in scholarly journals and chapters in anthologies. He was President of the Eastern Communication Association and is a member of the Speech Communication Association, the International Communication Association, the International Association of Public Participation Practitioners, and the Society for Professionals in Dispute Resolution.

Stephen W. Littlejohn is a communication consultant, mediator, and writer in Albuquerque, New Mexico. He is a Senior Consultant in the Public Dialogue Consortium. He received his doctorate in speech communication from the University of Utah and was Professor of Speech Communication at Humboldt State University in Arcata, California, for 26 years. He currently serves as Adjunct Professor of Communication and Journalism at the University of New Mexico. He is the author of *Elements of Speech Communication, Persuasive Transactions*, and *Theories of Human Communication*. He has authored numerous articles and papers on communication and conflict. He was President of the Western States Communication Association and is a member of the Speech Communication Association, the International Communication Association, the Society for Professionals in Dispute Resolution, and the International Association of Public Participation Practitioners.